Tom Reichert
Editor

Investigating the Use of Sex in Media Promotion and Advertising

Investigating the Use of Sex in Media Promotion and Advertising has been co-published simultaneously as *Journal of Promotion Management*, Volume 13, Numbers 1/2 2007.

Pre-publication REVIEWS, COMMENTARIES, EVALUATIONS . . .

"Excellent. . . Provides the reader with an overview of this robust area of social science inquiry. Each work draws us in for an ENLIGHTENING AND THOUGHT PROVOKING experience that CLEARLY STIMULATES ADDITIONAL DISCUSSION AND NO DOUBT, DEBATE . . . This collection of excellent works brings us all a step closer in our scientific journey."

Michael S. LaTour, PhD
Professor and Chair
Dept. of Marketing
College of Business
University of Nevada, Las Vegas

More pre-publication
REVIEWS, COMMENTARIES, EVALUATIONS . . .

"AN OUTSTANDING COLLECTION of examinations into the use of sexual content in advertising and media . . . Explores a range of timely issues of import to scholars and media professionals. Among the many strengths of this book are the diverse methodologies and approaches to the study of sex in advertising media. Readers will not only have a better understanding of how sex is used to sell, but also of the effectiveness and potential social consequences of sexual strategies and practices . . . Includes some of the best contemporary thinking on the complex realtionships between sexual imagery, advertising, and consumer responses to the use of sex to sell products, services, and people!"

Dwight E. Brooks, PhD
Professor and Chair
Department of Mass Communications
Jackson State University

"UNIQUE. . . . PROVIDES A GOOD OVERVIEW of the sexual content of global and American mass media editorial, entertainment and commercial messages in a variety of media. . . . Enables mass media effects and advertising scholars to develop a new appreciation of how research streams from several areas combine to provide a more complete picture of mediated sexual content and audience or consumer responses to that content. . . . Useful to teachers of mass media or advertising effects courses. . . . Provides a good introduction to the study of sexual content in different media and advertising using varying methodological approaches. . . . Could be used in a media effects course to show how and why sexual content is used in different media outlets.. . . . Provides examples and operationalizations of the major variables and methods often used in research on sexual content. Consumer and audience responses to sexual content are measured and explained. Thus, students learn to examine sexual content and its effects using a variety of approaches. For example, students learn about content analytic, case study and experimental research on sexual content and responses to that content in one volume."

Jan LeBlanc Wicks, PhD
Professor of Journalism (Advertising)
University of Arkansas (Fayetteville)

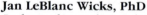

More pre-publication
REVIEWS, COMMENTARIES, EVALUATIONS . . .

"It is about time to talk about sex! As strange as it seems, only a few researches exist on this complex, controversial but appealing topic. This interesting collection of studies FILLS THE GAP AND PROVIDES A RARE INSIGHT INTO SEX IN MAINSTREAM MEDIA. A number of fundamental questions are explored regarding sexual information used as a promotional tool while practical advices for media and advertising practitioners are proposed. The variety of theoretical approaches enables useful references and perspectives as well as a multidisciplinary dialogue of great interest. . . . EXCITING AND ENRICHING READING. . . . INNOVATIVE, INFORMATIVE, CROSS CULTURAL AND CROSS MEDIA, this significant piece of scholarship is A MUST-READ!"

Esther Loubradou, PhD
Advertising, Law and Communication
Social Sciences University
of Toulouse, France;
Vice President
IAA New York Young Professionals

"Dr. Tom Reichert has once again compiled AN EXCELLENT COLLECTION OF STUDIES ON SEX IN THE MEDIA. His look at new and non-traditional media is especially helpful, including an analysis of sexual content on shock-jock radio and in music videos. I WOULD RECOMMEND THIS BOOK FOR STUDENTS OF MASS MEDIA AT ALL LEVELS—from undergraduates in survey courses to graduate students studying media effects."

Jami A. Fullerton, PhD
Associate Professor
Oklahoma State University
Tulsa

Best Business Books®
An Imprint of The Haworth Press

Investigating the Use
of Sex in Media Promotion
and Advertising

Investigating the Use of Sex in Media Promotion and Advertising has been co-published simultaneously as *Journal of Promotion Management*, Volume 13, Numbers 1/2 2007.

Monographic Separates from the *Journal of Promotion Management*™

For additional information on these and other Haworth Press titles, including descriptions, tables of contents, reviews, and prices, use the QuickSearch catalog at http://www.HaworthPress.com.

Investigating the Use of Sex in Media Promotion and Advertising, edited by Tom Reichert, PhD (Vol. 13, No. 1/2, 2007). *An insightful collection of case studies and essays that examines the prevalence and effects of sex in media promotion and advertising.*

Handbook of Product Placement in the Mass Media: New Strategies in Marketing Theory, Practice, Trends, and Ethics, edited by Mary-Lou Galician, EdD (Vol. 10, No. 1/2, 2004). *"COMPREHENSIVE. . . . A fascinating handbook for practitioners and students. . . . The content and presentation are superb." (Dr. Ronald A. Nykiel, CHA, CHE, Conrad N. Hilton Distinguished Chair, University of Houston)*

Investigating the Use of Sex in Media Promotion and Advertising

Tom Reichert, PhD
Editor

Investigating the Use of Sex in Media Promotion and Advertising has been co-published simultaneously as *Journal of Promotion Management*, Volume 13, Numbers 1/2 2007.

Best Business Books®
An Imprint of The Haworth Press, Inc.

www.HaworthPress.com

Published by

Best Business Books®, 10 Alice Street, Binghamton, NY 13904-1580 USA

Best Business Books® is an imprint of The Haworth Press, Inc., 10 Alice Street, Binghamton, NY 13904-1580 USA.

Investigating the Use of Sex in Media Promotion and Advertising has been co-published simultaneously as *Journal of Promotion Management*, Volume 13, Numbers 1/2 2007.

Cover design by Marylouise Doyle

Library of Congress Cataloging-in-Publication Data

Investigating the use of sex in media promotion and advertising / Tom Reichert, editor.
     p. cm.
     "Co-published simultaneously as Journal of Promotion Management, Volume 13, Numbers 1/2 2007."
     Includes bibliographical references and index.
     ISBN 978-0-7890-3728-2 (hbk. : alk. paper) – ISBN 978-0-7890-3729-9 (pbk. : alk. paper)
     1. Sex in advertising. I. Reichert, Tom. II. Journal of promotion management.

HF5827.85.I59 2007
659.1–dc22

           2007026738

The HAWORTH PRESS Inc.
Abstracting, Indexing & Outward Linking
PRINT and ELECTRONIC BOOKS & JOURNALS

This section provides you with a list of major indexing & abstracting services and other tools for bibliographic access. That is to say, each service began covering this periodical during the year noted in the right column. Most Websites which are listed below have indicated that they will either post, disseminate, compile, archive, cite or alert their own Website users with research-based content from this work. (This list is as current as the copyright date of this publication.)

Abstracting, Website/Indexing Coverage . . . . Year When Coverage Began

- **Academic Search Premier (EBSCO)**
  <http://search.ebscohost.com>. 2006

- **Business Source Complete (EBSCO)**
  <http://search.ebscohost.com>. 2006

- **Business Source Premier (EBSCO)**
  <http://search.ebscohost.com>. 2006

- **International Bibliography of the Social Sciences (IBSS)**
  <http://www.ibss.ac.uk>. 2004

- **MasterFILE Premier (EBSCO)**
  <http://search.ebscohost.com>. 2006

- **Professional Development Collection (EBSCO)**
  <http://search.ebscohost.com>. 2006

- *Academic Source Premier (EBSCO)*
  <http://search.ebscohost.com>. 2007

- *Academic Universe (Lexis/Nexis)* <http://www.lexisnexis.com/> . 2005

- *Banking Information Source (ProQuest CSA)*
  <http://www.proquest.com> 2007

(continued)

(continued)

Bibliographic Access

(continued)

- *MediaFinder <http://www.mediafinder.com/>*

- *Ulrich's Periodicals Directory: The Global Source for Periodicals Information Since 1932 <http://www.bowkerlink.com>*

*Exact start date to come.

Special Bibliographic Notes related to special journal issues (separates) and indexing/abstracting:

- indexing/abstracting services in this list will also cover material in any "separate" that is co-published simultaneously with Haworth's special thematic journal issue or DocuSerial. Indexing/abstracting usually covers material at the article/chapter level.
- monographic co-editions are intended for either non-subscribers or libraries which intend to purchase a second copy for their circulating collections.
- monographic co-editions are reported to all jobbers/wholesalers/approval plans. The source journal is listed as the "series" to assist the prevention of duplicate purchasing in the same manner utilized for books-in-series.
- to facilitate user/access services all indexing/abstracting services are encouraged to utilize the co-indexing entry note indicated at the bottom of the first page of each article/chapter/contribution.
- this is intended to assist a library user of any reference tool (whether print, electronic, online, or CD-ROM) to locate the monographic version if the library has purchased this version but not a subscription to the source journal.
- individual articles/chapters in any Haworth publication are also available through the Haworth Document Delivery Service (HDDS).

As part of Haworth's continuing commitment to better serve our library patrons, we are proud to be working with the following electronic services:

AGGREGATOR SERVICES

EBSCOhost

Ingenta

J-Gate

Minerva

OCLC FirstSearch **FirstSearch**

Oxmill

SwetsWise SwetsWise

LINK RESOLVER SERVICES

1Cate (Openly Informatics)

ChemPort (American Chemical Society) **ChemPort·**

CrossRef

Gold Rush (Coalliance) Gold Rush

LinkOut (PubMed) **LinkOut.**
LINKING TO A WORLD OF RESOURCES

LINKplus (Atypon)

LinkSolver (Ovid)

LinkSource with A-to-Z (EBSCO)

Resource Linker (Ulrich)

SerialsSolutions (ProQuest) **SerialsSolutions**

SFX (Ex Libris) $S·F·X$

Sirsi Resolver (SirsiDynix) SirsiDynix

Tour (TDnet)

Vlink (Extensity, formerly Geac) ((extensity))

WebBridge (Innovative Interfaces) WebBridge

Investigating the Use of Sex in Media Promotion and Advertising

CONTENTS

SHOCK JOCKS AND MUSIC VIDEOS

MAGAZINES

ADVERTISING

ABOUT THE EDITOR

Tom Reichert, PhD, is Associate Professor of Advertising at the University of Georgia's Grady College of Journalism and Mass Communication. Dr. Reichert's research focuses on sex in advertising and the media, social marketing, and political campaign communication. His books include *The Erotic History of Advertising*, *Sex in Advertising* (co-edited with Jacqueline Lambiase), and *Sex in Consumer Culture* (also co-edited with Jacqueline Lambiase).

Dr. Reichert is an active member of the American Academy of Advertising, Association for Education in Journalism and Mass Communication, and several other professional organizations. Before entering academia, Reichert sold advertising for *The Orange County Register* in southern California. He also served as deputy press secretary for U.S. Rep. Jim Kolbe's 1994 re-election campaign, and as a researcher for a political consulting firm. Reichert is a member of the editorial review boards of *Journalism Quarterly, Journal of Promotion Management, Journal of Current Issues and Research in Advertising,* and *Sexuality and Culture*. He was on the faculty at the University of Alabama and the University of North Texas, before joining UGA's Grady College in 2004.

Foreword

Sex in media has long been the subject of public dialogue and empirical inquiry. Everyone seems to have an opinion about sex in the media–the citizen on the street, the media pundit, the politician, and, of course, the social scientist. All too often these opinions have little or no scientific grounding; instead, speculation about such things as the prevalence of sex in media content or the effects of sexual stimuli on vulnerable media audiences are voiced based on selective attention to specific media or on limited exposure to the research literature on the content and effects of sexual stimuli in mediated messages. Even when scientific-grounded arguments are offered by the "more informed" among us, argumentation suffers from wide gaps in research-based knowledge on the subject.

The articles in this special volume figuratively-speaking shovel a little more "scientific dirt" into these knowledge gaps, with the end-effect of moving the public dialogue on sex in media a little further along. Authored by recognized experts on the subject, the collection of articles covers a wide "media waterfront" and provides informative and useful empirical evidence on media-conveyed sexual stimuli. For those interested in sex in media, this special volume edited by Tom Reichert, one of mass communication's leading experts on the subject, will be "must reading."

Leonard Reid

[Haworth co-indexing entry note]: "Foreword." Reid, Leonard. Published in *Investigating the Use of Sex in Media Promotion and Advertising* (ed: Tom Reichert), The Haworth Press, Inc., 2007, p. xv. Single or multiple copies of this article are available for a fee from The Haworth Document Delivery Service [1-800-HAWORTH, 9:00 a.m. - 5:00 p.m. (EST). E-mail address: docdelivery@haworthpress.com].

Preface

What do Howard Stern, Robin Meade of *CNN Headline News*, billboards for Hard Rock Hotel and Casino in Las Vegas, *Maxim* magazine covers, music videos, and coverage of the US female Olympic volleyball team have in common? If you guessed "sex," you guessed right. If you guessed that each are discussed and analyzed in this contributed volume, you again guessed correctly.

Yes, sex. It manifests in a variety of ways, but sexual information–that which evokes sexual thoughts, feelings, and responses in viewers–is present in each of these instances though it varies in intensity. For example, Howard Stern's dialogue is sexually gratuitous and explicit whereas Meade and her co-anchors are filmed in a manner that subtly accentuates their physical attractiveness. The authors in this volume are concerned with these forms of sexualized content, as well as the promotional effects of sexual content on audiences.

SEX IN THE MEDIA

It is obvious that sexual content is prevalent in the media. It is also obvious that the prevalence and intensity of sexual content have increased over the years. Less obvious, however, are the effects of the strategic uses of sexual content on viewership and consumption.

Does it work? Is it effective? Will sexual information attract viewers and enhance the viewing experience? Are people more likely to buy an issue of a magazine with a sexy coverperson or a music CD promoted with a sexually-graphic music video? Many individuals, especially those in the media professions, and even those in the academy, assume so. These assumptions may be based on personal experience and obser-

[Haworth co-indexing entry note]: "Preface." Reichert, Tom. Published in *Investigating the Use of Sex in Media Promotion and Advertising* (ed: Tom Reichert), The Haworth Press, Inc., 2007, pp. xvii-xviii. Single or multiple copies of this article are available for a fee from The Haworth Document Delivery Service [1-800-HAWORTH, 9:00 a.m. - 5:00 p.m. (EST). E-mail address: docdelivery@haworthpress.com].

vation, but very limited scholarship apart from advertising research exists to confirm these assumptions.

Mass communication research has been particularly helpful for answering some questions regarding sex. For one, the presence of sex in mainstream media content is well documented. And two, research shows that sex can *indirectly* influence viewers' sexual perceptions, attitudes, and actions. Indeed, media scholars have expertly measured and analyzed the incidence of sexual references and behaviors across media, as well as initiated effects research that examines the influence of sexual information on viewers, especially those who are young and the most vulnerable.

But, again, what are the *intentional* effects of sex on viewers and consumers? Regarding the promotion of media content, only a smattering of studies have addressed this question. More is known about the effects of sexual information when it appears in promotional messages for products (i.e., advertising), but even that knowledge base is small when compared to the volume of research on other emotional appeals such as humor and fear. An obvious opportunity exists for media and promotion scholars to come together–each with their respective theories and methods (e.g., uses-and-gratifications, entertainment theory, attitude-toward-the-ad) to better understand the strategic effects of sex on viewer/consumer response. This volume seeks to serve that purpose by bringing attention to relevant scholarship.

The articles in this special volume offer new directions in the study of sex and media (e.g., sex in the news, shock jocks, magazine covers) and timely findings that provide an indication of the nature, prevalence, and effects of sexual information when used as a promotional tool. I want to personally thank the contributors and reviewers for their insights and hard work. Much appreciation goes to the editors at The Haworth Press, Inc. and Richard Alan Nelson for seeing the value of–and supporting–this collection of research.

Tom Reichert

Introduction

You would think that after so many years of study and experience that all we need to know about sexual appeals in advertising and media would have been discovered by now. But, like much else in life, we still find ourselves learning something new about ourselves and what works to arouse and motivate us.

Sexual and erotic appeals are universal, although the U.S. continues to be the international focus of much spending. However, "despite polls indicating that the public would like to see less sex in advertising, Americans don't mean what they say," notes Tom Reichert. "They continue to respond to the lure of provocative marketing and, most important to business, they buy."

So I've asked Dr. Reichert, an international expert on research about sex and advertising, to serve as editor of this special volume. Tom, who is on the faculty at the University of Georgia and a member of *JPM's* editorial advisory board, is author or editor of several major books on this topic including *The Erotic History of Advertising* (2003), *Sex in Advertising* (2003, with Jacqueline Lambiase), and *Sex in Consumer Culture: The Erotic Content of Media and Marketing* (2006, also with Jacqueline Lambiase).

We'll continue to bring you top scholarship/interesting reading in the future. Please let me know what you think of the job we are doing.

Richard Alan Nelson
Rnelson@lsu.edu

[Haworth co-indexing entry note]: "Introduction." Nelson, Richard Alan. Co-published simultaneously in *Journal of Production Management* (The Haworth Press, Inc.) Vol. 13, No. 1/2, 2007, p. 1 and: *Investigating the Use of Sex in Media Promotion and Advertising* (ed: Tom Reichert), The Haworth Press, Inc., 2007, p. 1. Single or multiple copies of this article are available for a fee from The Haworth Document Delivery Service [1-800-HAWORTH, 9:00 a.m. - 5:00 p.m. (EST). E-mail address: docdelivery@haworthpress.com].

Available online at http://jpm.haworthpress.com
doi: 10.1300/J057v13n01_01

1

OVERVIEW

The Ageless Allure:
Sex, Media, and Marketing

Tom Reichert

SUMMARY. In this introductory article, Reichert argues that greater research attention should be paid to the area of strategic–or *direct*–effects of sexual information in the media. He begins by describing the nature of sexual information and the response it evokes in viewers. More important, Reichert outlines several ways that media organizations and advertisers use sex to promote their content and branded goods with the ultimate goal of enhancing revenue. Last, the author describes how the articles in this contributed volume advance the study of sex and promotion into new and important contexts (e.g., television news, sports coverage, magazine covers, shock-jock programming). doi:10.1300/J057v13n01_02 *[Article copies available for a fee from The Haworth Document Delivery Service: 1-800-HAWORTH.*

Tom Reichert (PhD, University of Arizona) is Associate Professor, Grady College of Journalism and Mass Communication, University of Georgia, Athens, GA 30602 (E-mail: reichert@uga.edu).

[Haworth co-indexing entry note]: "The Ageless Allure: Sex, Media, and Marketing." Reichert, Tom. Co-published simultaneously in *Journal of Production Management* (Best Business Books, an imprint of The Haworth Press, Inc.) Vol. 13, No. 1/2, 2007, pp. 3-11 and: *Investigating the Use of Sex in Media Promotion and Advertising* (ed: Tom Reichert) Best Business Books, an imprint of The Haworth Press, Inc., 2007, pp. 3-11. Single or multiple copies of this article are available for a fee from The Haworth Document Delivery Service [1-800-HAWORTH, 9:00 a.m. - 5:00 p.m. (EST). E-mail address: docdelivery@haworthpress.com].

E-mail address: <docdelivery@haworthpress. com> Website: <http://www. HaworthPress.com> © 2007 by The Haworth Press, Inc. All rights reserved.}

KEYWORDS. Advertising, effects, marketing, media, promotion, theory, sex

INTRODUCTION

The Federal Communications Commission recently fined CBS for airing a graphic scene that depicted a teenage orgy in the crime drama *Without a Trace*. Dolce and Gabanna's spring 2006 campaign featured svelte men in various levels of un-dress gazing longingly at each other's bodies. And, at last count, MSNBC anchor Chris Jansing was tied with CBS's Lara Logan as the "sexiest" female news anchor/reporter ("Sexiest Female News," 2006).

A visitor from just 10 years ago–watching a current television program or flipping through a recent issue of a magazine–is likely to notice these instances of sex-related strategic promotion. That person is also likely to notice that, in general, mediated sexual content in the form of images, frank discussions, and innuendo is more prevalent and more brazen than 10 years ago.

Media research would confirm the visitor's perceptions. As Farrar et al. (2003) reported in the third wave of their prime-time programming analysis, over 71% of programming contained sexual content in a variety of forms. The percentages increase as one moves to cable programming, most noticeably to paid programming. Television is a primary source of entertainment and information for most people, but sex has oozed into other media as the authors in this contributed volume demonstrate.

The purpose of this volume is to bring together several areas of research to better understand how sex is used to sell products; media products as well as branded goods and services. Much media research pertains to the nature and frequency of sexual content in mass media, as well as its *indirect* effects on individuals. On the other hand, much advertising and marketing research has been focused on the *direct* effects of sexual information on consumers, almost exclusively in the context of advertising. Each article uniquely attempts to weave these areas together to better understand why and how sex is used as a strategic promotional tool. To begin, however, it is important to understand the nature of sexual information.

SEEING AND RESPONDING TO SEXUAL INFORMATION

We may know it when we see it, but it is important to be clear about what sexual information is and the reactions it evokes in viewers. Sexual information is present in a variety of forms but it primarily consists of images and words with sexual meaning. In mainstream media, images of physically attractive people who are suggestively dressed, who behave in a sexually-suggestive manner, or who engage in sexual behavior with someone else represent what many people consider instances of sexual content (e.g., Reichert and Ramirez, 2000). In a music video, for instance, a dancer might move his/her hips in a provocative motion, be the object of a voyeur's gaze, passionately kiss the lead singer, and/or be attired in a revealing manner.

What the actors and models say can have sexual meaning as well. Farrar et al. (2003) elaborately recorded comments or "talk" about sexual behavior, sexual desires, sex-related crimes, and technical information about sex. They found that sex "talk" occurs in at least twice as many prime-time programs than instances of sexual behavior.

Therefore, we know that sexual information exists in today's media because of the work of Farrar et al. and many others who have expertly measured and analyzed the incidence of sexual references and behaviors across media (e.g., Greenberg and Busselle, 1996; Lambiase, 2003; Lin, 1998; Pardun, L'Engle, and Brown, 2005). Work in this volume extends the scope of what is known because the authors venture to new contexts. For instance, one article examines the nature and frequency of sexual discussion on shock-jock radio programming. Two articles examine how women are framed in completely different televised contexts: news and sports. Another article describes the sexualized formula for men's magazine covers, which invariably feature images of women as a dominant element. Within the advertising context, one article describes billboards in Las Vegas that offered the not-so-veiled promise of "getting lucky." And another article shows how female nudity in US advertising compares to advertising in other countries. Overall, these articles report the incidence and prevalence of sex in previously under- or unanalyzed contexts. As such, they represent advances into new domains with regard to the nature and prevalence of sex in the media.

How Sex Sells Products and Media

To truly assess the efficacy of sex in promotional contexts, it is important to understand the response it evokes in viewers. Work in sexology, medicine, and social psychology confirms that sexual information elicits what is referred to as a sexual response. According to the Sexual Behavior Sequence model (SBS) developed by Donn Byrne (1982; see also Fisher, 1986), this response can consist of one, some, or all of the following reactions: physiological (e.g., changes in heart rate, pupil dilation, and perspiration), affective (e.g., feelings), cognitive (e.g., sexual thoughts about the stimulus), and imaginative (e.g., imagining oneself in the narrative). Related work confirms that individuals experience these reactions when exposed to sexual information. For example, Lang and others (Lang, Greenwald, Bradley, and Hamm, 1993; LaTour, 1990) have demonstrated that sexual images evoke emotional responses generally characterized by positively-valenced arousal. In other words, viewers are–all things being equal–favorably energized by sexual information.

Obviously, there are many contextual factors such as prevailing tone, explicitness, tastefulness, and relevance that moderate reactions to sexual information. In addition, individual differences such as gender, age, religiosity, subculture, and personality (e.g., erotophobia, sex guilt, and sexual schema; e.g., Fisher, Byrne, White, and Kelley, 1988) play a role as well. If we consider the nature of the sexual response, and these moderating variables, the implications are obvious for the strategic uses of sex in media promotion and advertising.

Gaining Attention. From advertising research, it is clear that sex elicits attention. Research reliably demonstrates that sexual information, primarily because of its emotional nature, is able to pierce viewers' perceptional fields so that the message gets noticed (Severn, Belch, and Belch, 1990; Reichert, Heckler, and Jackson, 2001). When a commercial is surrounded by 17 minutes of competing commercials in a normal hour of prime-time programming–or 100 other ads in a magazine–standing apart from the field offers an advantage. The same is true for media. As busy consumers scan the newsstand while impatiently waiting for a train, magazine covers dominated by sexual information get noticed. As viewers flip channels, a sexually-laden scene (or close-ups of bikini-clad female Olympians) also get noticed. The same is true for radio and other forms of media. In sum, sex has the ability to attract and maintain the attention of audiences, which can increase ratings and circulation with the ultimate result of generating greater revenue for the organization.

Appealing to Needs and Wants. Aside from simply being used to generate attention, promoters use sex to appeal to viewers' interests. In television, for instance, research has shown that promotional announcements (i.e., promos) are apt to feature sexual scenes (Walker, 2000), even if those scenes represent a small portion of the program. In essence, promo creators imply to viewers: "If you want to see more of this, and we think you do, tune in to the program."

Similarly, it should not be forgotten that individuals seek out–and are willing to pay for–sexual content in mainstream media. Each month, for instance, over 2.5 million people pay for a copy of *Maxim*, either through a subscription or a single-copy purchase. Analyses have shown that there is little else in *Maxim*–and its "Playboy-lite" brethren *Stuff* and *FHM*–than "photo-essays" of up-and-coming panty-clad starlets and sex tips (Krassas, Blauwkamp, and Wesselink, 2003; Taylor, 2005). As Lawrence Soley points out in his analysis of shock-jock radio, Howard Stern's morning show is very popular among 18-34-year-old males. These listeners are seeking out and enjoying shock-jock entertainment that often is very crude, and, as Soley describes in his report, very sexual. As a result, Infinity Broadcasting was able to charge premium rates to advertisers wanting to reach that audience.

Because viewers, listeners, and readers desire exposure to sexual information because of its hedonic value, uses-and-gratifications approaches and entertainment theory can help to explain how and why psychological and physiological needs and wants translate into viewer choices (Rubin, 1994; Zillmann and Bryant, 1994). In a related sense, people develop and maintain parasocial relationships with media personalities. For example, viewers develop crushes on attractive news anchors and tune in regularly to watch them. In fact, viewers may engage in fantasy scenarios (i.e., imaginative responses) with the sexually attractive reporter, celebrity, or coverperson. As a promotional byproduct, these pleasurable experiences may result in increased ratings because viewers tune in to see their mediated "significant" others.

A similar principle is at work in advertising. Working with Jacqueline Lambiase, we discovered that sex is often used in advertising as a brand benefit as opposed to a simple attention-getting device (Lambiase and Reichert, 2006; Reichert and Lambiase, 2003). Common themes include: If you buy and use the product, you'll be more sexually attractive, have more sex, have better sex, or just feel sexier for your own sake. Consumers looking for these outcomes will be especially apt to notice, and perhaps respond to, sex-related appeals.

Enhancing the Association. Last, sexual information in ads–as long as it is not overly gratuitous or sexist–can evoke an emotional response that translates into favorable attitudes toward the ad and the brand.

LaTour (1990), for instance, reported that arousal generated by sexual images was a key determinant in participant responses to the ad and the featured product. Similarly, there is evidence that sexual content in music videos can influence the favorability of the music (Zillmann and Mundorf, 1987). In his report, R. Glenn Cummins describes this work and the mechanism behind it (e.g., excitation transfer). If this transference can occur for products and music, it is certainly likely to occur for other forms of media content.

In sum, sex can influence viewers, listeners, and consumers in obvious and not so obvious ways. There is little doubt given the prevalence of sexual content in mainstream media that advertisers and media organizations are using it for more than a simple plot device. The articles in this volume serve to advance what is known about sex in the media and to stimulate needed research in that direction. Perhaps, instead of just noticing sexual content in tomorrow's media, a visitor 10 years from now also will understand–and be able to be aware of–the promotional uses of sex in the media.

THE ARTICLES

The researchers' whose reports that appear in this volume are primarily concerned with the nature and effects of sex when it is used to attract audiences to media content. Additionally, two articles investigate the presence of nudity and highly suggestive content in advertising.

Several studies examine the nature of sexual information when it is used to promote television programming. To begin, Michael Nitz and his coauthors examine the prevalence of sexuality among anchors on cable news programs. Beyond physical attractiveness, they found that female newscasters often are dressed provocatively and filmed in a manner that accentuates their physical features. Similarly, Kimberly L. Bissell and Andrea M. Duke report that network cameras lingered on the bikini-clad bodies of US female volleyball players in the 2004 Olympics. Moving from content to effects, Yinjiao Ye and Shuhua Zhou report the results of their promotional announcement experiment. The investigation is one of a handful of studies that have examined the effects on sex on viewership. They found that sex enhances evaluation of the program and increases viewing intentions, thereby supporting the supposition that sex not only attracts viewers, but that it enhances how the program is perceived.

Shock jocks are popular for their use of attention-getting humor and discussions of sexual topics, but there has been very little investigation into the "shock jock" phenomenon. Lawrence Soley provides a much-needed history of shock-jock radio and the personalities that have shaped it. Soley also provides the first known content analysis of sexual content in shock-jock programming by comparing the *Howard Stern* and *Bob and Tom* shows. Moving from "talk" to music, R. Glenn Cummins provides a review of the sex in music video literature as it relates to music promotion. He convincingly argues that music videos are an essential piece of the music promotion puzzle, and that sex is a prominent promotional feature. As important, he reviews studies that use Excitation Transfer Theory to explain how sexual content influences perceptions of music.

Switching modalities, Jacqueline Lambiase provides an interesting case analysis of *Maxim* magazine covers and the adoption of its successful cover formula by competing men's titles such as *Details*, *GQ*, and *Esquire*. Working with Shuhua Zhou, I report the findings of an investigation that actually tested the influence of sexual information on magazine purchase intention. Specifically, we found that young adults were more likely to both find a magazine interesting and buy it if the cover featured a sexually attractive person.

The two remaining articles provide new insights into the use of sex when it is used to promote products and services. For example, Hye-Jin Paek and Michelle R. Nelson provide a content analysis of female nudity in advertising across five countries. Not only do the authors go beyond much cross-cultural research by comparing several countries, they also analyze television commercials and magazines, and include product congruence as a factor. Last, Erika Engstrom provides an interesting case analysis of the Hard Rock casino's attempt to brand itself as a sexual playground. Specifically, she describes how casino executives used billboard advertising to position the casino as a destination congruent with Las Vegas's recent ad campaign: "What happens here, stays here." In this instance, however, fairly explicit billboards were used to "arouse" the interest of patrons to the chagrin of local citizens.

REFERENCES

Brown, J. D., Steele, J. R., and Walsh-Childers, K. (eds.), (2002). *Sexual Teens, Sexual Media: Investigating Media's Influence on Adolescent Sexuality*. Mahwah, NJ: Lawrence Erlbaum Associates.

Byrne, D. (1982). Predicting human sexual behavior. In A. G. Kraut (ed.), *The G. Stanley Hall Lecture Series, Vol. 2* (pp. 207-254). Washington, DC: American Psychological Association.

Davies, J. (2003, August). Sexual content in promotional ads: Contributions of visual aspects to exposure. Paper presented at the annual meeting of the Association for Education in Journalism and Mass Communication, Kansas City, MO.

Farrar, K., Kunkel, D., Biely, E., Eyal, K., and Donnerstein, E. (2003). Sexual messages during prime-time programming. *Sexuality and Culture, 7*(3), 7-37.

Fisher, W. A. (1986). A psychological approach to human sexuality: The sexual behavior sequence. In D. Byrne and K. Kelley (eds.), *Alternative Approaches to the Study of Sexual Behavior* (pp. 131-171). Hillsdale, NJ: Lawrence Erlbaum Associates.

Fisher, W. A., Bryne, D., White, L. A., and Kelley, K. (1988). Erotophobia-Erotophilia as a dimension of personality. *Journal of Sex Research, 25*(1), 123-151.

Greenberg, B. S., and Busselle, R. W. (1996). Soap operas and sexual activity: A decade later. *Journal of Communication, 46*(4), 153-160.

Huston, A. C., Wartella, E., and Donnerstein, E. (1998). Measuring the effects of sexual content in the media: A report to the Kaiser Family Foundation (No. 1389). Menlo Park, CA: Kaiser Family Foundation.

Krassas, N. R., Blauwkamp, J. M., and Wesselink, P. (2003). "Master your Johnson": Sexual rhetoric in *Maxim* and *Stuff* magazines. *Sexuality and Culture, 7*(3), 98-119.

Lambiase, J. (2003). Sex online and in internet advertising. In T. Reichert and J. Lambiase (eds.), *Sex in Advertising: Perspectives on the Erotic Appeal* (pp. 247-269). Mahwah, NJ: Lawrence Erlbaum Associates.

Lambiase, J., and Reichert, T. (2003). Promises, promises: Exploring erotic rhetoric in sexually oriented advertising. In L. Scott and R. Batra (eds.), *Persuasive Imagery: A Consumer Perspective* (pp. 247-266) Mahwah, NJ: Lawrence Erlbaum Associates.

Lambiase, J., and Reichert, T. (2006). Sex and the marketing of contemporary consumer magazines: How men's magazines sexualized their covers to compete with *Maxim*. In T. Reichert and J. Lambiase (eds.), *Sex in Consumer Culture: The Erotic Content of Media and Marketing* (pp. 67-86). Mahwah, NJ: Lawrence Erlbaum Associates.

Lang, P., Greenwald, M., Bradley, M., and Hamm, A. (1993). Looking at pictures: Evaluative, facial, visceral, and behavioral responses. *Psychophysiology, 30*(3), 261-274.

LaTour, M., (1990). Female nudity in print advertising: An analysis of gender differences in arousal and ad response. *Psychology and Marketing, 7*(1), 65-81.

Lin, C. A. (1998). Uses of sexual appeals in prime-time television commercials. *Sex Roles, 38*(5/6), 461-475.

Pardun, C. J., L'Engle, K. L., and Brown, J. D. (2005). Linking exposure to outcomes: Early adolescents' consumption of sexual content in six media. *Mass Communication and Society, 8*(2), 75-91.

Reichert, T., Heckler, S. E., and Jackson, S. (2001). The effects of sexual social marketing appeals on cognitive processing and persuasion. *Journal of Advertising, 30*(1), 13-27.

Reichert, T., and Lambiase, J. (2003). How to get "kissably close": Examining how advertisers appeal to consumers' sexual needs and desires. *Sexuality & Culture, 7*(3), 120-136.

Reichert, T., and Ramirez, A. (2000). Defining sexually oriented appeals in advertising: A grounded theory investigation. In S. J. Hoch and R. J. Meyer (eds.), *Advances in Consumer Research, Vol. 27* (pp. 267-273). Provo, UT: Association for Consumer Research.

Rubin, A. (1994). Media uses and effects: A uses-and-gratifications perspective. In D. Zillmann and J. Bryant (eds.), *Media Effects* (pp. 417-436). Hillsdale, NJ: Lawrence Erlbaum Associates.

Sexiest Female News Reporters and Anchors (2006). *Wanderlist.* Retrieved April 24, 2006 from http://www.wanderlist.com/lists/lists.cgi?listid = 1117.

Taylor, L. D. (2005). All for him: Articles about sex in American lad magazines. *Sex Roles, 52*(3/4), 153-163.

Walker, J. R. (2000). Sex and violence in program promotion. In S. T. Eastman (ed.), *Research in Media Promotion* (pp. 101-126). Mahwah, NJ: Lawrence Erlbaum Associates.

Ward, L. M. (2002). Does television exposure affect emerging adults' attitudes and assumptions about sexual relationships? Correlational and experimental confirmation. *Journal of Youth and Adolescence, 31*(1), 1-15.

Williams, G. A. (1989). Enticing viewers: Sex and violence in *TV Guide* program advertisements. *Journalism Quarterly, 66*(4), 970-973.

Zillmann, D., and Bryant, J. (1994). Entertainment as media effect. In D. Zillmann and J. Bryant (eds.), *Media Effects* (pp. 437-461). Hillsdale, NJ: Lawrence Erlbaum Associates.

Zillmann, D. and Mundorf, N. (1987). Image effects in the appreciation of video rock. *Communication Research, 14*(3), 316-334.

doi:10.1300/J057v13n01_02

TELEVISION PROGRAMMING

All the News That's Fit to See?
The Sexualization
of Television News Journalists
as a Promotional Strategy

Michael Nitz
Tom Reichert
Adonica Schultz Aune
André Vander Velde

Michael Nitz (PhD, University of Arizona) is Associate Professor, Department of Communication, Augustana College, Sioux Falls, SD 57197 (E-mail: Michael.nitz@ augie.edu); Tom Reichert (PhD, University of Arizona) is Associate Professor, Grady College of Journalism and Mass Communication, University of Georgia, Athens, GA 30602 (E-mail: reichert@uga.edu). Adonica Schultz Aune (PhD, University of North Dakota) teaches for Continuing Education and the School of Communication, University of North Dakota, Grand Forks, ND 58202-7169 (E-mail: adonica.schultz@und. edu). André Vander Velde is an Undergraduate Student, Department of Communication, Augustana College, Sioux Falls, SD 57197 (E-mail: grapplerdre@hotmail.com).

The authors appreciate the assistance of Heather Berglove and Kelly Rolland.

[Haworth co-indexing entry note]: "All the News That's Fit to See? The Sexualization of Television News Journalists as a Promotional Strategy." Nitz et al. Co-published simultaneously in *Journal of Promotion Management* (Best Business Books, an imprint of The Haworth Press, Inc.) Vol. 13, No. 1/2, 2007, pp. 13-33; and: *Investigating the Use of Sex in Media Promotion and Advertising* (ed: Tom Reichert) Best Business Books, an imprint of The Haworth Press, Inc., 2007, pp. 13-33. Single or multiple copies of this article are available for a fee from The Haworth Document Delivery Service [1-800-HAWORTH, 9:00 a.m. - 5:00 p.m. (EST). E-mail address: docdelivery@haworthpress.com].

Available online at http://jpm.haworthpress.com
doi:10.1300/J057v13n01_03

SUMMARY. This formative investigation employed framing theory to content analyze the nature and extent of sexually appealing newscasters primarily on cable news programs. Overall, 62% of segments contained journalists with "high" sex appeal, and these were predominately female. Specifically, these journalists were physically attractive, suggestively dressed (e.g., open blouses, tight-fitting skirts), and filmed in ways that accentuated these features. Female newscasters on Univision's *Primer Impacto*, who double as models on its website, always exhibited "high" sex appeal compared to 93% of newscasters on MSNBC, 49% on Fox News, and 39% on CNN. doi:10.1300/J057v13n01_03 *[Article copies available for a fee from The Haworth Document Delivery Service: 1-800-HAWORTH. E-mail address: <docdelivery@haworthpress.com> Website: <http://www.HaworthPress.com> © 2007 by The Haworth Press, Inc. All rights reserved.]*

KEYWORDS. Content analysis, framing, journalist, news, newscaster, promotion, sex, television

INTRODUCTION

In 1989, political consultant and communication executive, Roger Ailes, was asked to explain the popularity of *The Wheel of Fortune*. "Vanna White," he answered, adding that viewers love to look at her while their minds solve word puzzles (LeBoutillier, 2002). Nine years later, while heading Fox News and losing ratings to CNN, Ailes hired attractive female newscasters such as Brigitte Quinn, Linda Vester, and Laurie Dhue. He also had the set altered so that viewers could see the journalists sitting in their chairs. According to LeBoutillier (2002), viewers saw plenty of legs and the program's ratings increased dramatically, thus demonstrating the "Vanna White-ing" of the news.

Fox is not alone, however. CNN hired attractive Fox News reporter Paula Zahn, and created controversy by promoting her as "a little bit sexy." CNN promptly pulled the promo amid complaints, but its actions reveal the network's strategy of using Zahn's looks to attract audiences (male in this case). Other news providers have followed suit, most notably *Primer Impacto*, a news program on Univision, with attractive newscasters and top ratings among 18-34-year-olds in New York City. Even local news is getting in on the act as a nude Ohio reporter delivered a story about an artist (LeBoutillier, 2002).

Despite the obvious presence of attractive newscasters, no systematic attempt has been made to determine the nature and extent of this phenomenon. This formative study seeks to address this inadequacy by first considering entertainment and personalization as a form of news promotion with particular focus on female newscasters, followed by an overview of framing theory and work on sexual images in the media as theoretical tools to explain the processes behind the promotion of news images. Second, the content analysis, relevant findings, and their implications for news and viewers are discussed.

LITERATURE REVIEW

The New News

One facet of *new* news identified in recent research is the increased personalization within traditional newscasts (Barney, 2001; Hollander, 1994; Johnson, 2004; Rosen and Taylor, 1992; Zelizer, 2001). Hollihan (2001), for instance, cites the increasing use of emotionally-intense narrative styles that emphasize images at the expense of official commentary and fact-based objectivism. The increased emphasis on entertainment, as some would argue, is the result of the desire to secure greater advertising revenue by attracting larger audiences (Eveland, 2002; Gans, 1979; Gorman and McLean, 2003; Powers, 1977; Sayre and King, 2003; Turow, 1978; Zillmann, 2000). As a result, the entertainment frame (e.g., titillating viewers) has led to greater an emphasis on marketing rather than journalistic values.

The pursuit of commercial values leads to an emphasis on individual preferences at the expense of substantive discourse (Redal, 1995). According to Cohen (2002), the selection of TV news personalities is an outcome of increased individualism. News managers, especially at the local level, package and promote their journalists (both anchors and reporters) as personalities with star power (Powers, 1977). Anchors adopt a conversational style by smiling and laughing, and engaging in banter with co-anchors or reporters. Also, the journalists are emphasized in promos and portrayed as attractive, smart, and insightful.

More recently, the packaging of news personalities appears to emphasize female correspondents. Not only have news consultants set the agenda for what reporters (at local and national levels) should cover (e.g., crime), but also what they should look like as well-young, attractive, pleasant, and usually white (Campbell, 1998, p. 404). As an example, Juliet Huddy, an anchor/reporter for the Fox News Channel, was recently pictured on a magazine cover (which was prominently displayed by her and her co-anchors) as the "Sexiest Woman in News." Gunter (2001) notes that women in the media are typically cast as decoration, or, in Huddy's case, as sex symbols.

Female Newscasters. As the Huddy example demonstrates, sexuality has made its way into the newsroom (Kieran, 1997). Sexual content is pervasive in most mainstream media, whether it be in television programs (Farrar et al., 2003; Greenberg and Hofschire, 2000), in music videos (Andsager, 2006), in or on magazines (Lambiase and Reichert, 2006; Taylor, 2005), and in advertising (Lin, 1998; Ramirez, 2006; Reichert and Carpenter, 2004). The "sexual" content in these instances predominately consists of images of women. Similarly, female journalists have come to represent sexuality in market-driven journalism (Carter, Brantson, and Allan, 2002).

According to Holland (2002), in the 1970s feminization began its transition to sexualization as the press attempted to lure the public with entertainment. Interestingly, it was media mogul Rupert Murdoch, with his purchase of *The Sun* in 1969, that heralded the invasion of breasts into news columns and entertainment pages. As could be expected, male-oriented perspectives dominated and the female body became more of a commodity and spectacle. With regard to television news, Buarque (2003) points to the promotion of beauty and strict body constructions as requirements for female journalists. Similarly, Shiflett (2001) asserts that a pretty face is more of a hiring credential than a graduate degree from Columbia Journalism School. Indeed, research has found that, compared to men, female newscasters are more likely to present trivial information and are more likely to have their bodies appear on screen (Capecchi and Demaria, 2001; Rakow and Kranich, 1991). As a result, female correspondents are concerned about aging in an environment where "a woman's appearance might mean the difference between getting an assignment or even keeping her job" (Foote, 1992, p. 40). The sexualization of female newscasters represents the increase of infotainment and aesthetics in news culture (Cupchik and Kemp, 2000; Weaver, 2000).

Framing Theory and Sex Appeal

Framing theory offers a useful and distinctive theoretical approach for analyzing news and its content (Kim, Scheufele, and Shanahan, 2002; Scheufele, 1999). The media can impact the construction of social reality by actively setting and creating frames of reference for the audience (Newhagen, 2002). Frames are organizing principles that are socially shared and persist over time, and work symbolically to meaningfully structure the social world (Reese, 2001, p. 11). Framing is a way of creating meaning by indicating which facts are important and implying a connection among those facts (Entman, 1993; Rendahl, 1995). In addition, news framing is a form of packaging that consists of various narrative devices and visual images (D'Angelo, 2002; McLeod, Kosicki, and McLeod, 2002).

Iyengar's (1991) approach to framing suggests that news reports may be usefully analyzed by their thematic or episodic content. Thematic news places events in a broader context of related events. Episodic framing, on the other hand, merely provides snapshots of an issue, with any explanation grounded in a sensational or emotional appeal. Research shows that episodic framing trivializes public discourse, discourages citizens from seeing links among issues, and leads to the exclusion of many important issues (Iyengar, 1991; Nitz and West, 2004). Graber (1994) suggests that news framing is intentionally dramatic and highlights entertainment features that focus on image over issues. The personalization and star-power of newscasters, as previously described, contribute to the emphasis on image frames and the entertainment value of news. As such, the focus of the present research is not the content of the news story per se, but on the messengers who introduce, report, and conclude the story. Specifically, we consider these messengers are packaged and presented with regard to their sex appeal.

Sexual Appeal. When considering the newscasters' sexual appeal, it is important to note that the present study is not concerned with extreme or even explicit forms of sexual content. Rather, the focus is on the framing of the newscaster with regard to his/her attire, physical attractiveness, and behavior, among other factors. Although each of these ingredients will be assessed separately, they often occur in tandem (Reichert and Ramirez, 2000). Regarding attire, the style and amount of clothing can contribute to sexual interpretations (e.g., LaTour, 1990). In content analyses of sex in popular media, clothing is generally categorized as ranging from demure (nonsexual) to suggestive (tight-fitting and revealing attire) to partial and full nudity (Farrar et al., 20003; Greenberg et al., 1980; Soley and Reid, 1988).

Physical attractiveness also is fundamentally linked to interpersonal attraction and sexual interpretations. For example, numerous studies document the role between physical beauty and initial attraction (Green, Buchanan, and Murr, 1984; Sprecher, 1989), liking (Byrne, London, and Reeves, 1968), dating (Walster, Aronson, Abrahams, and Rottman,

1966), and sexual interest (Cunningham, 1986). Although it is important to distinguish between people who are simply pleasing in appearance and those who are sexually attractive (Joseph, 1982), physical attractiveness is identified by viewers as a form of sexual content (Reichert and Ramirez, 2000). Behavior also evokes sexual responses. Media studies typically assess interpersonal behavior (e.g., kissing, intercourse), but subtle forms of behavior such as posing and facial expressions can contribute to sexual meaning as well (e.g., gazing, flirtatious expressions; Simpson, Gangestad, and Nations, 1996).

Sexually appealing newscasters are especially relevant when context and audience considerations are taken into account. For instance, hedonic responses are likely to occur when attractive females report to male audiences viewing financial news (Bloomberg, CNBC) and sports (ESPN). Skerski (2006) argues that female sports reporters in male-dominated athletics (NFL, MLB) often serve as little more than "cheerleaders with microphones." Women such as Jillian Barberie, Suzy Kolber, and Lisa Guerrero may know their sports knowledge, but are hired because of their appeal to a predominately male audience. This also appears to be the case in newsrooms as viewers focus their attention on talking heads– and bodies.

Camera Angle/Visual Presentation. Another factor that can contribute to sexual interpretation is how the object/person is filmed (Reichert and Ramirez, 2000). Producers have the potential to manipulate meaning by altering a variety of variables such as pacing, camera angles, music, and outtakes. For example, camera-angle variation can alter perceptions of credibility (Messaris, 1994), and research confirms that "intriguing" visual content maintains audience attention (Kraft, 1987; Mandell and Shaw, 1973; McCain, Chilberg, and Wakshlag, 1977; Olds and Seitz, 1995; Tiemens, 1970). Such elements have been analyzed in framing investigations on females in the news. For example, Archer, Irianti, Kimes, and Barrios (1983) found that men and women are framed differently during newscasts. Generally, the camera emphasizes men's faces while most camera shots tend to emphasize women's bodies. Similarly, Copeland (1989) found that men were framed with close-ups while women where shot in medium- to full-body positions. Last, Capecchi and Demaria (2001) reported that camera shots were more likely to pan over female newscasters and interviewees' bodies.

RESEARCH QUESTIONS/HYPOTHESES

This investigation is concerned with how television journalists, especially females, are framed on television news programs. More specifically, this paper examines the nature of sexualization as a particular aspect of framing. Because of the explorative nature of the present study, the following research questions and hypothesis are offered:

> *RQ1:* What is the nature and extent of sexualization as a frame in the presentation of journalists on television news programs (i.e., sexual appeal, clothing/dress, physical attractiveness, sexual behavior, referents, and facilitating factors)?
> *RQ2:* What stories are covered when female journalists are presented in a sexualized manner?
> *H1:* Overall, female journalists are more likely to be sexualized on news programs than are male journalists.

METHOD

Sample

Given the decline of traditional evening newscasts, this investigation assessed the presence and nature of sexualization in news programs. Research assistants recorded a convenience sample of segments from news programs airing during a two-week period in the fall of 2004 on CNN, Fox News, MSNBC, Univision's *Primer Impacto*, and an NBC network affiliate in Fargo, North Dakota. Segments were defined as content occurring between commercial breaks. Overall, 306 segments were coded ($N = 306$): CNN ($n = 84$), Fox News ($n = 84$), NBC affiliate ($n = 76$), Univision ($n = 35$), and MSNBC ($n = 27$).

Segments aired from morning to prime time, with most occurring during early-morning (44%). Evening or prime-time segments comprised 32%, and the remaining segments aired during late-morning (4%), noon or early-afternoon (11%), and late-afternoon (9%). Regarding types of programs, morning shows represented 33% of the sample, followed by interview-style programs (25%). Special reports or updates (i.e., breaking news) represented 20%, followed by traditional news programs (e.g., anchors in a studio reading the news) with 15%, and talk shows (e.g., Fox's *Dayside*) with 8%.

A wide range of news topics was covered in the sample. For instance, "other" was the largest category with 27%. Examples of stories in this area ranged from controversy over a Victoria's Secret ad to new electronic gadgets. The war in Iraq (17%), politics (13%), and the economy (10%) were big news items. Other domestic stories (e.g., agriculture, health care) were 12% of the sample, and a variety of other stories from sports (3%), war on terror (7%), foreign affairs (5%), and Hollywood/celebrity (6%) completed the sample. Regarding newscasters, only the most predominate newscaster was coded per segment. Demographically, the journalists were female (73%), and judged to be "adult" (73%; 31-50 years old). Young adults (under 30) represented 23% of the sample, and 5% of journalists where judged to be over 50 years old (mature adults).

Variables

The variables coded in this study were adapted from coding schemes utilized or described in related research (Farrar et al., 2003; Lin, 1998; Nitz, Cypher, Reichert, and Mueller, 2003; Olds and Seitz, 1995; Reichert, 2003; Soley and Reid, 1988). The components of the "sexualization" framing included: sex appeal, nudity/dress, physical attractiveness, sexual behavior, sexual referents, and facilitating factors (e.g., camera angles). Unless noted otherwise, each variable was measured on three ordinal levels of sexual content: low, medium, and high.

The overall "sex appeal" of the journalist was coded on a gestalt level that included several variables (e.g., clothing, physical attractiveness, demeanor, and overall appeal). "Nudity/dress" was represented in three levels: demure dress (typical business attire), suggestive dress (open blouses and shirts, miniskirts, tight clothing accentuating the figure, evening gowns, muscle shirts, hiked skirts), and partially clad dress (bathing suits, close-ups where shoulders are bare, photos or illustrations of legs including thighs but no clothing, men with no shirt). "Physical attractiveness" was coded on a gestalt level that included an overall assessment of the journalist's physical beauty (e.g., facial features, complexion, hair, and physique).

The sexual nature of journalists' nonverbal and verbal communication also was assessed. Sexual behavior was represented nonverbally and included the degree of suggestive/flirtatious individual and interpersonal behavior such as eye contact, posturing, and movement. Verbal communication was captured by assessing "sexual referents" (allusions to objects/events that have sexual meaning by use of innuendo and entendre). In addition, the sexual nature of the banter or crosstalk between journalists was coded, as was the seriousness of such banter (i.e., serious, not serious, or mixed). Facilitating factors (i.e., production elements that enhance or contribute to sexual meaning such as camera angles) were encapsulated into a gestalt item that assessed whether the following contributed to presence of sexual content: setting, music, lighting, design elements, camera shots, and editing; consistent with the argument that such elements comprise a package and cannot be analyzed separately (McLeod et al., 2003; Olds and Seitz, 1995). Descriptions were entered on the coding sheet if this variable was coded as "high."

Regarding coding, both female and male students were trained on the coding categories. Since none of the coders was fluent in Spanish, only the visual content of Univision segments was analyzed. Owing to coder error and technical malfunctions, some segments were not codable. To determine reliability, two coders independently coded a random sample of approximately 10% of the total instances. Intercoder agreement was acceptable with an agreement rate of 76% across all coding categories, and a Cohen's kappa of .66.

RESULTS

The first research question (RQ1) sought to determine the nature and extent of sexualization as a frame in the presentation of journalists on television news programs. To begin, over 62% of segments contained journalists with a "high" degree of sex appeal, with 38% representing moderate or "low" sex appeal (see Table 1). In many instances with female journalists, hairstyles and cosmetics contributed to a sensual image that was emphasized with fishnet stockings, slit miniskirts, and revealing blouses. The journalists' physical features were prominently displayed as cameras zoomed in on legs, faces, and in some cases, cleavages and backsides. Considering a composite of the contributing factors, most news segments contained images of sexually appealing journalists.

Focusing more specifically on clothing/dress, 46% of all journalists were dressed demurely compared to 54% who wore suggestive clothing or were partially clad. In some instances, the hems of female journalists' mini-skirts would rise as they shifted in their chairs or crossed their legs. Tight dresses that accentuated the journalists' figures were evident as were off-camera photos in evening gowns with plunging necklines. In

TABLE 1. Overall Sex Appeal of Television Journalists by Network (in Percent of Stories)

	Degree of Sex Appeal		
Network	High	Medium	Low
Overall	62	27	11
CNN	39	35	26
FOX	49	37	14
Local NBC affiliate	72	26	2
MSNBC	93	7	-
Primer Impacto	100	-	-

Note. Overall (*N*=306): *CNN* (*n*=84), *FOX*(*n*=84), Local (*n*=76), *MSNBC* (*n*=27), *Primer Impacto* (*n*=35).

TABLE 2. Degree of Overall Sexualization Variables (in Percent)

	Degree of Sex Appeal		
Sex Variables	High	Medium	Low
Physical Attractiveness	70	24	6
Clothing/Dress*	6	48	46
Sexual Behavior	20	33	47
Sexual Referents	11	13	76
Facilitating Factors	46	8	46
Crosstalk/Banter	24	32	44

Note. *N*=306.

* Clothing/dress was coded as either partially-clad (high), suggestive (medium), or demure (low).

addition, physical attractiveness was predominantly featured as 70% of journalists were highly attractive, with 30% of journalists coded as moderate to low on attractiveness. All the sampled networks featured highly attractive journalists, often in multi-anchor combinations.

Often clothing became more revealing if journalists displayed sexual behavior. Journalists were rated as exhibiting a high degree of sexual behavior in 20% of segments compared to 80% of moderate to low degrees of such behavior. Typical sexual behavior included outdoor segments where journalists engaged in flirtatious, interpersonal interactions such as one scene from *Fox & Friends* where Juliet Huddy sat on a bed in a camper with her two male co-hosts. Other activities included belly dancing, ballroom dancing, arm touches, and one scene where a female anchor on *Fox and Friends* was dunked in a dunk-tank wearing a spaghetti-strap mini-dress.

The incidence of sexual referents, innuendo, and entendre was low (11%). Occasionally, a female journalist was referred by to by a male counterpart as "hot." In one instance, Page Hopkins teased Juliet Huddy for wanting to be backstage with a male celebrity. Finally, assessment of facilitation factors (e.g., setting, camera angles) revealed an interesting finding: Overall, 46% of segments were rated as highly present with 56% exhibiting a moderate to low presence. In many instances, it appeared as if journalists, especially females, were posing for the camera. In news promos, often aired during a news program, for instance, female journalists were shown walking on stage in a mini-skirt or similarly revealing outfit. In addition, cameras would shoot from many angles seemingly to display a journalist's physical features. Also, sets were designed so that female anchors were inclined sit on a desk or to lean back in a chair or couch. Regardless of the network, facilitation factors were used to display female journalists' physiques.

The second question (RQ2) sought to determine the types of stories covered when journalists were presented in a sexualized manner. The intent was to observe whether sexualization was limited to "fluff" stories or whether it extended to serious topics. Overall, there was difference in story type. For example, the percentage of story types in the "high" sexual appeal condition approximated the distribution of stories previously described: 12% politics, 12% Iraq, 11% economy, and 6% war on terror. Again, sexualization was present in all types of news, regardless of the topic's seriousness.

Hypothesis: Female versus Male Portrayal

The hypothesis (H1) posited that female journalists would be depicted in a more sexualized manner than male journalists. Overall, this prediction was confirmed. With regard to sex appeal, 80% of females appearing in news segments were depicted as "high," compared to only 13% of males. Of all stories with journalists high in sexual appeal, 94% were women and 6% were men. Regarding dress/clothing, female journalists were depicted wearing suggestive clothing in 64% of all segments in which they appeared, and 8% were partially clad. Miniskirts were omnipresent, and photos would show the on-air personalities in evening gowns at social events. Blouses were open, particularly on Univision and Fox News. Coders observed that many female reporters on Fox News would wear a top (clearly visible under open jacket) that resembled a camisole. MSNBC's reporters could be seen in some segments wearing tight-fitting T-shirts and jeans. Partially clad female journalists included Fox News' Juliet Huddy in a bikini. Univision would show close-ups of their journalists' bare shoulders at social events.

Regarding physical attractiveness, cross tabulations indicated that in stories with journalists "high" in physical attractiveness, 93% were women and 7% were men. Overall, 88% of females appearing in news segments were rated as "high" in physical attractiveness compared to 12% of males who were similarly rated. In stories with journalists exhibiting "high" degrees of sexual behavior, 93% were females and 7% were males. Overall, 25% of females appearing in news segments engaged in sexual behavior, while only 5% of men engaged in such behavior.

Facilitation factors mainly emphasized female journalists' bodies and physical appearance. Of all stories that were coded as "high" for facilitating factors ($n = 140$), for example, 98.5% were of female newscasters. As previously noted, many stories utilized camera angles, studio settings, and other editing features to focus on female journalists' bodies and physical appearance. Coders noted camera shots that literally "peeked" under desks (whose fronts were removed as a design element) to offer glimpses of bare legs. Cameras would present close-ups of legs, tight fitting blouses, and faces, and shoot the journalists from all angles, including from behind. MSNBC, for example, would present a reporter sitting in a desk chair with the camera offering close-up shots of her back and legs. CNN's *Paula Zahn Now* would present the star leaning against (or sometimes even perched upon) a desk with the camera zooming in her legs and face. In other instances, Zahn would sit on a barstool-type chair while the camera rotated around her. This occurred regardless of whether the journalist was Zahn or a female substitute. *Primer Impacto*'s cameras zeroed in on cleavages and legs. Comparatively, male journalists were presented in suits and ties with the camera at face level.

In sum, females were much more likely to be highly attractive, provocatively dressed, and participating in behaviors such as flirting, eye contact, body posturing and other movements that connoted sexual behavior. Female journalists were shown belly dancing, participating in aerobics and yoga, roller-blading, leaning over to touch an interviewee or fellow journalist, and twisting in their chairs as if to accentuate their bodies. Male journalists were much less mobile. Generally, men remained in suits while observing their female counterparts.

Network Differences

Although our analysis and discussion implies that the networks presented newscasters in a similar sexualization frame, there were some differences. Following is a brief synopsis of notable findings for each network in turn.

CNN. The network of the Paula Zahn "sexy" promo had the most equal mix of female (71%) and male (29%) journalists among the sampled networks, yet, 56% of all journalists were still rated as highly attractive and 39% of journalists in all segments had a "high" degree of sex appeal. Dress was more modest than other networks with most journalists (57%) demurely dressed. CNN had a large percentage of male journalists in prime time, but when female journalists would substitute for these shows (*Aaron Brown, Lou Dobbs*), they mirrored the general findings in this report. Last, although Paula Zahn protested the sexy promo, an analysis of her segments indicates that she is prominently featured in miniskirts, tight dresses and blouses, and is positioned in studio locations that offer the camera easy access to her legs.

Fox News. As to be expected by the network accused of promulgating the "Barbification" of TV news, 62% of journalists were rated as physically attractive and 49% exemplified "high" sex appeal. Fox is the channel of miniskirts as 39% of journalists exhibited suggestive dress and nearly half of the partially clad segments. Fox also had the highest proportion of "high" sexual behavior (30%) and referents (21%).

NBC Affiliate. The local affiliate exhibited the typical morning-news banter. However, although the anchor team was mixed (male/female), the female was nearly always the interviewer. The female anchor was "high" in physical attractiveness (72% of all segments) and sex appeal (72%). In 60% of the stories, the female interviewer/reporter was suggestively dressed, typically in a miniskirt and revealing blouse. Sexual referents and behavior were almost non-existent, although facilitation factors were high (47% of all segments) as the camera zoomed in on her face and legs during the segments.

Primer Impacto. Univision's news exhibited the most sex appeal. Each segment was rated as "high," and nearly all (97%) of the journalists were rated as highly attractive. In addition, suggestive dress was evident with 70% of segments showing newscasters in miniskirts with tops with daring cleavage. Sexual behavior (i.e., posing and posturing) was "high" (51% of segments). Female journalists not only reported the news, but Carmen Dominicci and Barbara Bermudo doubled as evening gown models. In many segments, reporters' physical features were prominent as cameras shot them from head-to-toe.

MSNBC. On this network, a high proportion of journalists (92%) were rated as physically attractive, exuding sex appeal (93%), or suggestively dressed (72%). Comparatively, MSNBC was quite "high" in the incidences of sexual referents (25%) and behavior (21%). There was a high degree of interaction within its multi-anchor teams. Correspondingly, MSNBC had the highest rate of facilitation factors (77%, high) as reporters stood in front of maps and sat, miniskirt-clad, on stools.

DISCUSSION AND CONCLUSION

As the previous analysis indicates, television news places a heavy focus on journalists' sexuality. Journalists, especially females, are presented within a frame of sexualization that allows viewers the opportunity to observe newscaster sexual appeal and physical attractiveness. These elements are further emphasized by factors such as suggestive dress, suggestive behavior, and camera angles and design elements that emphasize the salience of the journalist's image, not the issues she might be presenting. Interestingly, this study confirms the work of Kieran (1997) who presents a metaphor of media when he says that news producers choose news much like a cartographer makes a map-only certain features can be emphasized. It appears as if producers are choosing to feature sexy messengers within the news mix.

News is one of the key institutions for dissemination of information about society and culture (Ziegler and White, 1990). Lessons learned from the news go beyond the content of stories as the presentation of stories can orient the public to a groups' social status, structural location, and other levels of their participation in society (Gans, 1979; Tuchman, 1978). Tuchman asserts news is a window on the world, and through news frames Americans learn of themselves and others (p. 1). In the case of this analysis, Americans learn about the news (or the news personalities) through frames emphasized with beautiful women in miniskirts. Instead of "talking heads," as a whole, female newscasters could be referred to a "talking bodies." In addition, media framing influences not only the stories and manner in which they are produced but also the thoughts and views of people watching them at home (Tewksbury, Jones, Peske, and Vig, 2000). This is especially important as media portrayals have the potential to shape young peoples attitudes about sexuality and gender (Barak, Fisher, Belfry, and Lashambe, 1999; Harris and Scott, 2002; Ward, 2002). A lesson to be drawn from watching network news is the tired theme that women's value (and role) is tied to their sexual appeal. A striking similarity exists between the presentation of female journalists and female celebrities and models in advertisements and magazine covers (Lambiase and Reichert, 2006; Reichert and Carpenter, 2004).

The results of this study serve as yet another indicator of the news as infotainment (Brant and Neijens, 1998). The *new* news (Rosen and Taylor, 1992) emphasizes the pressures of the new media economy that focuses on ratings over informative content. Networks, in today's age of cross-fertilization and new media technologies, are promoting their journalists as individual stars. Such emphasis on sex-appeal frames, while translating to more viewers (Dominquez, 2004), places the focus on the "sizzle" and not the "steak" in both news dissemination and reception. When the media focus less on issue analysis and more on sensational, image-based features, the long-term effect could be a "trivialization of public discourse" (Iyengar, 1991, p. 143). Despite this, Graber (1994) cautions critics who claim that such news is devoid of any informative value. She argues that such dramatic framing keeps the public informed and attracts otherwise disinterested viewers. Informative news is possible, "even without abandoning the sugarcoating of drama that makes today's news palatable" (p. 508). Meyer and Hinchman (2002) agree, yet warn that if one turns to the most abysmal standards as authoritative guidelines for deciding what fare should be the most widely available and accessible, then that is a serious concern for the entire community.

Although not hypothesized, a notable finding is that female journalists engage in more sexual referents than male journalists. While the number of segments in which sexual referents occurred was low (24%), within these stories females were more likely to espouse sexual referents: females used referents in 59 segments compared to 13 segments for males. Female journalists commented on the attractiveness of male celebrities and teased each other about boyfriends. Males also engaged in such banter, but were likely to comment on their female counterparts' appearance (especially on *Fox & Friends*). Males on Fox News would hold up pictures and encourage the camera to "look at her." Julian Edwards, in a story about which celebrities Fox reporters most resembled, told one female counterpart, "You're hot!"

FUTURE RESEARCH AND LIMITATIONS

As a first step, future research needs to confirm the present study's findings. Given the formative nature of this study, a comprehensive content analysis is needed to fully assess the sexualization of newscasters. Such research should sample the entire range of newscasts from news programs to the traditional newscast. In addition, this study revealed that journalists on the NBC affiliate exhibited a high degree of sex appeal. A content analysis of local newscasts in a range of markets would provide a more accurate view as to the sexual framing of local news.

Second, future research should combine the results of this study with experimental research to determine how sexualized newscasters influence viewer knowledge, beliefs, and attitudes. For example, advertising research has shown that sexual information can influence information processing and emotional responses to product messages (LaTour, 1990; Severn, Belch, and Belch, 1990; for review, see Reichert, 2002). A persistent finding is a distraction effect: Sexualized information is encoded and retrieved at the expense of detailed information about the product. Similarly, sexualized newscasters may be attracting more attention than the information they are presenting. In addition, emotion-evoking information such as sexual content also has been found to suppress analytical cognition (Reichert, Heckler, and Jackson, 2001). In other words, the emotional response evoked by a sexualized newscaster may decrease the likelihood of counter- or support-arguing that viewers may engage in when watching the news. In a related sense, sexualization may be seen as a new form of media discourse that has the potential to frame or construct reality for the public (Gamson, 1986; Gamson and Modigliani, 1989). Iyengar's (1991) classic work on framing indicates that the frames selected can have a significant impact on policy-making and an audience's view of the world.

Third, academic research should consider the promotional effects of sexy newscasters. Anecdotal evidence suggests that sexy newscasters enhance ratings, but that fact has yet to be confirmed. Related questions involve the presence and influence of parasocial relationships viewers may form with newscasters that can influence the likelihood of viewership over time. In addition, future work should investigate the role of hedonic arousal and viewership. As news is increasingly homogenized and becomes a parody product, the pleasing nature of a newscaster may represent a meaningful point of differentiation between news sources.

Several limitations should be noted. First, the findings did not include traditional evening newscasts (i.e., ABC, CBS, NBC) that still maintain relatively high ratings compared to most news programs. Therefore, the present study's findings cannot be generalized to all televised news. Second, although the coding scheme was adapted from previous research, simply categorizing aspects of sexuality as high, medium, and low has the potential to oversimplify subtle differences of presentation.

In conclusion, perhaps, as Meyer and Hinchman (2002) note, the worm does not have to taste good to the fisherman, only to the fish (p. 84). As Laurie Dhue, a reporter for Fox News, says, "Being good-looking and a good journalist are not mutually exclusive. TV is a visual medium and people flipping through channels will stop at good images" (Dominguez, 2004). Dominguez also cites Carmen Dominicci, a reporter for *Primer Impacto*, who asked: "If we were ugly, would you watch?" As the findings of this study suggest, news executives appear to believe the answer to Dominicci's question is a resounding, "No."

REFERENCES

Andsager, J. (2006). Seduction, shock, and sales: Research and functions of sex in music video. In T. Reichert and J. Lambiase (eds.), *Sex in Consumer Culture: The Erotic Content of Media and Marketing* (pp. 31-50). Mahwah, NJ: Lawrence Erlbaum Associates.

Archer, D., Irianti, B., Kimes, B., and Barrios, M. (1978). Face-ism: Five studies of sex differences in facial studies. *Journal of Personality and Social Psychology, 45*(4), 725-735.

Barak, A., Fisher, W., Belfry, S., and Lashambe, D. (1999). Sex, guys, and cyberspace: Effects of Internet pornography and individual differences on men's attitudes toward women. *Journal of Psychology and Human Sexuality, 11*(1), 63-91.

Barney, T. (2001). Celebrity, spectacle, and the conspiracy culture of Election 2000. *American Behavioral Scientist, 44*(12), 2331-2337.

Brant, K., and Neijens, P. (1998). The infotainment of politics. *Political Communication, 15*(2), 149-164.

Buarque, H. (2003). Telenovela and gender in Brazil. *Global Media Journal, 2*(2), 2-9.

Byrne, D., London, O., and Reeves, K. (1968). The effects of physical attractiveness, sex, and attitude similarity on interpersonal attraction. *Journal of Personality, 36*(2), 259-271.

Campbell, R. (1998). *Media and Culture.* New York: St. Martin's.

Capecchi, S., and Demaria, C. (2001). Gender representation in the news. Retrieved March 2, 2007 from http://orlando.women.it/cyberarchive/files/capecchi_ demaria.htm.

Carter, B., Brantson, G., and Allan, E. (2002). Setting news agenda. In B. Carter and E. Allan (eds.), *News, Gender, and Power* (pp. 17-31). London: Routledge.

Cohen, M. (2002, February). TV stalkers. *Columbia Journalism Review.* Retrieved February 11, 2007 from www.cjr.org/issues/2002/6/stalk-cohen.asp?printerfriendly=yes.

Copeland, G. (1989). Face-ism and prime-time television. *Journal of Broadcasting and Electronic Media, 33*(2), 209-216.

Cunningham, M. (1986). Measuring the physical in physical attractiveness: Quasi-experiments on the sociobiology of female facial beauty. *Journal of Personality and Social Psychology, 50*(5), 925-935.

Cupchik, G., and Kemp, S. (2000). The aesthetics of media fare. In D. Zillmann and P. Vorderer (eds.), *Media Entertainment: The Psychology of its Appeal* (pp. 249-265). Mahwah, NJ; Lawrence Erlbaum Associates.

D'Angelo, P. (2002). News framing as a multiparadigmatic research program: A response to Entman. *Journal of Communication, 52*(4), 870-888.

Dominguez, R. (2004, January 15). Sex appeal translates to more viewers. *Puerto Rico Herald.* Retrieved February 12, 2006 from http://www.puertorico-herald.org/issues/2004/vol8n17/SexAppeal.html.

Entman, R. (1993). Framing: Towards clarification of a fractured paradigm. *Journal of Communication, 43*(4), 51-58.

Eveland, W. (2002) The impact of news and entertainment media on perceptions of social reality. In J. Dillard and M. Pfau (eds.). *Persuasion Handbook* (pp. 691-729). Thousand Oaks, CA: Sage.

Farrar, K., Kunkel, D., Biely, E., Eyal, K., Fandrich, R., and Donnerstein, E. (2003). Sexual messages during prime-time programming. *Sexuality and Culture, 7*(3), 7-37.

Foote, J. (1992). Women correspondents' visibility on the network evening news. *Mass Communication Review, 19*(1/2), 36-40.

Gamson, W. (1996). Media discourse as a framing resource. In A. Crigler (ed.), *The Psychology of Political Communication* (pp. 111-132). Ann Arbor: University of Michigan Press.

Gamson, W., and Modigliani, A. (1989). Media discourse and public opinion: A constructivist approach. *American Journal of Sociology, 95*(1), 1-37.

Gans, H. (1979). *Deciding What's News: A Sstudy of the CBS Evening News, NBC Nightly News, Newsweek, and Time.* New York: Pantheon.

Gorman, L., and McLean, D. (2003). *Media and Society in the Twentieth Century.* London: Blackwell.

Graber, D. (1994). The infotainment quotient in routine television news: A director's perspective. *Discourse and Society, 5*(4), 483-508.

Green, S., Buchanan, D., and Murr, S. (1984). Winners, losers, and choosers: A field investigation of dating initiation. *Personality and Social Psychology Bulletin, 10*(4), 502-511.

Greenberg, B., and Hofschire, L. (2000). Sex on entertainment television. In D. Zillman and P. Vorderer (eds.), *Media Entertainment: The Psychology of its Appeal* (pp. 93-111). Mahwah, NJ: Lawrence Erlbaum Associates.

Greenberg, B., Graef, D., Fernandez-Collado, C., Korzenny, F., and Aitkin, C. (1980). Sexual intimacy on commercial TV during prime-time. *Journalism Quarterly, 57*(2),211-215.

Gunter, B. (2001). *Media Sex: What are the Issues?* Mahwah, NJ: Lawrence Erlbaum Associates.

Harris, R., and Scott, C. (2002). Effects of sex in the media. In W. Bryant and D. Zillman (eds.), *Media Effects: Advances in Theory and Research* (pp. 307-333). Mahwah, NJ: Lawrence Erlbaum Associates.

Holland, P. (2002). The politics of the smile. In B. Carter and E. Allan (eds.), *News, Gender, and Power* (pp. 87-101). London: Routledge.

Hollander, B. (1994). The new news and the 1992 presidential campaign: Perceived versus actual political knowledge, *Journalism and Mass Communication Quarterly, 72*(4),786-798.

Hollihan, T. (2001). *Uncivil Wars: Political Campaigns in a Media Age.* Boston: Bedford/St. Martin's.

Iyengar, S. (1991). *Is Anyone Responsible? How Television Frames Political Issues.* Chicago: University of Chicago Press.

Johnson, P. (2004, March 15). This just in: The future of news. *USA Today.* Retrieved February 12, 2006 from www.usatoday.com/life/2004-03-14-pew-report_x.htm.

Joseph, W. (1982). The credibility of physically attractive communicators: A review. *Journal of Advertising, 11*(3), 15-24.

Kieran, M. (1997). *Media Ethics: A Philosophical Approach.* Westport, CT: Praeger.

Kim, S., Scheufele, D., and Shanahan, J. (2002). Think about it this way: Attribute agenda-setting function of the press and the public's evaluation of a local issue. *Journalism and Mass Communication Quarterly, 79*(2), 7-25.

Kraft, R. (1987). The influence of camera angle on comprehension and retention of pictorial events. *Memory and Cognition, 15*(4), 291-307.

Lambiase, J., and Reichert, T. (2006). Sex and the marketing of contemporary consumer magazines: How men's magazines sexualized their covers to compete with *Maxim.* In T. Reichert and J. Lambiase (eds.), *Sex in Consumer Culture: The Erotic Content of Media and Marketing* (pp. 67-86). Mahwah, NJ: Lawrence Erlbaum Associates.

LaTour, M. (1990). Female nudity in print advertising: An analysis of gender differences in arousal and ad response. *Psychology and Marketing, 7*(1), 65-81.

LeBoutillier, J. (2002). Sexifying the news. Retrieved January 18, 2007 from www.newsmax.com/archives/articles/2002/1/9/131145.shtml.

Lin, C. (1998). Uses of sexual appeals in prime-time television commercials. *Sex roles, 38*(5/6), 461-475.

Mandell, L., and Shaw, D. (1973). Judging people in the news unconsciously: The effect of camera angle and bodily activity. *Journal of Broadcasting, 17*(3), 353-357.

McCain, T., Chilberg, J., and Wakshlag, J. (1977). The effect of camera angle on source credibility and attraction. *Journal of Broadcasting, 21*(1), 35-46.

McLeod, D., Kosicki, G., and McLeod, J. (2002). Resurveying the boundaries of political communication effects. In D. Zillman and J. Bryant (eds.), *Media Effects: Advances in Theory and Research* (pp. 215-269). Mahwah, NJ: Lawrence Erlbaum Associates.

Messaris, P. (1994). *Visual Literacy: Image, Mind, and Reality.* Boulder, CO: Westview.

Meyer, T., and Hinchman, L. (2002). *Media Democracy: How the Media Colonize Politics.* Cambridge, England: Polity Press.

Newhagen, J. (2002). The role of meaning construction in the process of persuasion for viewers of television images. In J. Dillard and M. Pfau (eds.), *The Persuasion Handbook* (pp. 729-748). Thousand Oaks, CA: Sage.

Nitz, M., Cypher, A., Reichert, T., and Mueller, J. (2003). Candidates as comedy: Political Presidential humor on late-night television shows. In L. Kaid, J. Tedesco, D. Bystrom, and M. McKinney (eds.), *The Millennium Election: Communication in the 2000 Campaign* (pp. 165-179). Lanham, MD: Rowman & Littlefield.

Nitz, M., and West, H. (2004). Framing of newspaper news stories during a Presidential campaign cycle: The case of Bush-Gore in Election 2000. In S. Senecah (ed.), *The Environmental Communication Yearbook* (pp. 205-227). Mahwah, NJ: Lawrence Erlbaum Associates.

Olds, A., and Seitz, C. (1995). Television technique revisited: The effect of camera angle on communicator credibility. Paper presented at the annual meeting of the Visual Communication Conference, Flagstaff, AZ.

Powers, R. (1977). *The Newscasters.* New York: St. Martin's.

Rakow, L., and Kranich, K. (1991). Women as sign in television news, *Journal of Communication, 41*(1), 8-19.

Ramirez, A. (2006). Sexually oriented appeals on the internet: An exploratory analysis of popular mainstream web sites. In T. Reichert and J. Lambiase (eds.), *Sex in Consumer Culture: The Erotic Content of Media and Marketing* (pp. 141-157). Mahwah, NJ: Lawrence Erlbaum Associates.

Redal, W. (1995, May). Marketing the news: Journalistic values in an era of changing newspaper identity. Paper presented at the annual conference of the International Communication Association, Albuquerque, NM.

Reese, S. (2001). Prologue-framing public life: A bridging model for media research. In S. Reese, O. Gandy, Jr., and A. Grant (eds.), *Framing Public Life: Perspectives on Media and Our Understanding of the Social World* (pp. 7-31). Mahwah, NJ: Lawrence Erlbaum Associates.

Reichert, T. (2002). Sex in advertising: A review of content, effects, and functions of sexual information in consumer advertising research. *Annual Review of Sex Research, 13*, 241-273.

Reichert, T. (2003). What is sex in advertising: Perspectives from consumer behavior and social science research. In T. Reichert and J. Lambiase (eds.), *Sex in Advertising: Perspectives on the Erotic Appeal* (11-38). Mahwah, NJ: Lawrence Erlbaum Associates.

Reichert, T., and Carpenter, C. (2004). An update on sex in magazine advertising, 1983 to 2003. *Journalism and Mass Communication Quarterly, 81*(4), 823-837.

Reichert, T., Heckler, S. E., and Jackson, S. (2001). The effects of sexual social marketing appeals on cognitive processing and persuasion. *Journal of Advertising, 30*(1), 13-27.

Reichert, T., and Ramirez, A. (2000). Defining sexually oriented appeals in advertising: A grounded theory investigation. In S. J. Hoch and R. J. Meyer (eds.), *Advances in Consumer Research, Vol. 27* (pp. 267-273). Provo, UT: Association for Consumer Research.

Rendahl, S. (1995, April). Frame analysis: From interpersonal to mass communication. Paper presented to the Central States Communication Association, Indianapolis, IN.

Rosen, J., and Taylor, P. (1992). *Perspectives on the News: The New News vs. the Old News. The Press and Politics in the 1990s.* New York: 20th Century Foundation.

Sayre, S., and King, C. (2003). *Entertainment and Society: Audiences, Trends, and Impacts.* Thousand Oaks, CA: Sage.

Scheufele, D. (1999). Framing as a theory of media effects. *Journal of Communication, 49*(4), 103-122.

Severn, J., Belch, G. E., and Belch, M. A. (1990). The effects of sexual and non-sexual advertising appeals and information level on cognitive processing and communication effectiveness. *Journal of Advertising, 19*(1), 14-22.

Shiflett, D. (2001, January). Foxy news: The Paula Zahn affair. *The National Review.* Retrieved November 15, 2006 from www.nationalreview.com/shiflett/shiflett011402. shtml.

Simpson, J. A., Gangestad, S. W., and Nations, C. (1996). Sociosexuality and relationship inititation: An ethological perspective of nonverbal behavior. In G. J. Fletcher and J. Fitness (eds.), *Knowledge Structures in Close Relationships: A Social Psychological Approach* (pp. 121-146). Mahwah, NJ: Lawrence Erlbaum Associates.

Skerski, J. (2006). From sideline to centerfold: The sexual commodification of female sportscasters. In T. Reichert and J. Lambiase (eds.), *Sex in Consumer Culture: The Erotic Content of Media and Marketing* (pp. 87-105). Mahwah, NJ: Lawrence Erlbaum Associates.

Soley, L., and Reid, L. (1988). Taking it off: Are models in magazine ads wearing less? *Journalism and Mass Communication Quarterly, 65*(4), 960-966.

Sprecher, S. (1989). The importance to males and females of physical attractiveness, earning potential, and expressiveness in initial attraction. *Sex Roles, 21*(9/10), 591-607.

Taylor, L. D. (2005). All for him: Articles about sex in American lad magazines. *Sex Roles, 52*(3/4), 153-163.

Tewksbury, D., Jones, J., Peske, M., and Vig, W. (2000). The interaction of news and advocate frames: Manipulating audience perceptions of a local public policy issue. *Journalism and Mass Communication Quarterly, 77*(4), 804-829.

Tiemens, R. (1970). Some relationships of camera angle to communicator credibility. *Journal of Broadcasting, 14*(4), 483-490.

Tuchman, G. (1978). *Making News: A Study in the Construction of Reality.* New York: Free Press.

Turow, J. (1978). *Media Industries: The Production of News and Entertainment.* New York: Longman.

Walster, E., Aronson, V., Abrahams, D., and Rottman, L. (1966). Importance of physical attractiveness in dating behavior. *Journal of Personality and Social Psychology, 4*(5), 508-516.

Ward, L. (2002). Does television exposure affect emerging adults' attitudes and assumptions about sexual relationships? Correlational and experimental confirmation, *Journal of Youth and Adolescence, 31*(1), 1-15.

Weaver, J. (2000). Personality and entertainment preferences. In D. Zillmann, and P. Vorderer (eds.), *Media Entertainment: The Psychology of its Appeal* (pp. 235-248). Mahwah, NJ: Lawrence Erlbaum Associates.

Zelizer, B. (2001). Popular communication in the contemporary age. In W. Gudykunst (ed.), *Communication Yearbook 24* (pp. 297-319). Thousand Oaks, CA: Sage.

Ziegler, D., and White, A. (1990). Women and minorities on television news: An examination of correspondents and newsmakers. *Journal of Broadcasting and Electronic Media, 34*(2), 215-223.

Zillmann, D. (2000). The coming of media entertainment. In D. Zillman, and P. Vorderer (eds.), *Media Entertainment: The Psychology of its Appeal* (pp. 1-21). Mahwah, NJ: Lawrence Erlbaum Associates.

doi:10.1300/J057v13n01_03

Bump, Set, Spike:
An Analysis of Commentary and Camera Angles of Women's Beach Volleyball During the 2004 Summer Olympics

Kimberly L. Bissell
Andrea M. Duke

SUMMARY. Content analysis was employed to examine the commentary and camera angles of six beach volleyball games from the 2004 Summer Olympic Games. Based on previous research in the area of gender and sport commentary, and based on pre-coverage of the Olympics, it was expected that a high level of sexualized talk and concentration on the athletes' body parts would be prevalent. While sexuality and sex difference were not found in audio coverage of the games, they were highly evident in the video coverage of the games. More than 20% of the camera shots were found to be tight shots of the players' chests and just over 17% of the shots were coded as buttock shots, which, it is argued, leaves

Kimberly L. Bissell (PhD, Syracuse University) is Associate Professor, Department of Journalism, University of Alabama, Box 870172, Tuscaloosa, AL 35487 (E-mail: bissell@jn.ua.edu). Andrea M. Duke is a Doctoral Student, College of Communication and Information Sciences, University of Alabama, Box 870172, Tuscaloosa, AL 35487 (E-mail: andreaduke1@gmail.com).

[Haworth co-indexing entry note]: "Bump, Set, Spike: An Analysis of Commentary and Camera Angles of Women's Beach Volleyball During the 2004 Summer Olympics." Bissell, Kimberly L. and Andrea M. Duke. Co-published simultaneously in *Journal of Promotion Management* (Best Business Books, an imprint of The Haworth Press, Inc.) Vol. 13, No. 1/2, 2007, pp. 35-53; and: *Investigating the Use of Sex in Media Promotion and Advertising* (ed: Tom Reichert) Best Business Books, an imprint of The Haworth Press, Inc., 2007, pp. 35-53. Single or multiple copies of this article are available for a fee from The Haworth Document Delivery Service [1-800-HAWORTH, 9:00 a.m. - 5:00 p.m. (EST). E-mail address: docdelivery@haworthpress.com].

viewers with lasting memories of players' bodies rather than of memories of athleticism. Such analysis of the visual coverage of the games confirms that sex and sexuality were used to not only promote the athletes but to sell the sport to viewers around the world. doi:10.1300/J057v13n01_04 *[Article copies available for a fee from The Haworth Document Delivery Service: 1-800-HAWORTH. E-mail address: <docdelivery@haworthpress.com> Website: <http://www.HaworthPress.com> © 2007 by The Haworth Press, Inc. All rights reserved.]*

KEYWORDS. Audio commentary, beach volleyball, camera angles, content analysis, Olympics, physical attractiveness, sex, sports, television

INTRODUCTION

Models, musical artists, or actresses, almost always lacking clothing and posing in provocative positions, typically grace the covers of men's magazines. Yet, in recent years, female athletes have begun to be featured on and in these magazines, as well as in ads and marketing campaigns with high levels of sex appeal. Such sex appeal is the basic foundation for advertising, defined as a persuasive appeal that contains sexual information integrated with the overall message (Reichert, Heckler, and Jackson, 2001). Sex appeal and sexual information can be subtle and blatant, verbal and non-verbal. Some argue the sexualization of female athletes in America is disturbing, rising out of the increased sexualization of women's sports in the Olympics (Woodroff, 2004). Research on the use of sexual appeals in advertising has shown that over the decades, the use of sexual appeals in advertising has increased (Soley and Kurzbard, 1986; Soley and Reid, 1989; Reichert and Carpenter, 2004), and the explicitness of these appeals has increased (Reichert, Lambiase, Morgan, Carstarphen and Zavoina, 1999; Piron and Young, 1996).

At the national and international level, the reliance on sex and/or sexualization to sell and promote sports to viewing audiences is further on the rise. In 2004, the Federation Internationale de Football Association (FIFA) president Joseph S. Baker suggested that female soccer players should consider wearing more revealing uniforms to bring increased interest and attention to the game (Millward, 2004). Female golfers on the Ladies' Professional Golf Association (LPGA) tour were told, "If you have it, flaunt it." Additionally, new tactics by sports and marketing companies view selling sex as a tactic to either save the sport (as with women's soccer) or enhance an athlete's image within the media. The use of sex to market and promote female athletes and sports was especially notable during the 2004 Summer Olympic Games. In the months before those games, numerous female athletes were featured in men's magazines–such as *FHM, Maxim, Playboy*, and *Stuff*–"posing provocatively in Victoria's Secret-meets-the-Sports-Illustrated-swimsuit-issue fashion" (Dillman, 2004). Many of the athletes competing for the United States received a tremendous amount of attention prior to, during, and after the Games, and some would argue that this attention was not related to skill or athleticism. One example of such attention was cut of the gold medalist beach volleyball team of Kerri Walsh and Misty May.

Beach volleyball has received its share of attention because of the purported sexual nature of the sport. During the coverage of the Games, one reporter wrote:

> Women's beach volleyball might be fraudulent, but it sure packs them in. It is the Olympic movement's equivalent of safe sex, sanitized for all the family . . . the Olympics were traditionally about faster, fitter, stronger, but now in the women's beach volleyball, it was all about browner, scantier, skimpier. It is a recurring theme . . . [The players] demand respect, yet they get very little attention. You can guarantee that one day soon, in desperation, they will plead to play topless, their country's badge tattooed on forearms. (Hopps, 2004, p. 2)

The use of sex as a marketing and promotional tool for female athletes and athletics has been clearly established (Woodroff, 2004; Millward, 2004), yet little empirical research exists to document these trends in women's beach volleyball. Subsequently, the goal of this project was to determine how or if the visual and audio components of televised coverage of 2004 Summer Olympic Games emphasized the sexuality of one U.S. beach volleyball team.

LITERATURE REVIEW

Since Title IX was implemented in the U.S., interest in female sports worldwide has grown at an amazing rate. As coverage of women's sports has increased over the last decade, viewership and fan support have increased as well. Historically, however, researchers have found that the media are more likely to cover female athletes in "socially accepted sports," and less likely to cover the athletes when women cross over into more male-dominated sports. Coverage of sports considered to be more feminine–ice-skating and gymnastics–tends to be much more prevalent compared to coverage of sports considered to be more masculine-soccer, hockey, and basketball. Along these lines, Alexander (1994) found that television furthered societal stereotypes suggesting the females should be graceful and glamorous and should not engage in sports that would include contact or sweating. Sports such as gymnastics and ice-skating have captivated audiences around the world for decades as a new "darling" garners accolades and trophies for her success. Such was the case for Mary Lou Retton and Carly Patterson in gymnastics, and Dorothy Hamill, Sarah Hughes, and Michelle Kwan in ice skating. Historically, it seems as if the media tried to create the "girl-next-door" image as a means of keeping the athlete as feminine as possible. More recently, the strategy appears to have changed, seemingly to create the image of a female athlete who is more sexual and/or sexualized than in the past.

For example, athletes such as Anna Kournikova, Jennie Finch, and Amy Acuff have been admired and adored by male fans arguably because of their physical appearance. The promotion of these female athletes focuses not only on their sports acumen, but on their bodies which serve as an obvious endorsement of sex and sexual appeal. Kournikova has earned an estimated $11 to $15 million through modeling and endorsement contracts and is viewed by some to be the most beautiful and photographed female athlete. Finch, Olympic Gold medalist in softball, was voted ESPN.com's "Hottest Female Athlete" and has become a model for numerous athletic and fashion companies. Acuff, an Olympic high jumper, has posed for *Playboy*, *Esquire,* and other men's magazines, and says, "I see the body as a miraculous machine and I don't see my sexuality when I see a woman's body. I see strength, athleticism, and beauty . . . We're promoting pride in our bodies" (Huang, 2004).

In addition, in this age of self-promotion, we are witnessing an increase in athletes promoting themselves alongside the networks. The 2004 Summer Olympics were broadcast on numerous affiliates of NBC, with promotional commercials and advertisements on all channels. Such promotional material has been shown to contain high levels of sexuality, especially when appearing on NBC. In an analysis of over 600 promotional announcements aired in prime time by ABC, CBS, and NBC during one week of the 1984 television season, Brown (1989) found that more than 25% of all promos contained sensuality expressed in either actions or words. Davis and Walker (1991) analyzed 1,204 promos in both non-prime time and prime-time shows and found NBC to have the most promotions with sexual behaviors (17.8%). Additionally, Sapolsky, Tarbarlet, and Kaye (1994) analyzed 171 hours of promotional materials in 1990, and also found NBC to have the most sexual content in its promos–4.56 hours, which was almost double that of the second-ranked network (ABC). Whereas such connection between programming materials for normal prime-time hours and programming for special sporting events such as the Olympics could be unrelated, the knowledge that NBC, over time, has been the leader in sexual promos might suggest an acceptance toward more sexualized camera angles, commentary, feature stories, and overall broadcasting at NBC. In addition, while the use and promotion of sexuality has been found in network programming and in promos for special events, the use of sexuality has also been found in rhetorical contexts.

Rhetoric in Sport Media

Carroll (1956) argued very early on that structures and traditions created by society can be seen and created through language. Parks and Robertson (1998) further advanced Carroll's observation in saying that "in the culture of the United States, females and males have traditionally been accorded differential treatment, with males enjoying privilege and status not extended to females. The prevalence of this tradition . . . is evident in the English language in the form of 'sexist language'" (p. 478). Henley (1987) argues that sexist language can be reduced to three types: language that ignores women, language that defines women narrowly, and language that depreciates women. Such language advances stereotypes and expectations for the genders and can be seen in the rhetoric of sport media. Some studies have revealed that the language commentators and reporters use when referring to male and female athletes in a sports media presentation emphasizes gender inequalities (Halbert and Latimer, 1994; Duncan and Hasbrook, 1988). Such research on rhetoric, along with promotion and advertising, spotlight the stereotypes and expectations for the genders in sport coverage. The general conclusion from research across several disciplines that examine the use of sex as a tool to market and promote sport suggests that televised coverage of female athletes competing in a physical sport emphasizes sexuality and sexual difference. Subsequently, the following research questions are addressed:

RQ1: Are female 2004 Olympic beach volleyball players gender stereotyped by attributions of personality, looks, and sexuality rather than by attributions of athleticism, mental toughness, or skill?

RQ2: Will the camera shot, body shot, and camera angle in the televised coverage of the volleyball players emphasize the athletes' athletic performance or appearance traits?

METHOD

Procedures

During the 17 days of the 2004 Olympic Game coverage, all beach volleyball games were recorded and saved on DVR to be analyzed and coded at a later date. Content analysis was used to analyze coverage of NBC's broadcast of women's beach volleyball. Specifically, the analysis was limited to play-by-play commentary, color analysis, and visual coverage of the USA women's gold-medal team of Misty May and Kerri Walsh.

Following the work of Billings and Eastman (2003) and Billings, Halone and Denham (2002), the on-air speech of NBC beach volleyball commentators during game play was analyzed. All commentary was coded, from the start of NBC's coverage of beach volleyball (prior to the first serve) to the end of the game (showing players' celebration after a win). It should be noted that six games were not coded because complete games were not always broadcast. While the study objective was to analyze coverage of complete games, the coders did analyze every minute of the televised broadcast of the women's games, which, in essence, means they coded all that viewers saw of each game.

The unit of analysis was the serve–all commentary and video from the start of one serve to the beginning of another serve was coded on a single line (the authors served as coders). The visuals were coded in a similar manner by recording the camera shot, the body shot, and the camera angle used between the start of one serve and the start of another. Coders recorded up to six camera shots, six body shots, and six camera angles per serve knowing that the camera shot would change during the serve. In order to achieve intercoder reliability on the coding instrument, the coders trained on an early Team USA game because it was thought that some of the commentary might be unique to games about the American players. The coding sheet was created, following the Billings and colleagues model, and then each coder independently analyzed segments of a game not included in the final sample. Intercoder reliability was checked and then modifications were made to the coding sheet and instructions. The authors independently coded another sample of televised beach volleyball not included in the final sample and reliability was checked again. Once acceptable reliability had been achieved on all variables, each coder independently coded 12% of the content from the final sample. While intercoder reliability was computed for each variable, the combined intercoder reliability score on all categories was .87 using Scott's pi.

Coding Categories

The variables coded for this project were similar to those analyzed by Billings and Eastman (2003). For each game included in the analysis, the following categories were assessed to better understand how, if, or when audio and visual coverage emphasized sexual difference or sexuality, and, if so, at what points in the game it was most evident: game status, game sequence, broadcast announcer gender, broadcast announcer ethnicity, play-by-play commentary, play-by-play valence, between-play commentary, between-play valence, camera shot, body shot, and camera angle.[1]

All broadcast comments (play-by-play and between-serve) were coded into one of 13 categories: physical/behavioral; mental/cognitive; affective; dominance; leadership; background 1; background 2; calling of the game; reporting of current or past score; other team; personal information; looks, personality, sexuality; attire.[2] While one objective of this project was to analyze the commentary during Team USA's beach volleyball play, a second objective was the analysis of the visual coverage of the game. Given the findings of Bissell and Holt (2005) in their analysis of still frames of the Olympic Games published on three websites, it was thought an analysis of three aspects of visual coverage of the games would yield interesting results with regard to an emphasis on sexuality. When the Olympic Games were initially televised during August 2004, a good deal of media hype and press coverage related to the athlete's attire was observed: Still frames of the game would focus on the backside of a player, as she bent down to receive serve (see Bissell and Holt, 2005). Therefore, the three visual variables that were coded included: camera shot, body shot, and camera angle. Specific analysis included the following: camera shot (*wide shot*–full court, *nar-*

row shot–half court including shots that would show the full body of the athletes, *close shot*–tighter shots of an individual athlete where the full body was not shown); body shot (*face*–a very tight shot of the face only, *chest*–a tight shot showing the athlete from the chest up, *buttock shot*–a tight shot of just the buttock, or a shot showing portions of the body including the buttocks, *full body*); camera angle (high-to-low, eye-level, low-to-high).

RESULTS

Six Team USA women's beach volleyball games played during the 2004 Olympic Games were coded, and play during these six games was against teams from the following countries: Czech Republic, Sweden, China, Canada, Brazil and the 2nd Team USA. As mentioned, the unit of analysis was the serve ($N = 185$), but researchers coded up to five comments during play and up to eight comments between play. A large percentage (20-35%) of the comments between serves was coded in the "calling of the game" or "reporting of the score" categories. This was one reason the audio and video coverage from the start of one serve to the start of another was used as the unit of analysis because it allowed the coders to get a better sense of the variety of comments. For example, as the ball was put into play, a commentator might update viewers on the current score, but as play progressed (all within the same serve), commentators might then discuss the physicality of the athletes, the speed of the athletes, or the athlete's ability to overwhelm other players.

While it was not surprising that commentary during play would vary based on how play was progressing, it was expected that some mention of body shape or size, attire, or sexuality in the play-by-play commentary from the games would be evident. The first research question (RQ1) pertained to the manner in which female players would be gender stereotyped by comments about appearance, sexuality, and attire. However, contrary to the findings of Billings et al. (2002) and Bissell and Holt (2005), the commentators making play-by-play and between-play commentary did not emphasize or even mention sexuality, appearance, or attire. While announcers made a few comments about Walsh's tattoo or the players' height, no comments were made about hairstyle, facial appearance, or body shape. Furthermore, the comments were not sexual or representative of gender stereotyping. As a whole, descriptive statistics indicate announcers' commented a great deal on physical strength, agility and athleticism, and very rarely made comments that were outside of the domain of the game.

The second research question (RQ2) examined the way the camera shot and camera angle emphasized the appearance traits of the athletes. Based on still frames published during the Olympic Games, it was expected that viewers would see a side view or behind the player view (buttock shot) with some degree of frequency (Bissell and Holt, 2005). Whether intentional or not on the part of the camera operator and producer, viewers did see players' backsides throughout all games, and these buttock shots included a large number instances when players made uniform adjustments. In the USA's first match of the Olympic Games (total camera shots = 56), 27% of the camera shots were full-court shots, 48% were half-court shots, and 25% were close shots of individual players; in a following game against Sweden ($N = 144$), 25% of the shots were full court; 44% were half-court shots and 31% were tight shots of individual players (see Table 1). Not only did the total number of camera shots almost triple, the number of tight shots of players increased as well. Most importantly, it was during tight shots when an athlete's body part rather than the whole athlete was seen with the greatest frequency.

When analyzing the specific body part seen during any given camera shot, a large percentage of chest shots and buttock shots were evident. For example, when Team USA was receiving serve, the players would bend at the waist anticipating the ball being put in play. At this point, the camera at the end of the court was used, and a tight shot of the players' backside was shown. Clearly, cameras were placed on all sides of the court because play from all angles and directions was seen, yet the director of the broadcast made the decision to frequently use the camera angle from behind the American players. It should be noted that on many occasions, the camera shot was a very tight shot of the player's buttock, cutting off the player's head and feet. On other occasions, the initial camera shot was a tight shot of the player's buttock with the camera panning back to show the full body of the player. While the director could argue that the behind-the-player angle was the most appropriate angle when the other team was serving (and Team USA was receiving serve), several tight shots of players' buttocks were shown after the point had ended and the players were walking elsewhere on the court. In this case, a wider shot of the players could easily have been used.

In addition to coding multiple buttock shots, many of the other close camera shots were tight shots of players' chests. After the point had been won and players returned to the backcourt to either receive serve or

TABLE 1. Camera Angle, Camera Shot and Body Shot During Televised Coverage of Beach Volleyball During the 2004 Olympic Games

Opponent	Camera Shot 1*		First camera shot of the serve Camera Angle 1**		Body Shot 1***	
	Freq.	%	Freq.	%	Freq.	%
Czech Rep						
Wide shot	6	30%	high-to-low angle 10	50%	face shot 1	5%
Narrow shot	8	40%	eye-level angle 9	45%	chest shot 10	50%
Close shot	6	30%	low-to-high angle 1	5%	buttocks shot 2	10%
					full body shot 7	35%
	N=20	100%	N=20	100%	N=20	100%
Sweden						
Wide shot	17	53%	high-to-low angle 21	66%	face shot 1	3%
Narrow shot	11	34%	eye-level angle 10	31%	chest shot 2	6%
Close shot	4	13%	low-to-high angle 1	3%	buttocks shot 7	22%
					full body shot 22	69%
	N=32	100%	N=32	100%	N=32	100%
China						
Wide shot	6	23%	high-to-low angle 11	42%	face shot 4	15%
Narrow shot	11	42%	eye-level angle 12	46%	chest shot 8	32%
Close shot	9	35%	low-to-high angle 3	12%	buttocks shot 10	38%
					full body shot 4	15%
	N=26	100%	N=26	100%	N=26	100%
Brazil						
Wide shot	4	14%	high-to-low angle 11	38%	face shot 5	17%
Narrow shot	11	38%	eye-level angle 12	41%	chest shot 5	17%
Close shot	14	48%	low-to-high angle 6	21%	buttocks shot 8	28%
					full body shot 11	37%
	N=29	100%	N=29	100%	N=29	100%

*The unit of analysis for this project was the serve. Within each serve, multiple camera shots, camera angles, and body shots could be recorded because the camera shot would change over the course of play following the serve. The data reported here represents the first camera shot following each serve.
**The camera angle data reported here represents the first camera angle recorded (within the first camera shot) following each serve.
***The body shot data reported here represents the first body shot recorded (within the first camera shot and within the first camera angle) following each serve.

serve, the camera shot would sometimes zero in on the Team USA players' chests. For example, during the early round game, 32% of the 56 camera shots were tight shots of Walsh or May's chest; 22% of the 144 shots in the game against Sweden were chest shots; 38% of the 138 camera shots against China were coded as chest shots, and 28% of the 152 shots in the final game against Brazil were chest shots (see Table 2).

Furthermore, in the analysis of camera angles used for each shot, it was found that the frequency of low-to-high shots increased as Team USA advanced (see Tables 1 and 2). Certainly, it could be argued that as the videographers and photographers became more familiar with the sport and the players, they quickly acclimated themselves to getting camera shots and camera angles that emphasized the athletes' body parts rather than the athletes' bodies as a whole.

It was also noted that at the start of each serve, the camera shot was almost always a wide shot showing Team USA's players' full bodies. This shot tended to be from a camera placed higher than the court, so the shot was coded as high-to-low. If the ball stayed in play for a few seconds, the camera tended to shift to a narrow shot or a shot of the half court. It was usually after the point was over when close camera shots of specific body parts were found shown. Misty May often slapped Walsh's buttock as a form of celebration or support, and the camera operators became quickly trained to capture this motion with a tight shot of Team USA's buttocks. The camera shot was also close and focused in on player's buttocks when adjustments to the swimsuits had to be made.

Finally, on a more observational note, when Misty May and Kerri Walsh beat the Brazilian team of Shelda Bede and Adriana Behar, Walsh and May embraced one another and eventually fell onto the sand on top of one another. This innocent celebratory embrace caught on video and still frames appeared to be sexually provocative. What followed were numerous replays of the moment on television on various networks and numerous reprints of the still frame on the web and in print media. For the United States and for the Walsh/May team, the win meant standing atop the gold medal podium; yet, the cutlines accompanying the still frame and the commentary used with the video deemphasized the athletic feat and focused on the tendency of women to react emotionally when good things happen. Since the Team USA men's team did not fare as well as either women's team, we were not able to compare reactions to a historic win based on gender. However, there were many images to choose from, all which would tell the story of the win, yet many media outlets chose to select the images that showcased the women as

TABLE 2. Camera Angle, Camera Shot and Body Shot During Televised Coverage of Beach Volleyball During the 2004 Olympic Games

Opponent	Camera Shot 2*		Second camera shot of the serve Camera Angle 2**		Body Shot 2***	
	Freq.	%	Freq.	%	Freq.	%
Czech Rep						
Wide shot / high-to-low angle / face shot	7 — 44%		7 — 44%		2 — 13%	
Wide shot	7	44%				
Narrow shot	7	44%				
Close shot	2	12%				
high-to-low angle			7	44%		
eye-level angle			8	50%		
low-to-high angle			1	6%		
face shot					2	13%
chest shot					2	12%
buttocks shot					8	50%
full body shot					4	25%
	N=16	100%	N=16	100%	N=16	100%
Sweden						
Wide shot	9	28%				
Narrow shot	12	38%				
Close shot	11	34%				
high-to-low angle			16	50%		
eye-level angle			11	34%		
low-to-high angle			5	16%		
face shot					2	6%
chest shot					7	22%
buttocks shot					6	19%
full body shot					17	53%
	N=32	100%	N=32	100%	N=32	100%
China						
Wide shot	4	16%				
Narrow shot	12	48%				
Close shot	9	36%				
high-to-low angle			10	40%		
eye-level angle			12	48%		
low-to-high angle			3	12%		
face shot					6	24%
chest shot					6	24%
buttocks shot					7	28%
full body shot					6	24%
	N=25	100%	N=25	100%	N=25	100%
Brazil						
Wide shot	10	34%				
Narrow shot	4	14%				
Close shot	15	52%				
high-to-low angle			10	34%		
eye-level angle			15	52%		
low-to-high angle			4	14%		
face shot					9	31%
chest shot					9	31%
buttocks shot					3	10%
full body shot					8	28%
	N=29	100%	N=29	100%	N=29	100%

*The unit of analysis for this project was the serve. Within each serve, multiple camera shots, camera angles, and body shots could be recorded because the camera shot, camera angle and body shot would change over the course of play following the serve. The data reported here represents the second camera shot following each serve.

**The camera angle data reported here represents the camera angle recorded (within the second camera shot) following each serve.

***The body shot data reported here represents the body shot recorded (within the second camera shot) following each serve.

sexual objects, not their strength, athleticism, or power (see Figure 1). One still picture widely circulated was by Associated Press photographer Adam Butler. This shows a jubilant Misty May celebrating Team USA's victory over Brazil in the golf medal final by grappling teammate Kerri Walsh and taking her to the ground in what could easily be

Photo by Christopher Hogg, www.digitaljournal.com. Reprinted with permission.

taken out of context as a lesbian sexual encouter. Television coverage also delighted in close-up buttock shots when women athletes cradle the volleyball between their legs.

While numerous instances of camera shots accentuating or highlighting the sexuality of the female players were found, it is important to acknowledge that there was no correlation between play-by-play commentary and the visual coverage of the games because comments were made independent of the camera shots as announcers watched the games live from a press box. So, while viewers may link the camera angles with specific comments made by announcers, it is important to note that any correlation between the two is spurious and not related to one another.

DISCUSSION

Pre-Olympic coverage of both the beach volleyball games and beach volleyball female athletes served a purpose for this research–such as coverage discussing the bodies of the female athletes, their clothing, tattoos, and physical attractiveness. This coverage occurred not only in sport and hard news outlets, but, as mentioned, in men's magazines such as *Maxim, Playboy, FHM*, and entertainment news shows such as *Access Hollywood*. More specifically, if one paid attention to the media during the Olympic Games, it would be difficult to avoid a story or photo of one of the two "hot" U.S. beach volleyball players–Misty May or Kerri Walsh. Based on the hype surrounding the sport, especially during the Olympics, it was expected that play-by-play commentary and video coverage of the game would highlight, to a large degree, the women's sexuality. Such hype included feature articles on the personal lives of the players, pictures of the duo in the new (more skimpy) volleyball uniforms, a VISA ad aired during the 2004 Super Bowl, and ads on cups and food wrappers at McDonald's. With beach volleyball being a highly visual and arguably sexy sport, it was expected that high levels of sexualized talk, with a concentration on the athletes' bodies, would be evident in audio coverage of the games. However, as indicated, the results from the analysis of the audio commentary did not support these propositions. The findings suggest that the announcers' calling of women's beach volleyball during the 2004 Olympic Games did not represent traditionally feminine traits and was literally devoid of language related to sexuality, appearance, and attire. Overall, the comments were overwhelmingly positive and focused on the physicality and athleticism of the Team USA women, with a strong emphasis on the domination of May and Walsh.

With regard to visuals, however, the camera shot, body shot and camera angles used during the games did tend to emphasize the athletes' sexual difference, sexuality, and feminine characteristics. While a 2-to-3 second shot of a player's buttock could be construed as unintentional on the part of the camera operator, it is difficult to believe that all the buttock shots were unintentional, especially given the great frequency of such shots during play. More important, because viewers were watching the game, it is very likely they saw these shots of May and Walsh's backsides as the women were walking on the court, bending to receive serve, or resting momentarily between serves. Because a slight increase in the number of buttock shots increased as Team USA advanced to the finals, it is speculated that the camera operators and/or show producers felt this angle was appropriate to use during the game. Given the presence of buttock and chest shots, it is evident that, overall, broadcast of women's beach volleyball was laden with less-than-positive portrayals of female athletes, even though the audio component was resoundingly positive.

Researchers are encouraged to continue analyzing broadcast coverage of women's sports so that the degree in which gender inequities still exist in the play-by-play commentary, color analysis, and video coverage of women's games can be better understood. Observationally, early press coverage of Misty May and Kerri Walsh suggested the media would continue to sexualize the sport and continue its pattern of treating male and female athletes differently. The findings suggest, however, that while other media outlets may have made references to body shape, attire, appearance, and other feminine traits, the broadcast announcers calling the beach volleyball games during the 2004 Olympic Games did so in non-objectified manner. What remains to be seen, however, is how commentary of the women's games differed from the men's beach volleyball games. Future research should systematically examine the commentary and camera shots of the men's and women's games so that a more solid basis of comparison can be made.

In consideration of the broader scope of beach volleyball during the Olympic Games and the promotion and hype of the sport and its athletes before, during, and immediately after the Games, it is likely that the media did rely on the attractiveness and sexuality of the Team USA players, Walsh and May, more so than their athletic skill, strength, or power. As has been seen historically, female athletes appear to get more coverage if they are physically attractive and scantily clad, which tends to deemphasize their athletic prowess. Gabrielle Reece Hamilton, a world famous beach volleyball player, commented that FIVA (International Federation of Volleyball) offers "this fantasy for people who say, 'I love the beach, I love the summer, I love sandy people,' Malibu Barbie stuff and they're trying to play off on that. The bottom line is, sex sells" (Brooks, 2001, p. 3). In other words, when it comes to marketing female athletes and sports, sex sells better than athletic skill. But, if an athlete such as Misty May or Kerri Walsh has both sex appeal and athletic ability, endorsers have an "easier" time marketing the athlete. Today's sports advertising seems to highlight the athletic capabilities and power of the female athlete's body, while, at the same time, overwhelmingly sexualizing the female body (Balsamo, 1996). Such attention-grabbing is known as borrowed interest (Brooks, 2001). "When borrowed interest is used to gain attention, the advertiser is taking advantage of an involving and arousing stimulus to 'borrow' the interest a consumer inherently has for this stimuli" (p. 1). These tactics are used to promote and sell products and companies, using the beauty and appeal of the female athletes. Such importance on looks (not necessarily skill) can be seen through the increased use of attractive and sexy athletes in the marketing and advertising fields.

In conclusion, achieving equity in sports may continue to be a challenge for female athletes in general, but especially when the uniform or competition clothing yields an opportunity for viewers and camera operators to focus on the athletes' body parts rather than their whole bodies (i.e., beach volleyball uniforms, swimsuits, leotards). That said, the findings of the present research reveal that several steps forward have been observed, at least in the manner that announcers call women's sports, even though the visual coverage of the game represents two steps backward. Because of the scope of the Olympic Games and the massive viewership during its two weeks of coverage, it is especially important to know that sports broadcasters took steps to cover the game without letting sexual difference and male bias seep into the commentary. More importantly, young girls watching coverage of women's beach volleyball may have watched the games and realized that they, too, could play sports and do what the boys do. Consider, for instance, the insight Jim Andrews, an editorial director of the IEG Sponsorship Report, imparted to *USA Today* regarding whether real athletic achievement has value for advertising sponsorships:

Winning just doesn't matter as much as it used to . . . There are other ways these athletes can capture the public's attention: by being gorgeous or by being a 'bad boy.' And getting the public's attention is all these companies really care about. ("Win or Lose", 2003, p. 1B)

NOTES

1. In the analysis of televised beach volleyball, the following coding scheme was used. The coding sheet contained 13 categories along the top. Game status was the first category on the coding sheet, and the coders recorded a 1 = round of sixteen, 2 = round of eight, 3 = semifinal, 4 = final, to represent the status of the game within the competition. The same procedure was followed for each variable. Each category represented a nominal variable. Each variable was coded as follows: game status (round of sixteen, round of eight, semifinal, final); game sequence (first of three, second of three, third of three); broadcast announcer gender (male, female); broadcast announcer ethnicity (White, Black, other); play-by-play commentary, which included commentary from the start of the serve to the end of the point (five columns were used so that each comment could be recorded separately); play-by-play commentary valence (positive, negative, neutral-five columns for valence so that each comment made during play could be coded); between-play commentary, which included all commentary made from the time the point was over until the next serve began (eight columns were used so that each comment could be recorded separately); between-play valence (eight columns were also used for this category to record the valence-positive, negative, neutral-of each comment made between serves); camera shot; body shot; and camera angle. Overall, for the unit of analysis, up to 13 different comments could be coded, and 18 data points could be entered for visual coverage.

2. Using the Billings and Halone coding categories for the analysis of commentary, each announcer play-by-play and between-play comment received one of the following codes: physical/behavioral (comments about individual players, "good athlete," "springs off the sand"); mental/cognitive (comments about intelligence, mental skill/mental toughness, "reads the line well"); affective (comments about hard work/effort, determination, i.e., "pushes herself through pain"); dominance (comments about the team as a whole rather than individual players, and comments related to a combination of attributes above); leadership (i.e., "strong leader" or "leads the team well"); background 1 (commentary about an athlete's background related to personal or family issues); background 2 (commentary as it relates to health, physical issues, training, practice, advantages, hardships as it relates to training, health, etc.); calling of the game (comments made regarding specific play, i.e., "Walsh serves," "May for the spike"); reporting of current or past score (comments updating viewers on score of current or earlier game); other team (all comments related to the other team); personal information (comments made regarding current personal life of an athlete); looks, personality, sexuality (comments about body shape, general looks and appearance, hairstyle, body art); and attire (comments specifically regarding the attire worn by athletes during play).

REFERENCES

Alexander, S. (1984). Newspaper coverage of athletes as a function of gender. *Women's Studies International Forum, 17*(6), 655-662.

Balsamo, A. (1996). *Technologies of the Gendered Body*. Durham, NC: Duke University Press.

Billings, A. C., and Eastman, S. T. (2003). Framing identities: Gender, ethic, and national party in network announcing of the 2002 Winter Olympics. *Journal of Communication, 53*(4), 569-586.

Billings, A. C., Halone, K. K., and Denham, B. E. (2002). "Man, that was a pretty shot"; An analysis of gendered broadcast commentary surrounding the 2000 men's and women's NCAA final four basketball championships. *Mass Communication and Society, 5*(3), 295-315.

Bissell, K., and Holt, A. (2005). Who's got game? Gender bias in coverage of the 2004 Olympic Games on the web. Paper presented at the national conference of the International Communication Association, New York, NY.

Brooks, C. M. (2001). Using sex appeal as a sport promotion strategy. *Women in Sport & Physical Activity Journal, 10*(1), 1-16.

Brown, D. (1989, November). Broadcast network television promotion during prime time of prime-time network programs. Paper presented at the convention of the Speech Communication Association, San Francisco, CA.

Carroll, J. B. (1956). *Language, Thought, and Reality: Selected Writings of Benjamin Lee Whorf*. Cambridge, MA: MIT Press.

Davis, D. M., and Walker, J. R. (1991, November). Sex, violence, and network program promotion: A content analysis. Paper presented at the annual meeting of the Speech Communication Association, Atlanta, GA.

Dillman, L. (2004, July 29). The wet look. *Los Angeles Times*. Retrieved July 25, 2005 from http://www.amandabeard.net/Articles/wet_look.htm.

Duncan, M. C., and Hasbrook, C. A. (1988). Denial of power in televised women's sports. *Sociology of Sport Journal, 5*(1), 1-21.

Halbert, C., and Latimer, M. (1994). "Battling" gendered language: An analysis of the language used by sports commentators in a televised coed tennis competition. *Sociology of Sport Journal, 11*(3), 298-308.

Henley, N. M. (1987). The new species that seeks new language: On sexism in language and language change. In J. Penfield (ed.), *Women and Language in Transition* (pp. 3-27). Albany, NY: State University of New York Press.

Hopps, D. (2004). Sun, sand, and a real bum deal for the men. *Guardian Unlimited*. Retrieved on July 10, 2005 from http://sport.guardian.co.uk/olympics2004/ballgames/story/0,14790,1291192,00.html.

Huang, T. (2004, August 30). Female athletes under scrutiny for modeling. *Dallas Morning News*. Retrieved on July 25, 2005 from http://www.kaleo.org.vnews/display.v/ART/2004/08/30/

Millward, R. (2004, January 17). FIFA head wants sexier women's uniforms. *Oakland Tribune*. Retrieved on August 2, 2005 from http://www.findarticles.com/p/articles/mi_qn4176/is_20040117/ai_n9721827

Parks, J. B., and Robertson, M.A. (2000). Development and validation of an instrument to measure attitudes toward sexist/nonsexist language. *Sex Roles, 42*(5/6), 415-438.

Piron, F., and Young, M. (1996). Consumer advertising in Germany and the United States: A study of sexual explicitness and cross-gender contact. *Journal of International Consumer Marketing, 8*(3/4), 211-228.

Reichert, T., and Carpenter, C. (2004). An update on sex in magazine advertising: 1983 to 2003. *Journalism and Mass Communication Quarterly, 81*(4), 823-837.

Reichert, T., Heckler, S. E., and Jackson, S. (2001). The effects of sexual social marketing appeals on cognitive processing and persuasion. *Journal of Advertising, 30*(1), 13-27.

Reichert, T., Lambiase, J., Morgan, S., Carstarphen, M., and Zavoina, S. (1999). Cheesecake and beefcake: No matter how you slice it, sexual explicitness in advertising continues to increase. *Journalism and Mass Communication Quarterly, 76*(1), 7-20.

Sapolsky, B. S., Tabarlet, J., and Kaye, B. K. (1994, August). Sexual behavior and references in program promotions aired during sweeps and nonsweeps periods. Paper presented at the annual convention of the Broadcast Education Association, Las Vegas, NV.

Soley, L., and Kurzbard, G. (1986). Sex in advertising: A comparison of 1964 and 1984 magazine advertisements. *Journal of Advertising, 15*(3), 46-54.

Soley, L., and Reid, L. (1988). Taking it off: Are models in magazine ads wearing less? *Journalism and Mass Communication Quarterly, 65*(4), 960-966.

Win or lose, drawing endorsements is key (2003, August 22). *USA Today*, 1B.

Woodroff, B. (2004, Oct 2). Olympic Centerfolds. *ABC News*. Retrieved on July 26, 2005 from http://abcnews.go.com/sections/WNT/Sports/olympic_centerfolds_040818-1. html

doi:10.1300/J057v13n01_04

Is It the Content or the Person?
Examining Sexual Content
in Promotional Announcements
and Sexual Self-Schema

Yinjiao Ye
Shuhua Zhou

SUMMARY. Sexual content is a prominent feature in television promotional announcements, but its effect has received little scholarly attention. This study tested the efficacy of both sexual content and a personality variable (sexual self-schema) on consumers' attitudes toward the promo, the advertised program, viewing intention, and self-reported arousal. Results showed that sex appeal had main effects on all dependent variables, and moderate sex appeal generally induced the most favorable responses. In contrast, sexual self-schema did not significantly affect participants' responses. Practical and theoretical implications are discussed. doi:10.1300/J057v13n01_05 [Article copies available for a fee from The Haworth Document Delivery Service: 1-800-HAWORTH. E-mail

Yinjiao Ye (PhD, University of Alabama) is Assistant Professor, Department of Communication Studies, University of Rhode Island, Kingston, RI 02881 (E-mail: yinjiao_ye@mail.uri.edu). Shuhua Zhou (PhD, Indiana University) is Associate Professor, Department of Telecommunication and Film, College of Communication and Information Sciences, University of Alabama, Tuscaloosa, AL 35487-0152 (E-mail: szhou@bama.ua.edu).

[Haworth co-indexing entry note]: "Is It the Content or the Person? Examining Sexual Content in Promotional Announcements and Sexual Self-Schema." Ye, Yinjiao and Shuhua Zhou. Co-published simultaneously in *Journal of Promotion Management* (Best Business Books, an imprint of The Haworth Press, Inc.) Vol. 13, No. 1/2, 2007, pp. 55-73; and: *Investigating the Use of Sex in Media Promotion and Advertising* (ed: Tom Reichert) Best Business Books, an imprint of The Haworth Press, Inc., 2007, pp. 55-73. Single or multiple copies of this article are available for a fee from The Haworth Document Delivery Service [1-800-HAWORTH, 9:00 a.m. - 5:00 p.m. (EST). E-mail address: docdelivery@haworthpress.com].

KEYWORDS. Advertising, perception, promotion, sex appeal, sexual self-schema, television

INTRODUCTION

It is an uncontested industry truism that the best TV program without promotion has no audience (Eastman, 2000). Fred Silverman, a celebrated network programmer in the 1970s, claimed that "fifty percent of success is the program and fifty percent is how the program is promoted" (Bedell, 1981, p. 141). Promotional announcements are clearly related to increased viewing, as demonstrated by robust positive correlations with Nielsen ratings (Eastman and Newton, 1999).

Promotions (promos) not only supply viewers information about the availability of a program, they also generate moods and attitudes toward those programs. While scholars have been interested in promotion functions and models, research on the effects of promotions for TV programs has been limited. Most promotions studies thus far deal with the content of promotions by looking at the prevalent strategies and practices, including language, visuals, sounds, and narrative structure. Very little research is available that directly examines the effects of promotions: how they affect viewers' perceptions, attitudes, and behaviors toward the promoted programs (Adams and Lubbers, 2000).

Research findings indicate that sex, next to violence, is the second most ubiquitous feature in promos (Walker, 2000). Oliver and Kalyanaraman (2002), for example, find that sexual portrayals are featured in more than half of promos. Apparently, the industry believes that certain types of content, such as sex and violence, are important elements for generating viewer interest. Consequently, one purpose of this study is to investigate the effects of sexual content in promotions on viewer perception of the promo, the promoted program, viewers' intention to view and discuss the program with others, and self-reported arousal after viewing the promo.

Most effects research to date has assumed that audiences are relatively homogenous (Eastman, 2000). However, not all promos have the same effects on all viewers. Therefore, to fully illustrate the effects of sexual portrayals on promotions, we consider a viewer's sexual self-schema—how one views his or her own sexuality—as a potential moderator.

LITERATURE REVIEW

Promotion Strategies

A successful promo is perceived as one that arouses interest in a program, informs schedule changes, or increases viewer satisfaction with television programs. Eastman (2000) reports that, on average, promotions occupy nearly 5 minutes of a prime-time hour. Walker and Eastman (2003) find that frequency of airing has a positive influence on program ratings. In addition, research demonstrates that sex and violence, as prevalent in televised offerings, are positively related to audience exposure (Williams, 1989). Shidler and Lowry (1995) assert that networks are using sex to attract audiences and that adult sitcoms consistently air high levels of sexual content.

Tallies of sexual content in network promos demonstrate that it is used often. For instance, Soley and Reid (1985) analyzed the content of 806 program ads in *TV Guide* in 1982 and 1983 and found that nearly 33% of such ads have sexual referents. Williams (1989) extends Soley and Reid's work to include promos from 1980 to 1985 in *TV Guide*, and report that 21% contain sexual content. The result differences in findings between the two studies may be due to sample choice as the former draws a sample from September to October and the latter from a sweep period (November and February).

It is widely assumed that "where there's sweeps, there's sure to be sex." For instance, Shidler and Lowry (1995) compared promos before and during sweeps period for sexual behavior in ABC, Fox, and NBC prime-time program promotions. They found that only ABC displayed a decrease of sexual referents in promotions from 7.48 (non-sweeps) to 2.80 (sweeps) per hour; in contrast, both Fox and NBC increase sexual referents in promotions from 2.10 to 4.63, and from 5.11 to 7.50, respectively. The practice of Fox and NBC in using more sex appeal in sweeps than in non-sweeps period provides support for the argument that networks are trying to attract audiences with sexual content.

More recent research reports an increase of sexual referents in prime-time promos from 1994 to 1998 (Walker, 2000). Specifically, the percentage of sexual behavior jumps from 13.3% to 21.5%, and sexual language also increases from 11.3% to 23.4% over the four years. A more recent study (Davies, 2003) shows that nearly 40% of the promos aired during the February 2003 sweeps contain verbal and visual sexual content. Davies' analysis also suggests that it is the visual intensity of sexual content rather than the duration of sexual content that predicts audiences' exposure to the program as measured by Neilsen ratings. Furthermore, survey results suggest that sexual content influences viewers' choice of television programs. For instance, Ward (1995) finds that the programs most viewed by adolescents contain significantly more sexual content than programs most viewed by pre-teens. Bahk (2000) finds that college-aged students are more likely to view television programs preceded by a sexual content advisory.

In sum, the prevalence of sexual content in promos suggests that network executives consider sex to be an effective means for attracting viewers. As important, research partially confirms executives' assumptions, at least with regard to the effect of sexual intensity in promos on audience size and program choice.

Effects of Sexual Portrayals in Advertising

Aside from the aforementioned research, studies of the effects of sexual promotional messages are largely nonexistent. One can, however, draw insight from studies on the effects of sexual content in advertising, as promotion is often considered a subset of marketing communication. Overall, studies show that sexual content in advertising attracts consumers' attention, and sexual ads are perceived as more engaging, entertaining, and interesting (Belch et al., 1981; Bello et al., 1983; Chestnut et al., 1977; Dudley, 1999; Judd and Alexander, 1983; Reichert and Alvaro, 2001; Reid and Soley, 1981, 1983). Sexual appeals also affect consumers' attitudes toward the ad, the product, and/or the brand. For example, Baker and Churchill (1977) found that ads with physically attractive models are rated more favorably than ads with unattractive models. Simpson et al. (1996) show when congruency between product type and nudity is present, respondents' attitudes toward the brand are more favorable in response to nudity. Last, Dudley (1999) found that brands advertised with sexual content are evaluated higher than those without sexual content.

However, the effects of sexual content do not exhibit a linear relationship. Research indicates that after some point, favorability diminishes as the level of nudity or sexiness increases (Alexander and Judd, 1978; LaTour et al., 1990). For example, Sciglimpaglia et al. (1979)

found that higher levels of nudity resulted in less positive evaluations of ads. Simpson et al. (1996) report that evaluations of male nudity increase until full nudity is present. Also, Peterson and Kerin (1977) observe that ads with nude models are rated as less appealing and featured products are of lower quality.

Studies also assess the influence of sex on consumers' behavioral intentions. Evidence shows that sexual content in ads can lead to a higher level of purchase intention compared to nonsexual ads (Dudley, 1999; Grazer and Keesling, 1995). For instance, Reidenbach and McCleary (1983) found that male nudity is effective in enhancing purchase intention among females. In addition, Severn et al. (1990) found that purchase intention is significantly higher in response to sexual ads than to nonsexual advertisements. In the area of social marketing, research indicates that sexual appeals can be more persuasive than nonsexual ads (Reichert et al., 2001).

Further, research indicates that moderate sex appeals are more effective than high-, low-, and no-sex counterparts with regard to purchase intention (Grazer and Keesling, 1995; LaTour and Henthorne, 1994). Specifically, LaTour and Henthorne (1994) found that a mild sex appeal generates significantly higher intention to purchase jeans than a strong, overt sex appeal. Nevertheless, inconsistencies are evident in other studies. For example, Bello et al. (1983) found that ads with controversial sexual content failed to generate intended purchase intention. Studies also show that the effectiveness of sexual appeals are dependent on the congruency of product type and sex. For example, Simpson et al. (1996) reported that for a body oil product, purchase intention is higher following a nude ad than that in response to a control, full dress, or suggestive ad. In contrast, in response to a wrench ad, purchase intention was highest after exposure to the control ad.

In spite of these inconsistencies, research on sexual appeals in advertising generally indicates overall sex is more effective than non-sex appeals in generating favorable attitudes toward the ad, product, and/or brand, as well as in eliciting higher purchase intention, providing that sexual content is appropriate for the product type.

A possible theoretical explanation for this pattern of findings is the affective experience generated by exposure to sex. Psychologists have long noticed the cognitive labeling effects of affective stimuli. For example, researchers find that, after exposure to an arousing sexual story, participants report increased attraction to a potential blind date (Stephan et al., 1971). Berscheid and Walster (1974) refer to this process as misattribution–attributing their experienced physiological arousal as positive affect for the romantic partner. More recent understanding of affect shows that such misattribution does occur, but in a more complex manner. Theorists note that affect consists of two components, valence and arousal (Bradley et al., 2001). Valence has the effect of coloring people's evaluations, whereas arousal tends to accentuate evaluation. In other words, when a stimulus is positively valenced, i.e., pleasant and/or happy, the target is evaluated more favorably than when it is negatively valenced, i.e., unpleasant and sad (Forgas, 1995; Goldberg and Gorn, 1987). In addition, the accentuating effects are more pronounced when the stimulus has high arousal potential compared to low arousal potential, as indicated in a study by Gorn et al. (2001).

Given that responses to sexual information are usually positively valenced (Bradley et al. 2001), exposure to sexual promos should induce favorable evaluations. It follows that the level of sex in an appeal also should correlate with arousal potential, such that highly sexual promos tend to yield the strongest accentuating effects. However, sexual content also is evaluated within a social context. For example, highly sexual material is often frowned upon, especially in a public sphere such as the mainstream media, which may explain why moderate sex appeals appear to be the most effective. Accordingly, the following hypotheses are proposed:

> H1a: The levels of sex appeal in a promo affect participants' perception of the promotion, its perceived entertainment value, perception of the advertised program, viewing intention, and self-reported arousal.

> H1b: Moderate sex appeal in promos generates the most favorable perception of the promotion, its perceived entertainment value, perception of the advertised program, viewing intention, and the highest level of self-reported arousal.

Sexual Self-Schema

Research on the effects of sex may be incomplete without the inclusion of sex-related personality measures, as all viewers may be dissimilar in their processing of sexual promos. Of particular interest to the present study is the concept of sexual self-schema, defined as a cognitive generalization of sexual aspects of the self (Andersen and Cyranowski, 1994; Andersen et al., 1999).

In the past decade, research has demonstrated this concept's ability to predict individual behavior such as condom use, risky sexual behavior, and sexuality in marriage. For instance, Yurek (1998) observes that females with negative sexual self-schemas more frequently experience avoidant behaviors (including avoidance of intercourse) and have greater distress in sexually-relevant situations (e.g., undressing in front of their partner) than females with positive sexual self-schemas. This concept has also been incorporated in advertising studies. For example, Reichert, Fosu, and Xue (2004) found that male respondents with positive sexual self-schemas evaluated a sexual ad more positively. Similar results are reported for females (Reichert and Fosu, 2005), although no relationship is evident between this sexual schema and purchase intention.

Beyond the recognition that men and women react to sexual stimuli differently, Andersen and colleagues also delineate the differences between men's and women's sexual self-schema. For example, if a person has a set self-schema they will not likely accept information that does not coincide with this; however, if one is aschematic he/she is likely to accept all types of information. Specifically, Andersen and co-researchers concluded that, for men, the construct is unidimensional: men can be arrayed along a continuum from schematic to aschematic (Andersen et al., 1999). For women, however, a bivariate model is necessary to capture the concept. Women are thought to have four self-views: positive, co-schematic, aschematic, and negative. Women with a positive self-schema view themselves as emotionally romantic and more open to sexual relationships and experiences. Conversely, women with a negative self-schema perceive themselves as cold or unromantic and are behaviorally inhibited in their sexual relationships. Aschematic women, however, demonstrate weak endorsements toward both positive and negative schema behaviors and emotion, whereas co-schematic women show strong endorsements towards both positive and negative schema behaviors and emotions. Accordingly, we propose the following hypotheses:

H2a: Schematic males will respond more positively toward sexual promos than aschematic males as measured by perception of the promo, the program, viewing intention, and self-reported sexual arousal.

H2b: Positive self-schematic and co-schematic females will respond more positively toward sexual promos than negative self-schematic and aschematic females, as measured by perception of the promotion, the program, viewing intention, and self-reported sexual arousal.

METHODOLOGY

Participants

A total of 147 undergraduate students enrolled at the University of Alabama were recruited for participation, and each was given a research credit. More females (65%) were recruited than males (35%) due to the multidimensional nature of female sexual self-schema. To ensure that participants in each sex appeal condition were comparable, they were also asked whether they were familiar with the promoted TV programs, as well as three viewing habit questions such as frequency of viewing TV shows and/or movies, of viewing promotions and movie previews, and of reading reviews. Analyses indicated that the groups showed no differences in these measures.

Stimuli

Nine color posters promoting three actual network programs (*Hollywood Wives, Likely Stories,* and *The Loss of Sexual Innocence*) were created and used in this study, with images captured from the Internet. These were programs about to be aired for the first time. For each program there were three promos created by the primary researcher, which were similar in all aspects except level of sexual imagery (i.e., low-, medium-, or high-sex). The manipulation of sexual imagery follows the definition of sex in advertising as well as the methods used in the literature. A review of sex in advertising (Reichert, 2003) indicates that the types of sexual content in advertising research often include nudity/ dress, sexual behavior, physical attractiveness, and sexual referents; further, nudity, sexual behavior, and physical attractiveness are the most common operationalization of sexual content in advertising (e.g., Dudley, 1999; Reidenbach and McCleary, 1983). Therefore, sex appeal was manipulated with variations of dress, sexual behavior, and physical attractiveness of models in the promos: Models in the low-sex condition were fully dressed, exhibited no sexual behavior, and were of average attractiveness; Models in the medium-sex condition wore revealing clothing, exhibited intimate forms of sexual behavior such as hugging and kissing, and were physically attractive; Models in the high-sex condition were nearly nude, exhibited very intimate behavior such as intercourse, and were highly attractive. Manipulation checks using participant ratings (11-point scale) indicated that the manipulation was successful, F (2, 144) = 82.66, p < .01. Pairwise comparisons also indicated that the groups were rated differently in degree of sexual content ($M = 1.52$, $SD = 2.22$, low-sex condition; $M = 6.43$, $SD = 2.15$, medium-sex condition; and $M = 7.13$, $SD = 2.70$, high-sex condition).

Within each condition there were three promos, each promoting one of the three programs. The purpose for using three promotions for each condition was to reduce random variance introduced by any uninteresting features of a particular promotion. The promotions were stored in a PowerPoint file, and were projected onto a screen.

Experimental Procedure

Participants were randomly assigned to one of three conditions (i.e., low, medium, or high sex) and were told that they would view some promos, and that they would be required to complete a questionnaire before and after viewing. Each participant signed a consent form before beginning.

Participants completed the sexual self-schema questionnaire first, with women and men using a different instrument for this scale. They were then shown three promotions, one for each of the three programs and all of representing the same sex level. Participants were given 20 seconds to view the promos in a dark room to ensure that attention was focused. After each promotion, the light was turned on and participants provided their feedback on the questionnaires. This procedure was repeated until all three promos were viewed. Once the questionnaires were completed, respondents were debriefed and thanked.

Other Variables

Sexual self-schema (IV). Female participants completed the 26-item schema scale from Andersen and Cyranowski (1994) while male participants used the 27-item scale from Andersen et al. (1999). The female scale has three factors, one negative and two positive whereas the male scale is a continuum. For the females, we followed Andersen and Cyranowski's instruction in first computing a score for each person on the negative factor of the scale, ranging from 2 to 32 ($M = 19.92$). A median split was conducted to separate the high and low scorers. The same procedure was conducted for the two positive factors in the scale, ranging from 60 to 101 ($M = 82.17$). Median split was used to separate high and low scores for both factors. These women's self-schema scores were then computed such that aschematic women were those low on both negative and positive factors; positive schematic women were those low on the negative factor but high on the positive factors; negative schematic women were those high on the negative factor but low on the positive factors; and co-schematic women were those high on both negative and positive factors (Andersen and Cyranowski, 1994). Male scores ranged from 82 to 139 ($M = 109.57$, $SD = 13.31$), and median split separated positive and negative schematics (Andersen et al., 1999).

Perception of promo (DV). Unless otherwise noted, all items were measured on 11-point scales anchored by "Not at all/Extremely." Ten items used to assess perception of the promos were drawn from previous research (Baker and Churchill, 1977; Belch et al., 1981; Bello et al., 1983; Dudley, 1999): involving, arousing, appealing, exciting, enjoyable, pleasant, good, sexy, boring, and disgusting. Reverse coding was applied to "boring" and "disgusting." Reliability for the scale was high ($a = .91$). Responses were therefore summed and divided by 10 to create a mean response for each participant.

Perceived entertainment value of promo (DV). Eight items measured the perceived entertainment value of the promotion. These items were adapted from those reported by Watson, Clark, and Tellegen (1988), and Watson and Clark (1991). Respondents were asked how likely they were to agree with the following: "It made me feel bad"; "It embarrassed me"; "I enjoyed it"; "It excited me"; "It made me feel good"; "I loved it"; "It relaxed me"; and "It bored me." Reverse coding was applied to the first two and last items. Reliability for the scale was acceptable ($a = .82$). Responses were summed and divided by eight to create a mean response score for each participant.

Perception of the promoted show (DV). Six Likert-type items measured the perception of the promoted show. Respondents were asked to rate each show on the following: appealing, interesting, enjoyable, sexy, exciting, and boring. Reverse coding was applied to the last item. Reliability was high for this scale ($a = .92$). Responses were summed and divided by six to create a mean response score.

Viewing intention (DV). Two items were created to measure participants' viewing intention. Participants were asked whether "I would consider watching the show when it's available," and "I would discuss and/or recommend the show to a friend."

Sexual arousal (DV). Respondents' subjective sexual arousal evoked by the promo was measured with three items by adapting two components of a sexual arousal scale created by Mosher, Barton-Henry, and Green (1988). The two components, sexual arousal and sexual interest, are subjective estimates of the participants' overall level of sexual arousal and the degree of present interest in sexual imagery or activities. Respondents rated how sexy the promotions were, how sexually enticing they felt about the promotions, and how sexually aroused they were ($a = .83$). A mean score was also created for each respondent by summing the items and dividing by three.

RESULTS

A series of MANOVAs were conducted to test the effects of sex and sexual self-schema on the dependent variables. Because of the incomparability between men and women's sexual self-schema, the first two hypotheses about the general effects of sex appeal were analyzed using the full data set. The last two hypotheses regarding the effects of sexual self-schema were analyzed separately for men and women.

Hypothesis 1a predicted that the level of sex in a promo would affect participants' perceptions of the promo, its entertainment value, and the advertised program, in addition to viewing intention and self-reported arousal. Overall, this hypothesis was supported. The main effect for level of sex appeal was significant in affecting participant perception of the promotion, $F(4, 140) = 4.75$, $p < .01$, $\eta^2 = .12$. Post hoc Bonferroni tests indicated that the medium-sex condition was significantly different from the low-sex condition ($p < .05$). Participants perceived the promotion in the medium-sex condition more favorably than the promotion in the low-sex condition. However, there was no significant difference between high- and medium-sex conditions, nor was there a difference between high- and low-sex conditions (see Table 1 for means on all dependent variables). For the perceived entertainment value of the promos, the main effect of sex also was significant, $F(4, 140) = 3.49$, $p < .05$, $\eta^2 = .09$. Post hoc analyses indicated that the medium-sex condition registered the highest mean, though the differences between groups were not statistically significant. The main effect of level of sex appeal also was significant in affecting participants' perceptions of the promoted program, $F(4, 140) = 5.89$, $p < .01$, $\eta^2 = .15$. Post hoc Bonferroni tests indicated that the medium-sex condition was significantly different from the low-sex condition ($p < .01$). Further-

TABLE 1. Mean Responses as a Function of Sex Appeal in Promotion

	Levels of Sex Appeal		
Dependent Variables	Low	Medium	High
1. Perception of promotion	4.38 (1.49) a	5.41 (1.45) b	5.08 (1.58) ab
2. Perceived entertainment value	4.70 (0.95) a	4.98 (1.14) a	4.71 (1.16) a
3. Perception of show	4.22 (1.77) a	5.47 (1.74) b	5.42 (1.78) b
4. Intention to watch	3.85 (2.95) a	4.45 (2.84) a	4.81 (2.74) a
5. Intention to discuss	2.87 (2.70) a	3.61 (2.56) a	3.98 (2.60) a
6. Sexual arousal	1.77 (1.38) a	4.10 (1.96) b	4.69 (1.66) c

Note: Means that do not share subscripts differ at $p < .05$ in the post hoc Bonferroni significant difference

comparison. Values in parentheses are standard deviations.

more, the low-sex condition was also significantly different from the high-sex condition ($p < .05$).

On the two behavioral intention measures, degree of sex also had significant main effects: viewing intention, $F(4, 140) = 3.07$, $p < .05$, $\eta^2 = .08$, and discussion/recommendation intention, $F(4, 140) = 2.64$, $p < .05$, $\eta^2 = .07$. The main effect of sex appeal also significantly affected participants' self-reported arousal, $F(4, 140) = 27.15$, $p < .01$, $\eta^2 = .45$. Post hoc Bonferroni tests indicated that the medium-sex condition was different from the low-sex condition as well as the high-sex condition. In addition, the high-sex condition also was significantly different from the low-sex condition ($p < .01$). In sum, level of sex appeal had main effects on all dependent variables, though effect sizes varied.

Hypothesis 1b predicted that the medium-sex appeal would generate the most favorable responses. From the post hoc analyses, it was evident that statistical differences existed between the medium conditions and other conditions for at least three dependent variables: perception of the promo, perception of the promoted show, and self-reported arousal. An examination of the data trend on all six dependent variables revealed an intriguing pattern, showing that the medium-sex condition peaked in three dependent variables related to the promotion and the promoted show (see Figure 1). However, the high-sex condition produced higher self-reported arousal and behavioral intention (see Figure 2), all of which relate to the self. Therefore, Hypothesis 1b is partially supported.

Hypotheses 2a and 2b made predictions about schematic males responding more positively toward sexual promos than aschematic males, whereas positive self-schematic and co-schematic females should respond more positively than negative self-schematic and aschematic females. However, none of the analyses showed that sexual self-schema, either for men or for women, was a significant factor in this investigation, nor did it interact with sex appeal.

DISCUSSION AND IMPLICATIONS

This study was designed to test the efficacy of sex appeals in network promos. Overall, the prediction that the level of sex appeal is influential on consumer responses is supported. However, the hypothesis that medium sex has optimal effects is supported only on the attitudinal measures related to perception of the promo, its entertainment value, and perceptions toward the promoted program, but not on measures related to the self: self-reported arousal, viewing intention and discussion intention. Also, sexual self-schema was found to have no effect on the dependent variables.

It is interesting to note that the medium-sex condition performed as predicted on variables pertaining to the perception of the promos and promoted programs, but not on individual variables. Because perception occurs from the interaction of what is being perceived and who the perceiver is, it is possible that social history of the perceiver plays a mediating role in this equation (Eysenk, 2001). Often society values the golden mean and discourages the extreme. As such, high-sex appeals are often considered inappropriate, resulting in disapproving attitudinal effects toward the promo and the promoted program. However, social influence diminishes when it encounters intensely personal variables

FIGURE 1. Mean Responses Pertaining to Perception

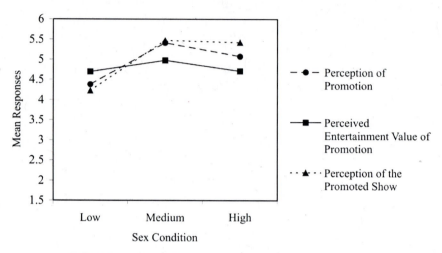

FIGURE 2. Mean Responses on Individual Variables

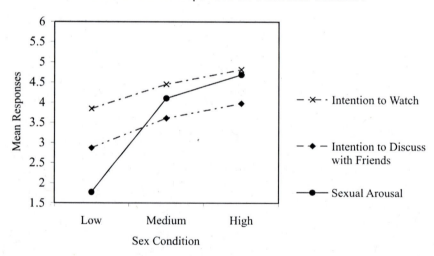

such as sexual arousal, and viewing and discussion intention. As the high-sex condition in this study contained only nudity and not extremely explicit sexual behavior, the boundary for offensive sexual content may not have been crossed, thereby resulting in a more direct transfer between the degree of sex appeal, the degree of sexual arousal, and behavioral intention.

Sexual self-schema affected none of the dependent variables, nor did it interact with sex appeal to affect the variables of interest. The creators of the scale consider it an unobtrusive and reliable measure for predicting how a person processes sexual information (Andersen and Cyranowski, 1994; Andersen et al., 1999). In the few advertising studies using the scale, researchers also reported moderate predictive power for this personality variable (Reichert and Fosu, 2005; Reichert et al., 2004). In light of the results in this study, it is possible to question either the validity of the scale in the context of promotion research or the robustness of the current study. It is possible that the scale is more conducive in predicting sexual attitudes and behaviors in unmediated situations. After all, the scale originates from survey data related directly to people's personal lives. In a mediated environment, its predictive power may fade. On the other hand, the small pool of participants in this study was limited to college students. As such, variation of the sample may not be large and diverse enough to allow full test of the concept.

Implications

The present study offers both professional and theoretical implications. As previously noted, sex is a prominent feature in TV program promos. The present findings support some of the decisions made by industry professionals regarding strategic decisions to promote a program. However, the results can only be generalized to short-term perceptions and viewing decisions, and nothing can be said about moderate to long-term effects on viewing behavior. As the findings suggest, sex influences perceptions of the promoted show as well as intention to view it.

There are two theoretical points to consider. First, the pattern of findings may be the result of cognitive labeling, as sexual appeal may influence subsequent evaluations. However, the duration of such an influence is unknown. Some promotions are aired several hours or days before the program airs. It would be interesting to find out the duration of such effects so that professionals can make informed decisions. Future research could incorporate multiple time points to test such effects. Second, the expectation of sexual content may be so high that if the program is inadequate or fails to match the implicit promise of "seeing more," consumers may feel cheated and reject the program. Underlying this conjecture, however, is the assumption that viewers expect to see sexual content after exposure to sexual promotions. The validity of such an assumption can be tested in future research by designing a study in which the program either provides what is promised (i.e., sexual content) or not (i.e., no sexual content).

Additionally, the arousal component of sexual information deserves further investigation. Judging by the effect size that sex had on self-reported arousal ($\eta^2 = .45$), and given the positive valence that sexual content evokes, it can be argued that a sizable portion of the perceptual effects can be attributed to arousal. Indeed, results of this study support a claim by previous research that arousal accentuates valence effects (Gorn et al., 2001), but only up to a point, as the high sex condition does not yield the highest perceptual evaluations. In other words, the accentuating function of arousal may not be linear. One shortcoming of this study is that the high-arousal condition is not sufficiently high ($M = 7.13$, 11-point scale), allowing only a limited range of examination. Regardless, future research can test the accentuating effects of arousal by sufficiently varying this component to test its validity and linearity. If enough arousal variations are manipulated, it is possible to pinpoint the level of arousal at which the accentuating effect peaks and begins to decline.

A second area of interest for future research is to examine the elicited arousal and the subsequent attention that viewers pay to the promotion, as arousal is strongly and positively correlated with attention (Lang et al., 1999). For example, one can measure participants' physiological arousal such as skin conductance under different levels of sexual content and measure attention using participants' heart rates to objectively correlate the two variables (see Grabe et al., 2000). At any rate, results of this study point to the effectiveness of sex in promos, even though sexual self-schema does not indicate predictive power. A fuller understanding of sex in network promos necessitates investigation into the valence and arousal components of sexual content.

REFERENCES

Adams, W. J., and Lubbers, C. A. (2000). Promotion of theatrical movies. In S. T. Eastman (ed.), *Research in Media Promotion* (pp. 231-264). Mahwah, NJ: Lawrence Erlbaum Associates.

Alexander, M. W., and Judd, B. (1978). Do nudes in ads enhance brand recall? *Journal of Advertising Research, 18*(1), 47-51.

Andersen, B. L., and Cyranowski, J. C. (1994). Women's sexual self-schema. *Journal of Personality and Social Psychology, 67*(6), 1079-1100.

Andersen, B. L., Cyranowski, J. M., and Espindle, D. (1999). Men's sexual self-schema. *Journal of Personality and Social Psychology, 76*(4), 645-661.

Bahk, C. M. (2000). College students' responses to content-specific advisories regarding television and movies. *Psychological Reports,* 87, 111-114.

Baker, M. J., and Churchill, G. A. (1977). The impact of physically attractive models on advertising evaluations. *Journal of Marketing Research, 24*(4), 538-555.

Bedell, S. (1981). *Up the Tube: Prime-time TV and the Silverman Years.* New York: Viking.

Belch, M. A., Holgerson, B. E., Belch, G. E., and Koppman, J. (1981). Psychophysical and cognitive responses to sex in advertising. In A. Mitchell (ed.), *Advances in Consumer Research, Volume 9* (pp. 424-427). Ann Arbor, MI: Association for Consumer Research.

Bello, D. C., Pitts, R. W., and Etzel, M. J. (1983). The communication effects of controversial sexual content in television programs and commercials. *Journal of Advertising, 12*(3), 32-42.

Berscheid, E., and Walster, E. (1974). A little bit about love. In T. Huston (ed.), *Foundations of interpersonal attraction* (pp. 24-42). Stanford, CA: Stanford University Press.

Bradley, M. M., Codispoti, M., Cuthbert, B. N., and Lang, P. J. (2001). Emotion and motivation I: Defensive and appetitive reactions in picture processing. *Emotion, 1*(3), 276-298.

Chestnut, R. W., LaChance, C. C., and Lubitz, A. (1977). The "decorative" female model: Sexual stimuli and the recognition of advertisements. *Journal of Advertising, 6*(4), 11-14.

Davies, J. (2003, August). Sexual content in promotional ads: Contributions of visual aspects to exposure. Paper presented at the annual meeting of the Association for Education in Journalism and Mass Communication, Kansas City, MO.

Dudley, S. C. (1999). Consumer attitudes toward nudity in advertising. *Journal of Marketing Theory and Practice, 7*(4), 89-96.

Eastman, S. T. (2000). Orientation to promotion and research. In S. T. Eastman (ed.), *Research in Media Promotion* (pp. 3-18). Mahwah, NJ: Lawrence Erlbaum Associates.

Eastman, S. T., and Newton, G. D. (1999). Hitting promotion hard: A network response to channel surfing and new competition. *Journal of Applied Communication Research*, 27(1), 73-85.

Eysenck, M. W. (2001). *Principles of Cognitive Psychology, 2nd ed.* East Sussex, UK: Psychology Press.

Forgas, J. P. (1995). Mood and judgment: The affect infusion model. *Psychological Bulletin, 117*(1), 39-66.

Goldberg, M. E., and Gorn, G. J. (1987). Happy and sad TV programs: How they affect reactions to commercials. *Journal of Consumer Research, 14*(3), 387-403.

Gorn, G., Pham, M. T., and Sin, L. Y. (2001). When arousal influences ad evaluation and valence does not (and vice versa). *Journal of Consumer Psychology, 11*(1), 43-55.

Grabe, M., Zhou, S., Lang, A., and Bolls, P. (2000). Packaging television news: The effects of tabloid on information processing and evaluative responses. *Journal of Broadcasting and Electronic Media, 44*(4), 581-598.

Grazer, W. F., and Keesling, G. (1995). The effect of print advertising's use of sexual themes on brand recall and purchase intention: A product specific investigation of male responses. *Journal of Applied Business Research, 11*(3), 47-58.

Judd, B. B., and Alexander, M. W. (1983). On the reduced effectiveness of some sexually suggestive ads. *Journal of the Academy of Marketing Science, 11*(2), 156-168.

Lang, A., Bolls, P., Potter, R. F., and Kawahara, K. (1999). The effects of production pacing and arousing content on the information processing of television messages. *Journal of Broadcasting and Electronic Media, 43*(4), 451-475.

LaTour, M. S., and Henthorne, T. L. (1994). Ethical judgments of sexual appeals in print advertising. *Journal of Advertising, 23*(3), 81-90.

LaTour, M. S., Pitts, R. E., and Snook-Luther, D. C. (1990). Female nudity, arousal, and ad response: An experimental investigation. *Journal of Advertising, 19*(4), 51-62.

Mosher, D. L.; Barton-Henry, M.; and Green, S. E. (1988). Subjective sexual arousal and involvement: Development of multiple indicators. *Journal of Sex Research, 25*(3), 412-425.

Oliver, M. B., and Kalyanaraman, S. (2002). Appropriate for all viewing audiences? An examination of violent and sexual portrayals in movie previews featured on video rentals. *Journal of Broadcasting and Electronic Media, 46*(2), 283-299.

Peterson, R. A., and Kerin, R. A. (1977). The female role in advertisements: Some experimental evidence. *Journal of Marketing, 41*(4), 59-63.

Reichert, T. (2003). What is sex in advertising: Perspectives from consumer behavior and social science research. In T. Reichert and J. Lambiase (eds.), *Sex in Advertising: Perspectives on the Erotic Appeal* (11-38). Mahwah, NJ: Lawrence Erlbaum Associates.

Reichert, T., and Alvaro, E. (2001). The effects of sexual information on ad and brand processing and recall. *Southwestern Mass Communication Journal, 17*(1), 9-17.

Reichert, T., and Fosu, I. (2005). Women's responses to sex in advertising: Examining the effect of women's sexual self-schema on responses to sexual content in commercials. *Journal of Promotion Management, 11*(2), 143-153.

Reichert, T., Fosu, I., and Xue, F. (2004). Examining responses to sex in advertising: Personality variables and sexy commercials. In P. Neijens, C. Hess, B. van den Putte, and E. Smit (eds.) *Content and Media Factors in Advertising* (pp. 91-99). Amsterdam, Netherlands: Het Spinhuis.

Reichert, T., Heckler, S. E., and Jackson, S. (2001). The effects of sexual social marketing appeals on cognitive processing and persuasion. *Journal of Advertising, 30*(1), 13-27.

Reid, L. N., and Soley, L. C. (1981). Another look at the "decorative" female model: The recognition of visual and verbal ad components. *Current Issues and Research in Advertising, 4*(1), 123-133.

Reid, L. N., and Soley, L. C. (1983). Decorative models and the readership of magazine ads. *Journal of Advertising Research, 23*(2), 27-32.

Reidenbach, R. E., and McCleary, K. W. (1983). Advertising and male nudity: An experimental investigation. *Journal of the Academy of Marketing Science, 11*(4), 444-454.

Sciglimpaglia, D., Belch, M. A., and Cain, R. F. (1979). Demographic and cognitive factors influencing viewers' evaluations of "sexy" advertisements. In W. L. Wilke (ed.), *Advances in Consumer Research, Vol. 6* (pp. 62-66). Ann Arbor, MI: Association for Consumer Research.

Severn, J., Belch, G. E., and Belch, M. A. (1990). The effects of sexual and non-sexual advertising appeals and information level on cognitive processing and communication effectiveness. *Journal of Advertising, 19*(1), 14-22.

Shidler, J. A., and Lowry, D. T. (1995). Network TV sex as a counterprogramming strategy during a sweeps period: An analysis of content and ratings. *Journalism and Mass Communication Quarterly, 72*(1), 147-157.

Simpson, P., Horton, S., and Brown, G. (1996). Male nudity in advertisements: A modified replication and extension of gender and product effects. *Journal of the Academy of Marketing Science, 24*(3), 257-262.

Soley, L., and Reid, L. (1985). Baiting viewers: Violence and sex in television program advertisements. *Journalism Quarterly, 62*(1), 105-110, 131.

Stephan, W., Berscheid, E., and Walster, E. (1971). Sexual arousal and heterosexual perception. *Journal of Personality and Social Psychology, 20*(1), 93-101.

Walker, J. R. (2000). Sex and violence in program promotion. In S. T. Eastman (ed.), *Research in Media Promotion* (pp. 101-126). Mahwah, NJ: Lawrence Erlbaum Associates.

Walker, J. R., and Eastman, S. T. (2003). On-air promotion effectiveness for programs of different genres, familiarity, and audience demographics. *Journal of Broadcasting and Electronic Media, 47*(4), 618-637.

Ward, L. M. (1995). Talking about sex: Common themes about sexuality in the prime-time television programs children and adolescents view most. *Journal of Youth and Adolescence, 24(5),* 595-615.

Watson, D., and Clark, L. A. (1991). Self- versus peer ratings of specific emotional traits: Evidence of convergent and discriminant validity. *Journal of Personality and Social Psychology, 60*(6), 927-940.

Watson, D., Clark, L. A., and Tellegen, A. (1988). Development and validation of brief measures of positive and negative affect: The PANAS scales. *Journal of Personality and Social Psychology, 54*(6), 1063-1070.

Williams, G. A. (1989). Enticing viewers: Sex and violence in *TV Guide* program advertisements. *Journalism Quarterly, 66*(4), 970-973.

Yurek, D. L. (1998). Surgical treatment of breast cancer: Sexual self-schema, stress reactions, and sexuality outcomes. Unpublished Doctoral Dissertation, Ohio State University.

doi:10.1300/J057v13n01_05

Sex and Shock Jocks:
An Analysis of the *Howard Stern* and *Bob & Tom* Shows

Lawrence Soley

SUMMARY. Studies of mass media show that sexual content has increased during the past three decades and is now commonplace. Research studies have examined the sexual content of many media, but not talk radio. A subcategory of talk radio, called "shock jock" radio, has been repeatedly accused of being indecent and sexually explicit. This study fills in this gap in the literature by presenting a short history and an exploratory content analysis of shock jock radio. The content analysis

Lawrence Soley (PhD, Michigan State University) is Colnik Professor, Diederich College of Communication, Marquette University, Milwaukee, WI 53233 (E-mail: lawrence.soley@marquette.edu).

The author would like to thank Holly DeShaw and Aaron Smith for their assistance.

[Haworth co-indexing entry note]: "Sex and Shock Jocks: An Analysis of the *Howard Stern* and *Bob & Tom* Shows." Soley, Lawrence. Co-published simultaneously in *Journal of Promotion Management* (Best Business Books, an imprint of The Haworth Press, Inc.) Vol. 13, No. 1/2, 2007, pp. 75-93; and: *Investigating the Use of Sex in Media Promotion and Advertising* (ed: Tom Reichert) Best Business Books, an imprint of The Haworth Press, Inc., 2007, pp. 75-93. Single or multiple copies of this article are available for a fee from The Haworth Document Delivery Service [1-800-HAWORTH, 9:00 a.m. - 5:00 p.m. (EST). E-mail address: docdelivery@haworthpress.com].

doi:10.1300/J057v13n01_06

compares the sexual discussions of two radio talk shows: Infinity's *Howard Stern Show* and Clear Channel's *Bob & Tom Show*. doi:10.1300/ J057v13n01_06 *[Article copies available for a fee from The Haworth Document Delivery Service: 1-800-HAWORTH. E-mail address: <docdelivery@haworth press. com> Website: <http://www.HaworthPress.com> © 2007 by The Haworth Press, Inc. All rights reserved.]*

KEYWORDS. Advertising, content analysis, Federal Communications Commission (FCC), indecency, radio, sex, shock jock

INTRODUCTION

The quantity and explicitness of sexual content in mass media has steadily increased during the past three decades. Greenberg and Busselle (1996) found that sexual activities depicted in soap operas increased between 1985 and 1994, rising from 3.67 actions per hour in 1985 to 6.64 per hour in 1994. Kunkel et al. (2001) found that the percentage of television programs with sexual content increased from 56% during the 1997/1998 season to 68% during the 1999/2000 season. In a study of 2001 television programming, Fisher et al. (2004) found that 78.8% of broadcast network programming contained sexual content. Over 95% of the movies airing on premium cable channels contained sexual content, as did feature films shown on the commercial television networks.

Sommers-Flanagan and colleagues (1993) found that nine-tenths of the 30-second intervals in a sample of MTV music videos contained sexual materials. In a study of sexual content in media to which adolescents were exposed, Pardun et al. (2005) found that music contained the most sexual content, outstripping television, movies and magazines. The majority of the sexual content dealt with romantic relationships, but 15% concerned sexual intercourse. Pardun et al. (2005) also found a significant relationship between exposure to sexual materials and adolescents' sexual activity.

Sexual content on the internet is also pervasive. For example, studies conducted for the US General Accounting Office and House Committee on Government Reform showed that over 50% of the video files retrieved on file-sharing servers such as Kazaa using seemingly innocent search terms such as "Britney" and the "Olsen twins" contained pornography (Krim, 2003). The use of sexual appeals in advertisements has also increased over time. Reichert et al. (1999) showed that the percentage of magazine ads portraying intimate sexual behavior more than doubled between 1983 and 1993.

These studies demonstrate that sexual content in the media has increased, and is abundant on the internet, music, music videos, television, films, and magazine advertisements, but no study has yet systematically studied the sexual content of talk radio shows, particularly "shock jock" shows. Shock jocks have been criticized for their sexual-and some say, obscene-discussions. The term "shock jocks" originated with critics employed by other media, who developed the term to describe radio shows containing "a panoply of sexual and scatological references" and cultural and ethnic insults (Feldman, 2004, p. 1261).

This study fills in the gap in the research by presenting a short history of shock jock radio shows and a content analysis of one week of the *Howard Stern Show* and the *Bob & Tom Show*. Both drive-time radio programs receive high ratings where they air, and may well set the standards for sexual content of other media. Stern says, "I changed the way people speak on TV. I changed the way people talk on the radio. . . . When I first got into radio, TV never used the word 'penis' on the air" (Stern, 2002). Stern is regarded as a shock jock, whereas Bob and Tom are not.

ORIGINS OF "SHOCK JOCK" RADIO

The direct predecessor of shock jock radio is the "topless radio" format that developed in the early 1970s. This format originated in Los Angeles with Storer Broadcasting-owned station KGBS-AM/FM, which assigned nighttime disk jockey Bill Balance as host of a live, daytime call-in show titled *Feminine Forum* (McLellan, 2004). Women were invited to call the *Feminine Forum* and discuss that day's issue, which was usually a romantic or sexual topic (Carlin, 1976; McLellan, 2004).

Although originally targeted to women, the show attracted many men, and after a year-and-half captured the number one rating in the city. The show's popularity led to its being syndicated and imitated. Similar shows appeared in New York, Detroit, Cleveland, Washington, DC, Dallas, and Chicago (Shipler, 1973; Carlin, 1976). Some imitators, such as the *Feminine Forum* program carried on Sonderling Broadcasting Co.'s WGLD-FM in Chicago, had far more sex-laden discussions than Balance's show.

Federal Communications Commission (FCC) chairman Dean Burch listened to tapes of these broadcasts and the following month at the National Association of Broadcasters convention excoriated "the prurient trash that is the stock-and-trade . . . of the smut-hustling host" (Krebs, 1973, p. 94). Burch was not just responding to what he heard on the tapes, but to a reported 3,000 obscenity complaints received by the FCC about the programs. Two weeks later, the FCC fined WGLD-FM for airing indecent programs focusing on oral sex, where callers were invited to discuss their experiences on-air (FCC, 1973). Rather than challenge the fine, Sonderling paid it and then halted the talk show. Other stations also dropped their programs.

The radio industry's rapid submission to the FCC was due to several factors: First, fears that industry expansion would be hurt if the programs continued; second, topless radio's contribution to station profits was small; and third, industry executives believed that the Nixon-appointed FCC would revoke station licenses for the continued airing of these shows. A radio station manager summed up the first factor, saying, "We are a member of a group that operates a number stations and are going to cable TV, and our growth depends on FCC approval." Another noted, "We didn't feel it was a big enough part of our format to be worth the hassle" (Krebs, 1973, p. 94). Lastly, the FCC had a decade earlier refused to renew the license of a Kingtree, South Carolina station for programming that was "course, vulgar, suggestive and of indecent double meaning." The FCC's decision was upheld in court (*Robinson v. FCC*, 1964).

Don Imus

Don Imus, host of the syndicated *Imus in the Morning Show*, is considered the pioneer of "shock jock" radio (White, 1995), but the format is actually a fusion of "topless" and insult radio, which was pioneered by Joe Pyne. Imus's radio career began in Sacramento in 1968, where he developed a reputation for, and increased his popularity by, making prank phone calls, hurling insults and making lewd comments. This strategy was copied by subsequent shock jocks, who continuously increased the sexual content of their shows. Imus's success in Sacramento allowed him to move to larger markets, first Cleveland then New York, where the same combination of antics attracted high ratings (Goldstein, 2000).

Imus's national prominence is linked to Infinity Broadcasting Corp.'s purchase in 1992 of WFAN-AM in New York. The station was purchased to ensure that Infinity had a major presence in the New York market, and because Infinity chairman Mel Karmazin viewed Imus's show as an established "franchise" that could be nationally syndicated. When added to Infinity's rock station, WXRK-FM, which carried Howard Stern in the morning, Infinity captured nearly 16 percent of 25-54 olds, the largest percentage being male (Colford, 1992). Infinity's strategy was to attract younger, "rock and roll" males with Stern on the rock station, and older, better-educated males with Imus on WFAN, and to then syndicate the shows to other stations.

In order to attract a better-educated audience, and to attract celebrities to interview, Imus abandoned the crudest elements of his show, leading some commentators to describe him as a "former shock jock" (Feldman, 2004). This, in turn, attracted higher profile celebrities, and made the program more palatable for Midwestern markets, such as Sioux City and Fargo, where stations have carried the program (Marcotty, 1995). An example of Imus's toned-down comments are typified by a 2005 interview with conservative Sen. Rick Santorum (R-PA), who appeared on *Imus in the Morning* to discuss his book, *It Takes a Family: Conservatism and Common Good*. Imus said to Santorum, "You have six kids. Can I ask you a personal question?" Santorum said, "Yes," and Imus asked, "Have you had sex with Mrs. Santorum more than six times?" Santorum replied "yes" again, and the interview continued as before (Eisele and Dufour, 2005).

Imus views his show as competing with news and classic rock programs for better educated males, in contrast with Stern's program. "By the nature of what we do, you're limiting the audience . . . It's a high-end audience," unlike the one attracted to Stern, Imus says (Ostrow, 1995). Imus reportedly dislikes Stern not just because of Stern's higher ratings, but because he views Stern as a vulgar imitator.

Howard Stern

Like Imus, Stern is a product of Infinity Broadcasting. He began as a radio personality in Connecticut, and then moved to larger stations in Detroit and Washington, DC. Stern returned to his hometown of New York in 1982, after landing a show on NBC's flagship station, WNBC-AM. He was fired from there in 1985 for broadcasting a skit, "Bestiality Dial-A-Date," but was quickly picked up by Infinity's WXRK-FM. The following year, Infinity Broadcasting started syndicating Stern's show, which featured interviews with strippers, pornographers, prostitutes and second-tier celebrities (Flint, 1992).

In the Los Angeles, Philadelphia and Washington, DC markets, where his show has been syndicated, Stern was number one in ratings among men 18-34 during the early 1990s. After putting Stern on KLSX-FM in Los Angeles, the station was able to quadruple its morning drive-time rates (Viles, 1992). Although Stern's ratings faltered over the years, he returned to the number one spot in New York and Los Angeles in 2004 (Pugh, 2004). These ratings have created for Stern a loyal advertising base, including Anheuser-Busch, Cingular Wireless and Toyota, which have been reluctant to terminate advertising on his show despite pressure from such groups as the American Decency Association (American Decency Association, 2004).

The profitability and popularity of Stern's show explains why the radio industry responded differently to FCC complaints about indecency in the 1990s than to complaints about "topless radio" in the 1970s: The profits generated by shock jock programming exceeded the fines levied by the FCC. Thus, stations continued to air, and Infinity continued to distribute, the *Howard Stern Show* even after the FCC repeatedly fined Infinity Broadcasting for Stern's indecency (Ahrens, 2005). Moreover, Clear Channel decided to carry Stern's show on their stations after the FCC concluded that the show's content had been indecent (Petrozello, 1996; Stern, 1995), suggesting the corporation was less interested in decency than profits.

Other reasons for the different response was that the industry had consolidated, creating much larger, more secure corporations; shock jock programming had become a bigger and more profitable part of radio programming than "topless" radio was; and the industry was more willing to challenge the FCC on First Amendment grounds. The largeness of the radio industry, and the importance of shock jocks, is exemplified by Infinity Broadcasting, which acquired Westwood and Unistar networks, in part to distribute its talk shows, which included shock jocks Don Imus, Howard Stern, and Doug "The Greaseman" Tracht (Vilas, 1993a, 1993b). Infinity is now part of Viacom, one of the world's largest media companies.

Broadcasting companies assert that shock jocks are protected by the First Amendment because of the increased protection accorded indecent speech by court decisions such as *Reno v. ACLU* (1997), and because many shock jocks espouse political philosophies on their shows. For example, shock jocks Howard Stern and "Mancow" Muller espouse libertarianism, leading them to criticize "politically correct" Democrats like former President Bill Clinton.

Part of Stern's appeal to 18-34 year-old males is because of his opposition to "political correctness." As one listener put it, "I like the fact that that with all the political correctness in the world, he is anti-pc"

(Pugh, 2004, E8). In contrast with Imus, who interviews but neverthe-less criticizes Democrats and Republicans, Stern has used his show to promote anti-pc political candidates, whose laissez faire attitudes Stern favors. Stern endorsed such candidates as President Ronald Rea-gan, gubernatorial candidates George Pataki, Christine Todd, and Ar-nold Schwarznegger, and mayoral candidate Rudolph Giuliani (Marinucci, 2004; Ferguson, 2004). Despite his favoring Republican candidates, traditional conservative organizations have been Stern's most vocal critics.

Stern shifted political allegiances in 2004, announcing that he op-posed President George W. Bush's re-election. The major reason for the shift was that Bush appointee Michael Powell led a FCC crackdown on indecent broadcasting, which Stern viewed as an attack on him (Fergu-son, 2004). Several days after Stern's announcement, Clear Channel suspended and then dropped Stern's show from six stations, saying that its decision was based on Stern's refusal to abide by FCC indecency rules or the corporation's new "zero tolerance" policy, adopted after Clear Channel was fined for indecency by the FCC. Stern claimed the decision was based on his opposition to Bush.

In 2004, Stern signed a $500 million, five-year contract with Sirius Satellite Radio to appear on that network beginning in 2006, claiming that being on satellite would allow him to escape FCC "censorship" (Klaassen, 2005). Stern repeatedly mentioned his impending move to Sirius during broadcasts, causing a displeased executive with Citadel Broadcasting Corp., whose stations carried Stern's show, to plead with Stern's producer "to get Howard back to the T and A and the filth, and off satellite" (Day, 2005). When Stern did not stop, Citadel dropped him from its stations and temporarily replaced him with the shock jock *Opie & Anthony Show* under an agreement with Sirius's rival, XM Satellite Radio (Reuters, 2005; Bachman, 2004).

Mancow

After Stern announced his move to satellite, Infinity Broadcasting began looking for a substitute for Stern. One of the individuals Infinity courted was Eric "Mancow" Muller, another politically conservative shock jock (Feder, 2005). Muller, a San Francisco area shock jock in the early 1990s, gained notoriety by stopping Bay Bridge traffic for a hair-cut to ridicule President Clinton for allegedly tying up Los Angeles air traffic while getting a $200 trim (Kettmann, 1993). Using similar stunts, Mancow earned a reputation and following, which allowed him to move to Chicago, a larger market. In Chicago, Mancow hosts *Mancow's Morning Madhouse* on Emmis Communications' WKQX-FM, an album-oriented rock station. The show is syndicated to 20 stations by Talk Radio Network.

Mancow's show appeals to male virility with a combination of conservatism, militarism and sex. His followers are described as members of Mancow's Militia, and his website (www.Mancow.com) includes images of partially nude women holding weapons. T-shirts sold by Mancow read, "Kill a Satanist for Christ." An example of the way that Mancow mixes patriotism and sex is exemplified by an interview with statutory rapist Joey Buttafuoco, who discussed the Moonlight Bunny Ranch, a legal brothel (Q-101, 2003). The Bunny Ranch's owner, Dennis Hof, offered free sex to American soldiers who finished a tour of Iraq. As a result of broadcasts such as these, Mancow has succeeded in generating higher ratings in some markets than Stern (Smith, 2005).

Like Stern, Mancow was been cited by the FCC for indecent broadcasting, including one segment where a porn star graphically described "fisting" and another where women were interviewed about whether they "spit or swallowed" after engaging in oral sex (FCC, 2002, 2004). Also like Stern, Mancow has been the target of conservative critics, despite his self-professed conservatism. As an example, David Smith of the Illinois Family Institute filed 66 complaints about Mancow's indecency with the FCC (Feder, 2004).

Despite paying $42,000 in fines for the indecent content of Muller's show, Emmis Communications continued to air it, suggesting that the company is less interested in morality than money. However, Muller claims that he is changing the content of the show to more accurately reflect his Christian outlook. "When I was 22, it was interesting to talk to porn stars . . . I'm just not there anymore," Muller claims (Smith, 2005).

The "Bob & Tom Show"

The *Bob & Tom Show* is hosted by Bob Kevoian and Tom Griswold, who have been doing the show for over twenty years. The program is classified as a comedy program and has been syndicated to radio stations since 1995 by Premiere Radio Networks, a Clear Channel subsidiary (Premiere Radio Networks, 2003). The program originates on classic rock station WFBQ in Indianapolis, a Clear Channel station. The *Bob & Tom Show* is syndicated in the morning to over 150 stations nationwide and is targeted to somewhat older males who listen to classic rock, but is also carried by alternative rock stations that target younger males, Stern's target market. Although not usually classified as a "shock jock" program, the show has been cited by the FCC for indecency (FCC, 2000).

Bob and Tom are joined on-air by Kristi Lee, the program's female "news director," and Chic McGee, the program's "sports director." Other personnel call the show and pretend to be Larry King, Bill Clinton, George Bush, Dr. Phil, and other, less well-known characters. The show consists of humorous songs and skits, news segments that are interrupted with comments and jokes, and telephone interviews with celebrities or near-celebrities, such as Mark Vancil, co-author of Michael Jordan's autobiography, and former talk show host Dick Cavett. The show usually includes having stand-up comics present in the studio, who integrate their comedy routines into the show.

The format is similar to that of the *Howard Stern Show*, which also has a female news announcer, Robin Quivers. Quivers joins Stern on-air with an assortment of other talking heads, who have included comic Artie Lange, John Melendez, Gary Dell-Abatte, and KC Armstrong, who was fired in 2004 after fabricating a story to generate publicity for a gambling website. Stern takes calls from listeners and does celebrity interviews.

The *Bob & Tom Show* is scripted with the skits, songs and phone calls that revolve around daily themes, to which the personalities repeatedly return. The themes of the day are inspired by news stories and listeners' comments or questions.

The *Howard Stern Show* is scripted, but far less so than the *Bob & Tom Show*, making it appear more spontaneous and less predictable than its competitor. Like the hosts of the *Bob & Tom Show*, Stern frequently has a daily theme to which the personalities repeatedly return, or around which the program is focused.

The *Bob & Tom Show* was selected for comparison with shock jock Howard Stern's broadcasts because it is one of the most widely-syndicated talk shows targeted to males, and originates on a station operated by Clear Channel, which now claims to have a "zero tolerance" policy toward indecency. The program should therefore serve as a benchmark, with which to compare the sexual content of the *Howard Stern Show*, as well as serving as a measure of the sexual content on large, corporate-owned programs.

METHOD

This study consists of an exploratory content analyses of the *Howard Stern Show* and the *Bob & Tom Show*, comparing the two for sexual content. A week of *Howard Stern Show* broadcasts from June 24-28, 2002 was obtained from the American Decency Association, which has a library of taped Stern broadcasts. Over one hour of the programming on the tapes was inaudible. Thus, under 19 hours of the show were actually analyzed.

The researchers asked for these broadcasts because they: (1) Pre-dated the FCC's attempts to curb indecency following the bearing of Janet Jackson's breast during the 2004 Super Bowl half-time show; (2) preceded Stern's decision to move to Sirius; and (3) preceded Stern's about-face on supporting President Bush. Thus, the broadcasts should be typical of Stern broadcasts during the late 1980s, 1990s and early 2000s.

Stern's show is on the air five hours each weekday morning, but just under four hours is actual programming. The Stern show employs 13-minute cut-aways, during which commercials and news segments are aired by the radio stations. The show was also carried for 11 years by the *E!* cable channel, and was that network's highest rated program until ending its run in July 2005 (*Broadcasting and Cable*, 1994; Wallenstein, 2005).

The *Bob & Tom Show* is on the air weekdays between 6 and 10 a.m. EST. The content of this show was analyzed by randomly sampling shows airing between October 25 and November 15, 2005. This time period follows Clear Channel's dropping Stern from their stations, and follows the FCC's reported attempts to curb indecency on radio. It should therefore be indicative of the content of radio in the "post-2004 Super Bowl" era.

Coding

An attempt was made to code the radio shows using coding catego-ries developed in previous studies (e.g., Greenberg and Busselle, 1996, p. 155), where references to "prostitution, rape, homosexual-ity, intercourse among individuals married to each other" and other sexual activities were coded, but these categories proved inadequate and unreliable, given the varied nature of sexual discourse on the radio shows. As an example of the difficulties, *Bob & Tom Show* daily themes included a report about a woman who glued her ex-boyfriend's "manhood" to his stomach; nude beach behavior; a vibrator that can be attached to an iPod; and a life-size, nude blow-up doll of news director Kristi Lee, all of which elicited numerous comments that did not reliably fit previously-used categories.

Consequently, a much simpler, but reliable method was used for the coding, which consisted of coding ten-minute segments of each broadcast as to whether they contained or did not contain sexual content. Sexual content was described as references to breasts, genitals and anuses; nudity and partial nudity; intercourse, oral sex, anal sex, intimate touching and arousal; prostitution and stripping; masturbation; semen; menstruation; adult bookstores, theaters, toys and pornography, including references to blow-up dolls; and double entendres for these, which the FCC has ruled can be indecent (FCC, 2000). Although it might be argued that anal references are not necessarily sexual, comments on the radio shows demonstrate they are. For example, during a discussion of clothing on the *Bob & Tom Show*, a male described some young women as wearing "little teeny sweatpants that say 'juicy' right above their buttocks" (November 11).

References such as "giving the finger" or referring to someone as a "bitch" or "queer" were not coded as sexual, unless combined with any of the above sexual references. However, referring to a woman as a "nut cracker" was, because the term includes a reference to male genitals. Similarly, words such as "friggin" were not coded as sexual.

Using this definition, three different judges analyzed 18 ten-minute segments of the *Howard Stern Show*. At least two coders analyzed each segment, producing 88.8% agreement. Disagreements focused primarily on whether epithets such as "whore" constituted sexual content. The coding nevertheless proved reliable (Scott's pi = .82). Another 79 ten-minute segments of the *Howard Stern Show* and 87 ten-minute segments of *Bob & Tom Show* segments were analyzed by a single judge.

RESULTS

Of the *Howard Stern Show* segments, 73.2% (i.e., 71 of 97) had sexual content. A slightly higher percentage of segments on the *Bob & Tom Show* (78.6%) contained sexual content. These two percentages do not differ significantly ($z = -.85$, using a difference of proportions test), suggesting that the number of segments containing sexual materials on both shows is similar.

Although the number of segments containing sexual references does not differ, a qualitative analysis shows that the programs differ in terms of their focus on sex. First, interviews conducted on the *Howard Stern Show* focus heavily on the sexual activities of the interviewee, as shown by the following questions asked of *JAG* television actress Catherine Bell (June 28):

> HS: When did you start having sex? How old were you?
> HS: (about being taught by nuns): The school you went to, did they discourage you from masturbating?
> HS: (about Bell's husband): How long did it take you to bang him after you met him?
> HS: (about Bell's relationship with her husband): Would you ever bring another woman in the sack?
> HS: Is size important to you? Size, yeah, men's size–penis size?
> HS: You ever made a made a home porno with him?

Bell answered some questions, such as about her first sexual encounters, and answered, "It's not my thing," to questions about bisexuality and home pornography. The only time she became indignant was when Stern ridiculed her belief in Scientology.

Similarly, actor David Arquette was asked the following questions about his relationship with his wife, actress Courteney Cox (June 25):

> HS: Have you ever banged her without a rubber?
> HS: Have you ever done anal with her?
> HS: Do you ever take home porno of Courteney? Like, do you guys ever make your own porno?
> HS: Would you ever give Courteney an enema . . . I'm talking about a sexual enema?

Stern's questions are designed to make interviewees engage in explicit sexual discussions. *Bob & Tom Show* interviews are the opposite–they usually avoid sexual discussions, although Mark Vancil's interview about Michael Jordan ended with a request for Jordan's email address, and a quip about sending him a spam email for a "penis extender."

Second, the news segments on the two shows are the opposite: The *Bob & Tom* news segments usually focus on sexual topics, which lead to short sexual discussions, whereas the *Howard Stern Show* news reports are usually about non-sexual matters that may or may not lead into sexual discussions. As examples, news segments on the *Bob & Tom Show* included reports about Lauren Hutton posing in the nude at 61 years of age; a sex party on Lake Minnetonka sponsored by Minnesota Vikings players; a Serbian physician's claim that he can induce temporary infertility in men by transmitting a mild electrical current through testicles; a report about an adult video producer being sued in Great Britain for false advertising; and two Carolina Panthers cheerleaders being arrested after engaging in sex acts in a restroom at a Tampa bar, all of which are real news stories. Such stories led to numerous sexual comments, such as referring to Minnesota Vikings quarterback Dante Culpepper as "Cul-pecker"; and discussions of lesbianism in sports, dotted with comments such as the Women's National Basketball Association not wanting "to use the phrase, 'Take it to the hole'" (October 26).

In contrast, news reports on the *Howard Stern Show* are usually, but not always, about popular culture, celebrities and entertainment, which Stern or his co-hosts often turn toward sexuality. For example, a news report that actress Daryl Hannah was dating magician David Blaine led Stern to complain, "David Blaine is banging Daryl Hannah . . . Who's he to be banging her?" (June 24). A discussion about a forthcoming calendar featuring Stern's girlfriend, model Beth Ostrosky, led KC to comment, "I had this calendar with hot Asian chicks. I must have pleasured myself three times a week to that calendar" (June 28). A report and discussion about the death of The Who bassist John Entwhistle resulted in a remark about Peter Townsend's friendship with Beth Ostrosky. This led Artie to comment, "The guy must be trying to get in her pants" (June 28).

Not all Stern news reports are about celebrities. A June 28 broadcast concerning a report that most women are wearing the wrong sized bra led to a 45-minute discussion about bras and breasts, during which Stern reportedly measured a female college student for a bra, commenting about the size of her "boobs" and observing, "In college, I would have banged you so hard you wouldn't have known what hit you." Stern also interviewed the woman about her sex life, and after learning that she shaved all over, offered her money and other inducements to remove her bikini bottom, saying, "Do you totally shave? Everything shaved off? Boy, that's hot. What kind of money does it take to get those bottoms off?" She reportedly removed them.

These and the previously quoted statements demonstrate a major difference between the sexual content of the *Stern* and the *Bob & Tom* shows: *Stern* broadcasts usually concern personal sexual gratification, whereas *Bob & Tom*'s do not. Paying a woman to remove her bikini bottom produces sexual excitement for Stern–and titillation by audio voyeurism for listeners–and little else. Discussions of nude beach decorum as were carried on the *Bob & Tom Show* do not focus on individual sexual gratification, and might even produce the opposite. For example, "Larry the Cable Guy" said that most young men go to nude beaches with false expectations, saying, "Let's go see some boobies." Bob commented that their expectations are that all the women will "look like *Playboy* centerfold models." "Instead, there are old women bending over with their boobs hanging down like a 7-11 split," Larry says (October 25). Thus the comments, while sexual, do not concern individual sexual gratification, but disappointment. This distinguishes much *Howard Stern Show* content from *Bob & Tom Show* airings, and may well distinguish indecency from crudity.

Third, the analysis shows that Kristie Lee and Robin Quivers serve different functions on the two radio shows. Kristie serves as a tempering voice, often claiming to be embarrassed about discussions of sexuality, such as her comments about the nude Kristie Lee blow-up doll shown on the *Bob & Tom* website. "It isn't funny if my 7 year-old daughter sees it," she said. On the other hand, Robin Quivers' comments differ little from the males' comments on the Stern show, and often encourage sexual discussion. As an example, Artie commented about actress Jaime Bergman, "What kind of lens do you have to use to get Jaime Bergman's breasts on screen . . . They're enormous." Quivers concurred, saying with a laugh, "I've never seen a bra top for a bikini that big" (June 24).

DISCUSSION

Approximately three-fourths of the 10-minute segments analyzed for this study contained sexual content. The percentages were nearly the same for shock jock Howard Stern's program and the comedic *Bob & Tom Show*, which raises the question: What is the difference between shock jocks and other morning radio talk show personalities? A qualitative analysis of the content suggests that they are distinguishable only by degree: Shock jock programming focuses more on individuals' sexual gratifications, whereas the other programming does so to a far lesser degree. There is a difference between asking David Arquette if he engages in anal intercourse with his wife, as Stern did, and airing a segment about "Herbie the Love Hummer," a homosexual vehicle, who "slams on his brakes" and says, "Hey, What does a guy have to do to be rear-ended around here?" as the *Bob & Tom Show* did. Stern's approach gives one a personal look–make that a leer–into the sexual activities of individuals, which Bob and Tom's sexual comments do not.

Both broadcasts use a variety of synonyms for breasts (i.e., "boobies" and "cans"), penises (i.e., "peckers" and "weiners"), female pubic areas ("beavers" and "fur burgers"), semen ("DNA" and "mayonnaise") and nearly every other sexual activity. Although both shows use similar terminology, the terms are used differently on the shows: Howard Stern individualizes the terms, whereas Bob and co-host Tom do not. An example of this is provided by Stern's interview with Catherine Bell: Stern says that her breasts are large and inquires, "Are they real?" Stern then says, "That's a D-cup bra" and laughing says, "I'll measure you." During a discussion of a nude photograph of Catherine Bell, Stern asserts he can see her "fur burger." In contrast, the *Bob & Tom* duo refer to the "huge, heaving breasts" and "big breasted women" that can be seen wearing Birbiglia brand tank tops on their website.

The frequency with which sexual comments are made on both radio programs undoubtedly exceeds the frequency of sexual discourse in everyday life, suggesting that programs do not merely reflect sexual norms, as some theorists have suggested. The frequency with which sexual content appears in the programs suggests that it is used to attract and maintain male listeners, creating an unreal, sex-filled environment. On Stern's show, this fantasy world is taken to an extreme, where men are allowed to make comments to a woman about her breasts, ask a woman to remove her bikini bottom, or ask whether she has "orgied" or had lesbian experiences. This conclusion about a sex-filled, male fantasy world is supported by the terms used on the programs, such as "beaver," "hole" and "fur burger," that is part of the vocabulary of younger men, not women, and by the way that sexual material on the show's websites are mentioned to induce listeners to go to the websites.

Last, the analysis shows that explicit sexual content is common, even on radio shows originating on Clear Channel, which has adopted a "zero tolerance" policy toward indecency. Although Clear Channel and Infinity might claim that their program content is not indecent, this is something that the FCC determines, largely based on listener complaints.

CONCLUSIONS

The sexual content of talk radio shows is far more graphic than the sexual content of other broadcast or major print media, providing support for Stern's contention that he and other radio hosts set the standard for sexual permissiveness in other media. As an example of this graphicness, Stern opened his show on June 26, complaining about the underwear he was wearing, having switched from boxers to briefs to look sexier. About the briefs, Stern complained, "I want to hang free . . . I want to arrange it so my wiener isn't so stifled . . . My balls feel stifled, all crunched together. I like everything to loosely hang." Clearly, Stern engages in far more graphic, on-air sexual discussions than found in other media, establishing a standard of what is legally acceptable for broadcast discourse.

Other radio programs, such as the *Bob & Tom Show*, also engage in considerable, graphic sexual discussion, even using words that violate the "seven dirty words" standard. As an example, Bob spelled out the name of a Thai newspaper on air, "The P-h-u-k-e-t Gazette," and challenged his co-hosts to pronounce it (November 11). One readily volunteered, "It's 'fuck it.'"

These types of discourse occur on a daily basis and are found in nearly three-fourths of all ten-minute radio segments, this study shows. Although Stern and other radio hosts complain about FCC censorship, the number of fines levied by the FCC for indecency have been few compared to the number of graphic, and potentially indecent, sexual discussions in which radio talk show hosts have engaged. As an example, Stern and his co-hosts use words such as "wiener," "prick" (June 26), and "penis" (June 27) without hesitation. The FCC apparently does not consider this language indecent.

When the FCC does determine that shock jocks' language has been indecent, it does not vigorously pursue the cases (McConnell, 1997). A study by the *Washington Post* of the 93 proposed indecency fines levied by the FCC found that most were "undermined by plodding investigations, insufficient fine amounts and inconsistent follow-up" (Ahrens, 2005, p. A1). The FCC levies fines, but does not collect them. It also willingly renegotiates and lowers the fine, and then allows broadcasters to pay the reduced amount without admitting guilt. As an example, a 1996 Stern interview with adult film actress Jenna Jameson was cited by the FCC for indecency a full year after it was broadcast, and fined just $6,000. Four years later, the fine was never paid, so the FCC rescinded it due to "passage of time" (Ahrens, 2005).

Despite the FCC's reluctance to levy and collect fines for indecency, Stern nevertheless claims that the FCC heavily censors what he and others say. During one broadcast, Stern contended, "Censorship is running rampant when it comes to me . . . What kills me now is because of the FCC scrutiny of me, I can't say things" (June 27). Despite this assertion, Stern or his co-hosts on June 27 nevertheless referred to a woman as "giv[ing] great oral," used words such as "penis" and "balls" repeatedly, said that he had run "into my dad at a gang bang, a whorehouse," and discussed motel etiquette, which called for "pleasur[ing] yourself in the shower." Stern and other radio personalities appear to be free from FCC censorship, despite claiming that their speech has been sharply curtailed by the FCC. By claiming to be censored, they can appear to be confronting and challenging "big brother."

Given the content of Stern's terrestrial radio show, it is difficult to imagine how it will be change in the "unregulated" environment of satellite radio. A future study should examine whether Stern's "unregulated" satellite show is markedly different from his broadcast radio show, or whether Stern's claims of being heavily censored on terrestrial radio were just that–mere claims.

REFERENCES

Adelson, A. (1996, June 21). Man behind the scenes at Infinity Broadcasting. *New York Times*, D5.

Ahrens, F. (2005, November 10). Delays, low fines weaken F.C.C. attack on indecency. *Washington Post*, A1.

American Decency Association (2004, June). Toyota: Hardcore advertiser of the *Howard Stern Radio Show. ADA Newsletter*, 1, 3.

Bachman, K. (2004, December 6). Stern cut short on Citadel affils after plugging Sirius. *Media Week, 14*, 4.

Carlin, J. C. (1976). The rise and fall of topless radio. *Journal of Communication, 26(1)*, 31-37.

Colford, P. D. (1992, July 22). Mel who? That's megawatt Mel Karmazin, head of Infinity Broadcasting. *Newsday*, 56.

Day, J. (2005, January 6). Citadel turns off "bad-mouthing" Stern. *The Guardian*, 19.

Eisele, A., and Dufour, J. (2005, August 3) Under the dome. *The Hill* (Washington, DC), 3.

Fast track. (2004, May 3). *Broadcasting and Cable, 134,* 6.

Feder, R. (2004, August 3). Mancow ends legal beef with indecency crusader. *Chicago Sun-Times*, 55.

Feder, R. (2005, August 30). How Infinity stumbled on the road to Mancow. *Chicago Sun-Times*, 57.

Federal Communications Commission (1973, April 11). In re the apparent liability of station WGLD-FM (73-401). 41 *F.C.C. 2nd* 919.

Federal Communications Commission (2000, April 28). Notice of apparent liability for forfeiture (DA 00-951). 15 *F.C.C. Record* 13624.

Federal Communications Commission (2002, October 31). In the matter of Emmis Radio License Corporation: Forfeiture order (DA 01-2937). 17 *F.C.C. Record* 21697.

Federal Communications Commission (2004, February 18). In the matter of Emmis Radio License Corporation: Memorandum opinion and order (DA 04-386). 19 *F.C.C. Record* 2701.

Feldman, C. (2004). Shock jocks. In C. Sterling (ed.), *Encyclopedia of Radio* (p. 1261). New York: Fitzroy Dearborn.

Ferguson, A. (2004, July 18). Stern's anti-Bush crusade shouldn't be casually dismissed. *Pittsburgh Post-Gazette*, B2.

Fisher, D. A., Hill, D. L., Grube, J. W., and Gruber, E. L. (2004). Sex on American television: An analysis across program genres and network types. *Journal of Broadcasting and Electronic Media, 48*(4), 529-553.

Flint, J. (1992, November 2). FCC's Stern fine: Record $105,000. *Broadcasting, 122,* 55-56.

Goldstein, R. (2000, July 12-18). Celebrity bigots. *Village Voice*, 12.

Greenberg, B. S., and Busselle, R. W. (1996), Soap operas and sexual activity: A decade later. *Journal of Communication, 46(4),* 153-160.

Kettmann, S. (1993, November 14). Return of the personality that can stop traffic. *San Francisco Chronicle*, 58.

Klaassen, A. (2005, August 22). Sirius asking top dollar for spots on Stern show. *Advertising Age, 76,* 6.

Krebs, A. (1973, March 29). Burch scores fad of "topless radio." *New York Times*, 94.

Krim, J. (2003, March 13). Pornography prevalent on file-sharing services. *Washington Post*, E1.

Kunkel, D., Cope-Farrar, K., Biely, E., Maynard-Farinola, W. J., and Donnerstein, E. (2001). *Sex on TV (2)*. Menlo Park, CA: Kaiser Family Foundation.

Lorek, L.A. (2004, July 22). Clear Channel fires back at lawsuit. *San Antonio Express-News*, 1E.

Marcotty, J. (1995, June 5). Tiny KCFE radio adds shock jock Don Imus to its morning lineup. *Star Tribune*, 1D.

Marinucci, C. (2004, July 1). Stern mobilizes shock jock bloc. *San Francisco Chronicle*, A1.

McConnell, C. (1997, January 27). FCC indecency review yields few fines. *Broadcasting and Cable, 127,* 26.

McLellan, D. (2004, September 25). Obituary: Bill Balance, 85, legendary host of provocative radio talk show. *Los Angeles Times*, B14.

Nguyen, D. (2004, November 24). 4 letters spell end for DJ. St. *Petersburg Times*, 1B.

Ostrow, J. (1995, October 2). Offending with a smile is old stuff for Don Imus. *Denver Post*, F1.

Pardun, C. J., L'Engle, K. L., and Brown, J. D. (2005). Linking exposure to outcomes: Early adolescents' consumption of sexual content in six media. *Mass Communication and Society, 8*(2), 75-91.

Petrozzello, D. (1996, October 21). Stern generates indecency fine against Richmond station. *Broadcasting and Cable, 126*, 23.

Premiere Radio Networks (2003, November 24). Premiere Radio Networks renews "The Bob and Tom Show" (press release).

Pugh, C. (2004, July 18). We're in for a rude awakening. *Houston Chronicle*, E8.

Q101-FM (2003, July 7). Mancow radio interview with Joey Butafuoco, digital archive. Retrieved October 20, 2005 from www.q101.com/interviews/mancow.aspx.

Rahner, M. (2000, August 13). Churning up the radio. *Seattle Times*, L1.

Reichert, T., Lambiase, J., Morgan, S., Carstarphen, M., and Zavoina, S. (1999). Cheesecake and beefcake: No matter how you slice it, sexual explicitness continues to increase. *Journalism and Mass Communication Quarterly, 76*(1), 7-20.

Reno v. ACLU. 117 *S. Ct.* 2329 (1997).

Reuters (2005, January 2). Stern off four more stations. *Houston Chronicle*, A2.

Robinson v. F.C.C. 334 *F. 2nd* 534 (1964).

Shipler, D. K. (1973, April 24). Sexually explicit radio shows wilt under criticism by F.C.C. *New York Times*, 1.

Smith, L. (2005, June 19), Catching the Mancow fever. *Los Angeles Times*, E26.

Sommers-Flanagan, R., Sommers-Flanagan, J., and Davis, B. (1993). What's happening on music television? A gender role content analysis. *Sex Roles, 28*(11/12), 745-753.

Stern, E! strike deal. (1994, June 6). *Broadcasting and Cable, 124, 24.*

Stern, C. (1995, July 17). FCC to butt heads with Stern. *Broadcasting and Cable, 125*, 48.

Stern, H. (Producer). (2002, June 27). *The Howard Stern Radio Show*. Radio broadcast. New York: Infinity Radio.

Viles, P. (1992, November 2). Stern builds a loyal advertiser following. *Broadcasting, 122*, 53-54.

Viles, P. (1993a, January 18). Infinity eyes Unistar. *Broadcasting and Cable, 123*, 8.

Viles, P. (1993b, October 18). A new network giant: Infinity to run Westwood and Unistar. *Broadcasting and Cable, 123*, 40.

Wallenstein, A. (2005, June 23). Shock jock to depart E! channel. *Chicago Sun-Times*, 43.

White, K. (1995, May 17). Shock jock pioneer holds no punches. *Las Vegas Review-Journal*, 1E.

doi:10.1300/J057v13n01_06

Selling Music with Sex: The Content and Effects of Sex in Music Videos on Viewer Enjoyment

R. Glenn Cummins

SUMMARY. Sexual content in music videos has long been the focus of attention within communication research, although few communication scholars have illuminated the relationship between sex in a music video, viewer enjoyment, and actual product purchase intention. This article examines the presence of sexual content in music videos as well as the relationship between sexual content and enjoyment. The paper challenges scholars from communication, advertising, and marketing to establish links among their disciplines to develop a thorough understanding of how sex in music videos may increase liking of a video and subsequent purchase intention. doi:10.1300/J057v13n01_07 *[Article copies available for a fee from The Haworth Document Delivery Service: 1-800-HAWORTH. E-mail address: <docdelivery@haworthpress.com> Website: <http://www.HaworthPress.com> © 2007 by The Haworth Press, Inc. All rights reserved.]*

R. Glenn Cummins (PhD, University of Alabama) is Assistant Professor, Department of Electronic Media and Communications, College of Mass Communications, Texas Tech University, Box 43082, Lubbock, TX 79409-3082 (E-mail: glenn.cummins@ttu.edu).

[Haworth co-indexing entry note]: "Selling Music with Sex: The Content and Effects of Sex in Music Videos on Viewer Enjoyment." Cummins, R. Glenn. Co-published simultaneously in *Journal of Promotion Management* (Best Business Books, an imprint of The Haworth Press, Inc.) Vol. 13, No. 1/2, 2007, pp. 95-109; and: *Investigating the Use of Sex in Media Promotion and Advertising* (ed: Tom Reichert) Best Business Books, an imprint of The Haworth Press, Inc., 2007, pp. 95-109. Single or multiple copies of this article are available for a fee from The Haworth Document Delivery Service [1-800-HAWORTH, 9:00 a.m. - 5:00 p.m. (EST). E-mail address: docdelivery@haworthpress.com].

Available online at http://jpm.haworthpress.com
© 2007 by The Haworth Press, Inc. All rights reserved.
doi:10.1300/J057v13n01_07

KEYWORDS. Content analysis, media effects, music video, promotion, purchase intention, sex

INTRODUCTION

Since MTV debuted more than two decades ago, music videos have become a staple of the recording industry. Although some critics examine the form for its aesthetic and/or cultural value (e.g., Dancyger, 2002; Feineman and Reiss, 2000), the music video remains at its core a three-and-a-half-minute advertisement designed to sell everything from the actual artist and records, to clothing and lifestyle, to motion pictures (Smith, 1985). Recent examinations of the music video position it as a part of the "complete musical artist package; it creates face recognition" (Andsager, 2006, p. 37). Although the success of the form as an advertising vehicle has been in doubt for years (e.g., Bronstein, 1986), the recording industry continues to operate under the implicit assumption that music videos are an effective means of promoting an artist.

Despite recent complaints that MTV and its progeny have abandoned their focus (i.e., music videos), ample evidence exists to support the argument that music videos remain a vital part of the recording industry's marketing mix. MTV continues to expand its brand on-air and online through spin-off channels and proprietary online portals like MTV Overdrive that serve up music videos on demand (Ouellette, 2005; Umstead, 2005). In addition, virtually all major record labels are actively pursuing alternate means of content delivery such as video on demand via digital cable (Hay, 2005), or through popular online music portals such as Yahoo Music, which reported streaming 3 billion music videos online in 2005 (Bruno, 2005b). One author noted, "Label executives equate featured placement of a video on AOL or Yahoo with appearing on the cover of *Rolling Stone*, in terms of exposure" (p. 18). As a result, the recording industry is producing more videos than ever before (Bruno, 2005b). Finally, consumer electronics has also allowed fans to download music videos to their cellular telephones or other handheld devices such as Apple's video iPod, providing other potential avenues for music video distribution (Bruno, 2005a; McCarthy, 2005).

A second implicit assumption regarding music videos is that one way to enhance the appeal of a music video is through the use of sexual content. From Madonna's landmark performance of "Like a Virgin" on MTV, to Jessica Simpson's controversial video for "These Boots Are Made for Walkin'," music videos and music video channels have been the target of vocal criticism over the use of all manner of sexual imagery (e.g., Gardner, 2003; Vancheri, 2005). One of the key reasons for concern over the use of sex is because of the target audience for music videos, primarily teens and adolescents, and a wealth of research has demonstrated the potentially harmful effects that such sexual content can have (see Andsager and Roe, 2003, or Hansen and Hansen, 2000, for a review).

Although these concerns are well founded, this research has ignored the intended purpose of sex in music videos, to increase their enjoyment and effectiveness as a marketing tool. Thus, the focus of this article is first, to review the literature demonstrating that sexual content is a common feature in music videos, and second, to explore the few empirical studies that have examined its effectiveness in enhancing viewer enjoyment.

MEASURING SEX IN MUSIC VIDEOS

Soon after the development of music videos in the 1980s, activist groups such as the National Coalition on Media Violence began expressing concern over the presence of sexual and violent content in music videos and particularly the combination of these elements (Kaplan, 1984; Sweeny, 1984). Fueled by these concerns, scholars quickly launched empirical examinations of the new form to determine just how pervasive such content was. A number of early content analyses justified some public fears and demonstrated that sexual content of varying levels of explicitness could readily be found on MTV.

Measuring Sexual Content

The earliest examinations of sex in music videos revealed scholars' struggles to understand and accurately capture the essence of music videos. In short, the unique and complex mix of visual and aural elements made music videos difficult to examine, and some scholars elected to ignore certain dimensions of music videos and quantify other parts that were perhaps easier to gauge. In one of the earliest content analyses of music videos, Baxter et al. (1985) stated that traditional coding schemes could not be readily applied to music videos. Therefore the authors developed an exhaustive list of content categories and examined 62 videos recorded in April, 1984, for the presence or absence of these themes.

Their analysis found sexual content in nearly 60% of the videos analyzed. However, the authors noted that most of the sexual content "was understated, relying on innuendo through clothing, suggestiveness, and light physical contact rather than more overt behaviors" (p. 336). The presence of more unusual sexual behaviors such as sadomasochism and sexual bondage was rare.

Sherman and Dominick's (1986) examination of the content of music videos also illustrated scholars' early struggles to thoroughly classify and analyze music videos. The authors discussed whether music videos should be approached as a musical or a visual phenomenon, stating that the "still-emerging 'language' of music television stretches the content analysis model to its limits" (p. 82). As a result, the authors coded only the visual elements of music videos, ignoring the musical dimension. The authors also sought to account not only for the presence or absence of sexual content, but also the frequency with which it appeared, and the explicitness of each sexual act. Finally, the analysis examined whether the sexual behavior represented heterosexuality, homosexuality, transvestitism, prostitution, exhibitionism, voyeurism, or bondage.

Results showed that sexual behavior could be found in more than 75% of the videos coded, with an average of 4.78 sexual acts per video. In addition, the analysis showed that 81% of the videos containing violent behavior also contained sexual behavior. Furthermore, most of the sexual acts coded (more than 70%) represented heterosexual behavior. As with the previous analysis, the study suggested that nontraditional sexual acts were rare, and sexual content such as non-intimate touching was the norm. Moreover, the data also showed that half of the female characters in the videos were dressed provocatively.

Greeson and Williams (1986) conducted a less detailed content analysis of the types of sex found in videos, as well as an early examination of the effects of exposure to sexual content in music videos. Similar to previous findings, the authors noted that the theme of love and romance was present in 50% of the videos examined, and sexual references were present in 47% of the videos examined. In addition, the authors conducted perhaps the only research examining the effects of sex in music videos on actual product purchase intentions, which will be discussed shortly. Overall, these early analyses indicated that sexual content was a common feature in the world of music videos.

Music Videos and Gender-Role Stereotypes

Later analyses of sex in music videos represent a shift away from capturing baseline measures of sexual content in favor of examining how characters were portrayed within music videos. For example, Seidman (1992) looked at how music videos portrayed gender role stereotypes. His analysis of 182 music videos showed that videos overwhelmingly reinforced these stereotypes. In addition, much like Sherman and Dominick (1986), Seidman (1992) also found that women were much more likely to be shown in revealing clothing than men. The author states that more than one-third of female characters were depicted in revealing clothing, versus only four percent for men.

Gender roles were also the focus of another content analysis of music videos by Somers-Flanagan et al. (1993). The authors examined 40 music videos and examined the gender roles portrayed in the videos. Results indicated that women engaged in significantly more sexual behavior than men, and women were more often the object of sexual aggression than men. Inspired by the popular notion that 1997 was the "year of the woman" in country music, Andsager and Roe (1999) also sought to examine how women were portrayed in country music videos. Their findings contradicted that notion. Data indicated that women were portrayed as men's equals only when the artist in the video was female, and for the most part, "women have not reached an equal footing with male artists" (p. 78).

Most current research into content trends in music videos has sought to link various content elements to specific genres of music and music video channels. Jones (1997) examined a variety of content features in music videos and the videos' associated genre. That analysis revealed a link between hip-hop and R&B music and sexual content. Within the same vein, Hansen and Hansen (2000) reported that women are much more likely than men to be shown in revealing clothing and as sexual objects, especially on BET.

The overall picture generated by these numerous content analyses shows that sexual content remains a staple of music videos, and these videos continue to reinforce negative gender role stereotypes. If the implicit assumption that content producers used sex to enhance enjoyment of music videos is true, then ample evidence exists to suggest that they used such content liberally. However, updated research is clearly needed that examines current content trends in music videos. One of the most evident shortcomings of this body of literature is the lack of holistic analyses of music videos that measure both visual and lyrical dimensions of the form. In addition, longitudinal analyses comparing past research with updated findings would also illuminate content trends over the now decades-old history of music videos.

THE EFFECTS OF SEX IN MUSIC VIDEOS

Just as scholars have failed to engage in holistic analysis of music videos, they have likewise failed to recognize music videos as a vehicle for promoting an artist. Only recently have scholars begun to explore how musical artists (and particularly female artists) may strategically employ sex to craft a public persona (e.g., Andsager, 2006). Instead, scientists have been primarily focused on the negative consequences of sex in music videos. For example, a host of studies have examined the effects of sex in music videos on viewers' attitudes about sex and relationships. Calfin and co-authors (1993) found that exposure to sexual content of varying levels of explicitness resulted in the endorsement of more liberal sexual beliefs. Additionally, Kalof (1999) reported that exposure to the sexual music videos results in greater support for adversarial sexual beliefs. Hansen and Hansen (1988) also found that viewing music videos that portrayed women as sex objects primed stereotypical thoughts in subsequent scenarios. Similarly, Gan et al. (1997) indicated that exposure to sexual rap videos primed negative attitudes toward black women in other contexts. Thus, research has demonstrated a variety of effects on viewer attitudes about sexual relationships, but it sheds little light on how viewers react to the actual viewing experience or their attitudes about the music video itself, much less on the effectiveness of music videos as a form of artist promotion.

Effects on Purchase Intentions

Greeson and Williams (1987) conducted one of the few, if not the only, published empirical studies within the field of communication that examined the effects of sex in music videos on viewers' purchase intentions, although that was not the primary goal of the research. The study actually sought to address a number of research questions, including the effects of sexual content on teenagers' attitudes about pre-marital sex and drug use. Within that context, the authors also asked research participants to indicate their agreement with the statement, "I buy clothes, tapes, records, or other items that I see on MTV" (p. 182). Half of the research participants answered that question prior to watching one of two specially prepared collections of music videos, and the other half answered that question after watching the videos. The two versions of the stimulus materials contained either high-impact or a random assortment of music videos. The authors stated that the high-impact videos were chosen "for their reference to sex, violence, and antiestablishment overtones" (p. 181).

The results suggested that viewing music videos in general did increase purchase intention, although those results did not suggest that the increase was a product of the sexual content of the videos. When compared with research participants who completed the experimental survey before viewing the videos, those who completed the survey after watching the music videos reported that they were more likely to buy music from artists featured on MTV, although the findings only approached statistical significance. No difference regarding purchase intention was found between participants viewing the high-impact videos and those viewing the random collection of videos.

These limited findings do suggest that music videos can be used as an effective promotional tool, although they do not suggest that the use of sexual content can enhance this effect. However, cursory review of the high-impact videos that were utilized (e.g., "Jump" by Van Halen, or "That's Why They Call It the Blues" by Elton John) suggests that they would likely be considered quite tame by contemporary standards. Thus, despite this research, we still know precious little about the relationship between music videos, sex, and purchase intention.

Sex, Music Videos, and Excitation Transfer

Although the assertion that using sex could help enhance liking of a music video seems plausible, a deeper understanding of exactly how this relationship functions has not been thoroughly illuminated. Scholars investigating media effects have developed numerous theoretical perspectives, such as cultivation theory (Gerbner, Gross, Morgan, Signorielli, and Shanahan, 2002), or social cognitive theory (Bandura, 2002), to explain how sex in any media content can subsequently affect viewer attitudes and behavior. Although these theories may be adept at explaining the negative effects of media sex, they do little to address how sex may increase enjoyment *per se*.

Zillmann's excitation transfer theory (1971, 1983, 2006; Bryant and Miron, 2003) does, however, address both the potentially negative outcomes of exposure to sex as well as how it may lead to the increased enjoyment of media content. In-depth analysis of the theory and its applications is beyond the scope of this discussion. Nonetheless, the basic premise of the theory is that residual arousal from an initial stimulus may contribute to the arousal elicited by a subsequent stimulus in an additive fashion. The theory holds that cognitive appraisal of the arousal decays faster than the physiological dimension of arousal. Thus, viewers remain in an excitatory state despite having forgotten about the initial stimulus. Lastly, the theory holds that viewers are not consciously aware of this additive process or the exact source of their arousal due to the cognitive demands of processing the message at hand. Overall, the effect is that the second stimulus is perceived as more emotionally intense than it would otherwise be. To the extent that the second stimulus is positive, viewers will find it to be more positive (liked) due to the prior stimulus. To the extent that the second stimulus is negative, viewers will find it to be more negative (disliked).

Effects of Sex in Music Videos on Enjoyment

Admittedly, enjoyment of a music video and product purchase intention are distinct phenomena. Moreover, record sales are based upon a myriad of factors, and viewer enjoyment of a music video is only part of a marketing mix for any given artist (Andsager, 2006). Nonetheless, music videos remain vital promotional tools for a product (e.g., the musical artist), and enjoyment of a music video would clearly be the goal of record industry executives in order to cultivate a positive attitude toward their product/artist. Thus, enjoyment is a highly beneficial although not essential factor in creating product purchase intention. Until future research examines music videos explicitly as a form of promotion, we may substitute the concept of viewer enjoyment as a temporary proxy.

Only a few studies have examined the effects of utilizing sexual content in music videos on viewer enjoyment. In fact, only two studies have focused on sex, music videos, and entertainment proper, and their findings are somewhat inconclusive. Zillmann and Mundorf (1987) conducted the earliest published study examining the effect of sexual content in music videos on viewer enjoyment. The authors argued that within the context of music videos, excitation transfer theory (Zillmann, 1971, 1983, 2006) holds that the use of sexual content in a music video creates arousal for the viewer, which subsequently contributes to the increased enjoyment of the musical content. To test this theory, the experimenters inserted eight sex scenes depicting pre-coital and coital behavior from an R-rated film into a rock music video. Research participants were then assigned to view either the original unedited video, the edited video containing the sexual content, or a music-only condition where participants heard only the song with no visual accompaniment. After viewing the music video, research participants were asked to rate the stimulus presentation on three dimensions: music, lyrics, and visuals. The dependent measures asked participants to indicate how exciting, arousing, creative, or sensual they found each dimension of the presentation.

The authors reported that the inclusion of sexual content had a mixed result, divided largely upon gender lines. Sexual content significantly increased participants' overall appreciation for the musical dimension of the music video when compared to the other experimental conditions, regardless of participant gender. In addition, male participants also rated the musical dimension of the video to be significantly more sensual when compared to their female counterparts. Moreover, the authors noted that the use of sexual content in the music video resulted in females judging the music to be less sensual, which was in direct contrast with male participants.

With respect to the visual dimension of the video, results were also mixed. The authors reported that female research participants rated the version containing sexual elements as significantly less pleasant than did their male counterparts. Moreover, both men and women reported greater disapproval of the sexual version of the video when compared to the unedited version. Finally, the use of sexual content also made the video appear less romantic to the female research participants, whereas the male participants found the sexual version more romantic. Overall, these findings only partially support excitation transfer theory, as the use of sexual content did result in more positive evaluations of the musical aspect of the music video, but the effects of sex on viewers' evaluations of the visual elements were divided along gender lines.

Based on this initial study, the tentative answer to the question of whether sex enhances enjoyment of a music video is a resounding "maybe." However, a few caveats must be tendered before accepting the results of Zillmann and Mundorf's (1987) experiment. First, scholars have questioned the approach of much media effects research–including that of Zillmann and Mundorf–for utilizing single-message stimulus materials to represent conditions in experimental designs (e.g., Jackson and Jacobs, 1983). Second, the R-rated sex scenes inserted into the stimulus video were likely not representative of the type of sexuality present in most music videos, thus potentially reducing the study's ecological validity.

Hansen and Hansen (1990) addressed both of these shortcomings in a later series of experiments examining the effects of sexual and violent content on the enjoyment of music videos. Rather than use more sexually explicit content utilized by Zillmann and Mundorf (1987), the authors selected 15 music videos that already contained various levels of sexual content, thus making the experiment more naturalistic since the videos were not artificially edited in any way. Moreover, the videos were also assigned to one of three levels of sexual content–high, moderate, and low–via content analysis in order to create the experimental manipulation. Finally, the selection of multiple music videos controlled for potentially idiosyncratic effects caused by a single stimulus video. After viewing the stimulus video, research participants were asked to complete several dependent measures designed to gauge their evaluations of a number of dimensions of the music video.

The results indicated that as hypothesized, the videos containing the greatest amount of sexual content were rated as significantly more visually appealing than either the moderate- or low-sex videos. No significant differences were found between the moderate- and low-sex videos. Findings for musical appeal mirrored that of the visual appeal, with participants in the high-sex condition reporting the greatest level of musical appeal. Finally, the music videos in the high-sex condition also elicited the strongest emotional response when compared to the other experimental conditions. Thus, their study wholeheartedly supported the notion that the use of sex can enhance viewer enjoyment of a music video.

Hansen and Hansen (1990) offered a number of potential explanations for the contrast between the overwhelmingly positive reception to sexual content demonstrated by their research and the previous findings from Zillmann and Mundorf (1987). The most plausible explanation offered by the authors is that viewer enjoyment of sexual content in music videos is curvilinear, with the greatest level of appeal resulting from moderate levels of sexual content. They note, "Beyond some point, more explicit sexual material becomes intrusive and detracts from, rather than enhances, appeal" (Hansen and Hansen, 1990, p. 229). This hypothesis is supported by Zillmann and Mundorf's findings, given the more explicit sexual content utilized in their stimulus video and the less graphic material commonly found in the videos utilized in the second study. Nonetheless, this *post-hoc* explanation has never been explicitly tested in a single laboratory experiment. Unfortunately, these two studies remain the only empirical studies within communication examining the effects of sex in music videos on viewer enjoyment, as scholars later turned their attention to the negative consequences of sex in music video.

DIRECTIONS FOR FUTURE RESEARCH

These two studies (Hansen and Hansen, 1990; Zillmann and Mundorf, 1987) suggest that the implicit assumption that sexual content can be used to increase the enjoyment of music videos is at least partially valid. Thus, music video producers seeking to create positive feelings regarding an artist in order to enhance enjoyment and ultimately increase record sales would be wise to utilize limited amounts of sexual content. Research indicates that an optimal level of sexual content exists to elicit the greatest sense of enjoyment, which content producers may have stumbled upon through practice and intuition. Nonetheless, drawing final conclusions based solely upon two studies would be unwise at best. Much like the literature on the sexual content found in music videos, updated research is needed to determine if and how much sex can make a video more attractive to viewers.

One clear shortcoming of past research is that neither of the experiments that were reviewed addressed the sexual content of the lyrics, which have become increasingly explicit in recent years (Hansen and Hansen, 2000). As stated earlier, the unique mix of visual, lyrical, and musical elements found in music videos makes the form distinct, and experimental research has yet to fully address this mix. For example, the Busta Rhymes' music video "Light Your Ass on Fire" unquestionably depicts sexual content of varying degrees of explicitness. However, do the lyrics of the song enhance the perceived level of sexual content found in the music video, and if so, what is the effect of this holistic viewing experience?

An additional research question involves the centrality of the sexual content to the music video. Advertising scholars have explored the use of sexual appeals in advertisements where the appeal was functionally related to the product (e.g., condoms) versus similar appeals that were not centrally relevant (e.g., Richmond and Hartman, 1982). Although an imperfect analogy, scholars examining sexual content in music videos have failed to consider the impact of content that is more central to the video versus more peripheral.

Some scholars argue that the mere association of sexual imagery with an artist makes it difficult for viewers to disassociate the two, and that feelings of enjoyment generated by sexual content will naturally transfer (Andsager and Roe, 2003). By this logic, to enhance enjoyment of a video by an all-male band, producers should also feature an attractive woman in revealing clothing. For example, the video for "Stacy's Mom" by Fountains of Wayne features relatively little footage of the band and instead provides abundant footage of supermodel Rachel Hunter disrobing, dancing on a table, and in a bikini. However, what is the effect on enjoyment when the woman in the revealing clothing is the actual artist, such as Faith Hill, Britney Spears, or Christina Aguilera? One such example would be Mariah Carey's 2005 video for "Shake It Off," which begins with a tantalizing shot of the performer in a bathtub, contains additional footage of the performer in revealing clothing, and closes with Carey disrobing as she walks away from the camera. Empirical research is needed to determine if the use of sexual content is an equally effective marketing strategy for both female and male artists, and if there is a difference when the sexual content directly involves the artist.

This article has argued that research examining sex in music videos has two significant shortcomings: the failure to account for the interaction of all elements present in a music video, and the failure to recognize the intended purpose of music videos, that is to promote a product. With respect to the latter, a multidisciplinary approach to understanding sexual content in music videos is needed to fully understand the phenomenon. The aforementioned research examined the effects of sex on viewer enjoyment with little or no regard for future purchase intention. Future research should borrow from advertising research and examine concepts such as attitude toward the ad, attitude toward the brand, and brand recall when examining music videos (e.g., Severn et al., 1990; Reichert et al., 2001). Finally, media practitioners and industry professionals have developed practical wisdom in how best to use sexual content, and they have knowledge of whether these practices result in actual consumer behavior through market data such as record sales, video airplay, or video requests.

Combining the wisdom of parties from all three fronts presents the opportunity to fully understand how utilizing sexual content in a music video can operate as a marketing tool. Clearly, the recording industry has not abandoned the format. Observers have recently noted that new technology and the legal download and purchase of individual tracks has revived the market for music "singles" (Gallo, 2006), and music videos could play a key role in promoting new songs and encouraging fans to purchase these tracks or even the videos themselves. Record labels continue to use music videos to attract audiences (and consumers), and the use of sex remains one of the primary means to do so. The opportunity for further research into music videos as promotional tools, how much sex is found in music videos, and how that content relates to enjoyment and consumer behavior is evident, presenting a clear need and agenda for renewed research.

REFERENCES

Andsager, J. (2006). Seduction, shock, and sales: Research and functions of sex in music video. In T. Reichert and J. Lambiase (eds.), *Sex in consumer culture: The erotic content of media and marketing* (pp. 31-50). Mahwah, NJ: Lawrence Erlbaum Associates.

Andsager, J. L. and Roe, K. (1999). Country music video in country's year of the woman. *Journal of Communication, 49*(1), 69-82.

Andsager, J., and Roe, K. (2003). "What's your definition of dirty, baby?": Sex in music video. *Sexuality and Culture, 7*(3), 79-97.

Bandura, A. (2002). Social cognitive theory of mass communication. In J. Bryant and D. Zillmann (eds.), *Media effects: Advances in theory and research, 2nd ed.* (pp. 121-153). Mahwah, NJ: Lawrence Erlbaum Associates.

Baxter, R. L., DeRiemer, C., Landini, A., Leslie, L. Z., and Singletary, M. W. (1985). A content analysis of music videos. *Journal of Broadcasting and Electronic Media, 29*(3), 333-340.

Bronstein, S. (1986, July 6). Music videos hit a sour note. *The New York Times*, p. C3. Retrieved on August 23, 2005 from LexisNexis database.

Bruno, A. (2005a, October 22). Apple plays the video game. *Billboard, 117*, 12.

Bruno, A. (2005b, November 5). Music video audience migrates to web. *Billboard, 117*, 18.

Bryant, J., and Miron, D. (2003). Excitation-transfer theory and three-factor theory of emotion. In J. Bryant, D. Roskos-Ewoldsen, and J. Cantor (eds.), *Communication and emotion: Essays in honor of Dolf Zillmann* (pp. 31-60). Mahwah, NJ: Lawrence Erlbaum Associates.

Calfin, M. S., Carroll, J. L., and Schmidt, Jr., J. (1993). Viewing music-videotapes before taking a test of premarital sexual attitudes. *Psychological Reports, 72*(2), 475-481.

Dancyger, K. (2002). *The Technique of Film and Video Editing: History, Theory, and Practice.* London: Focal Press.

Feineman, N., and Reiss, S. (2000). *Thirty Frames Per Second: The Visionary Art of the Music Video.* New York: Harry N. Abrams.

Gallo, P. (2006, January 5). Digital boom, CD gloom. *Daily Variety*, 1. Retrieved January 9, 2006 from LexisNexis database.

Gan, S. L., Zillmann, D., and Mitrook, M. (1997). Stereotyping effect of black women's sexual rap on white audiences. *Basic and Applied Social Psychology, 19*(3), 381-399.

Gardner, E. (2003, August 29). MTV video music awards: Equal parts risqué and cliché. *USA Today*, p. D10. Retrieved on August 23, 2005 from LexisNexis database.

Gerbner, G., Gross, L., Morgan, M., Signorielli, N., and Shanahan, J. (2002). Growing up with television: Cultivation processes. In J. Bryant and D. Zillmann (eds.), *Media effects: Advances in theory and research, 2nd ed.* (pp. 43-67). Mahwah, NJ: Lawrence Erlbaum Associates.

Greeson, L. E., and Williams, R. E. (1986). Social implications of music videos for youth: An analysis of the content and effects of MTV. *Youth and Society, 18*(2), 177-189.

Hansen, C. H., and Hansen, R. D. (1988). How rock music videos can change what is seen when boy meets girl: Priming stereotypic appraisal of social interactions. *Sex Roles, 19*(5/6), 287-316.

Hansen, C. H., and Hansen, R.D. (1990). The influence of sex and violence on the appeal of rock music video. *Communication Research, 17*(2), 212-234.

Hansen, C. H., and Hansen, R.D. (2000). Music and music videos. In D. Zillmann and P. Vorderer (eds.), *Media entertainment: The psychology of its appeal* (pp. 175-196). Mahwah, NJ: Lawrence Erlbaum Associates.

Hay, C. (2004, May 29). On-demand channel offers music videos. Billboard, 116, 63. Retrieved January 3, 2006 from Academic Search Premiere database.

Jackson, S., and Jacobs, S. (1983). Generalizing about messages: Suggestions for design and analysis of experiments. *Human Communication Research, 9*(2), 169-191.

Jones, K. (1997). Are rap videos more violent? Style differences and the prevalence of sex and violence in the age of MTV. *Howard Journal of Communications, 8*(4), 343-356.

Kalof, L. (1999). The effects of gender and music video imagery on sexual attitudes. *Journal of Social Psychology, 139*(3), 378-385.

Kaplan, P. W. (1984, December 15). Measuring violence in rock 'n' roll videos. *The New York Times*, A46. Retrieved on May 1, 2003 from LexisNexis database.

McCarthy, S. L. (2005, August 28). Hold the phone: Viewers find new ways to get their music video fix. *The Boston Herald*, 31. Retrieved on August 23, 2005 from LexisNexis database.

Ouellette, D. (2005, October 3). Niche movement. *MediaWeek*, 16-20.

Reichert, T., Heckler, S. E., and Jackson, S. (2001). The effects of sexual social marketing appeals on cognitive processing and persuasion. *Journal of Advertising, 30*(1), 13-27.

Richmond, D., and Hartman, T.P. (1982). Sex appeal in advertising. *Journal of Advertising Research, 22*(5), 53-61.

Seidman, S. A. (1992). An investigation of sex-role stereotyping in music videos. *Journal of Broadcasting and Electronic Media, 36*(2), 209-216.

Severn, J., Belch, G. E., and Belch, M.A. (1990). The effects of sexual and non-sexual advertising appeals and information level on cognitive processing and communication effectiveness. *Journal of Advertising, 19*(1), 14-22.

Sherman, B. L., and Dominick, J. R. (1986). Violence and sex in music videos: TV and rock 'n' roll. *Journal of Communication, 36*(4), 79-93.

Smith, S. B. (1985, March 10). There's no avoiding music videos. *The New York Times*, B29. Retrieved on August 23, 2005 from LexisNexis database.

Somers-Flanagan, R., Somers-Flanagan, J., and Davis, B. (1993). What's happening on music television? A gender role content analysis. *Sex Roles, 28*(11/12), 745-753.

Sweeny, L. (1984, May 22). Look quick, it's music video. *The Christian Science Monitor*, 16. Retrieved on August 23, 2005 from LexisNexis database.

Umstead, R. T. (2006, January 2). The future of content distribution. *Multichannel News*, 22.

Vancheri, B. (2005, August 5). Singing a new tune: Jessica Simpson injects charisma into 'Dukes of Hazard.' *Pittsburgh Post-Gazette*, D1. Retrieved on August 23, 2005 from LexisNexis database.

Zillmann, D. (1971). Excitation transfer in communication-mediated aggressive behavior. *Journal of Experimental Social Psychology, 7*(4), 419-434.

Zillmann, D. (1983). Transfer of excitation in social behavior. In J. T. Cacioppo and R. E. Petty (eds.), *Social Psychophysiology: A Sourcebook* (pp. 215-240). New York: Guilford Press.

Zillmann, D. (2006). Dramaturgy for emotions from fictional narration. In J. Bryant and P. Vorderer (eds.), *Psychology of entertainment* (pp. 215-238). Mahwah, NJ: Lawrence Erlbaum Associates.

Zillmann, D., and Mundorf, N. (1987). Image effects in the appreciation of video rock. *Communication Research, 14*(3), 316-334.

doi:10.1300/J057v13n01_07

MAGAZINES

Promoting Sexy Images:
Case Study Scrutinizes *Maxim*'s Cover Formula for Building Quick Circulation and Challenging Competitors

Jacqueline Lambiase

SUMMARY. *Maxim* features a scantily dressed woman on its cover each month, persuading readers to buy its erotically branded magazine with a repetitive cover formula. Based on descriptive and ethnographic analyses, this exploratory case study addresses *Maxim*'s cover formula and the competitive response from other men's lifestyle magazines. The formula has influenced several new men's magazines, and *Maxim*'s success tempted at least one existing men's magazine to switch its own

Jacqueline Lambiase (PhD, University of Texas-Arlington) is Associate Professor, Department of Journalism and Mayborn Graduate Institute of Journalism, University of North Texas, P.O. Box 311460, Denton, TX 76203 (E-mail: lambiase@unt.edu).

[Haworth co-indexing entry note]: "Promoting Sexy Images: Case Study Scrutinizes *Maxim*'s Cover Formula for Building Quick Circulation and Challenging Competitors." Lambiase, Jacqueline. Co-published simultaneously in *Journal of Promotion Management* (Best Business Books, an imprint of The Haworth Press, Inc.) Vol. 13, No. 1/2, 2007, pp. 111-125; and: *Investigating the Use of Sex in Media Promotion and Advertising* (ed: Tom Reichert) Best Business Books, an imprint of The Haworth Press, Inc., 2007, pp. 111-125. Single or multiple copies of this article are available for a fee from The Haworth Document Delivery Service [1-800-HAWORTH, 9:00 a.m. - 5:00 p.m. (EST). E-mail address: docdelivery@haworth press.com].

identity to the lad-mag style, but without *Maxim*'s success. The predictable formula presented complex challenges for men's titles, in terms of creating brand identity, building circulation, and maintaining advertising revenue. doi:10.1300/J057v13n01_08 *[Article copies available for a fee from The Haworth Document Delivery Service: 1-800-HAWORTH. E-mail address: <docdelivery@haworthpress.com> Website: <http://www.HaworthPress.com> © 2007 by The Haworth Press, Inc. All rights reserved.]*

KEYWORDS. Advertising revenue, branding, case study, lad-mag, magazine covers, *Maxim* magazine, men's lifestyle magazines, sexual appeals, women

INTRODUCTION

Maxim, the hottest star of North American men's lifestyle magazines in the last decade, simulates and stimulates the sexual revolution every month on its cover. On the outside, the magazine features a scantily dressed B-list actress, surrounded by headlines that promise "Tonight's the Night," "Expert Sex," and an "All-Sex Workout." On the inside–true to its advertised promises–are photo spreads, advice, erotic ads, innuendo, and graphic party narrative. *Maxim*'s brand works to create and to target American male macho culture, using an eroticized marketing strategy to sell magazines. McLuhan (1964) links consumption and photography, especially repetitive pictures of Hollywood iconography. It is precisely this mixture of iconography and consumption that *Maxim* uses so successfully each month in its cover photograph. "The movie stars and matinee idols are put in the public domain by photography," McLuhan writes, and "they become dreams that money can buy. They can be bought and hugged and thumbed more easily than public prostitutes" (1964, p. 170).

Borrowing a formula from Great Britain's "lad mags," *Maxim*'s consistent sales pitch through its sexualized covers has proven successful and has inspired imitators across North America and in other parts of the world. *Maxim* called itself in June 2004 "the best-selling men's lifestyle magazine in the nation and the world," claiming a total worldwide readership of more than 12.8 million ("Maxim continues," 2004). This case study, through descriptive analysis, studies the production of *Maxim*'s covers by analyzing its repetitious use of idealized female models and its corollary construction of an idealized audience embedded in male macho culture. To make this exploratory study relevant to both professional and academic audiences, ethnographic analysis is also used to track the competitive actions and results of men's lifestyle magazines, both old and new, after *Maxim*'s U.S. debut.

BACKGROUND

Maxim, launched by Dennis Publishing in spring 1997, might be described as the quintessential "successful magazine." The magazine guarantees its own success through a time-proven formula that matches its brand with its readers.

Maxim*'s Success*

Just three years after its launch, *Maxim*'s monthly circulation had surpassed long-time men's magazines such as *Esquire*, *GQ*, and *Details*, whose circulations remain steady between 400,000 and 800,000 (see Table 1). Industry observers continue to credit *Maxim* with the increased use of sex to sell other men's magazines, namely *GQ*, *Details*, *Esquire*, and even *Rolling Stone* (Gremillion, 1997; Munk, 2001; Sullivan, 2000; Turner, 1999; Walker and Golden, 2001; Warner, 1997). *Maxim* itself seems to be profiting from the cover formula the most. With its rate base at about 2 million in 2000, *Maxim*'s circulation increased 127%, ad pages were up 52%, and revenue was up $31 million over 1999 ("Upstarts," March 6, 2000). Since then, *Maxim*'s circulation has consistently stayed around 2.5 million, just as its cover formula has consistently advertised the magazine's brand (Cyr, 2003; Itzkoff, 2007; Reuters, 2007).

While those in industry circles may believe sexy covers translate into higher circulation for magazines, scholarly research on covers remains limited (Johnson, 2002). One historical study found that depictions of "playful women" appeared on magazine covers to attract younger male readers in the early 20th century, with "playful" defined as "sin—whether in the form of alcohol or illicit sex" (Kitch, 2001, p. 58). Another study of men's and women's magazine covers asserted that strategies for these depictions had changed little for mainstream magazines over the 20th century (Malkin et al., 1999).

According to Gremillion, *Maxim* has achieved success because it has "devoted its covers to B-list female celebs" (1997, p. 28). One industry analyst wrote that many men's magazines are "slapping cleavage on their covers" in homage to *Maxim* (Handy,

1999, p. 75). *Maxim* did not invent this formula in the United States, because a mainstream magazine for women, *Cosmopolitan,* had fine-tuned the formula for decades, albeit for a different audience. Yet *Maxim* most consciously simulates IPC's *Loaded,* the leading men's lifestyle magazine in the United Kingdom in the mid-1990s, with an editorial format focusing on sex, beer, and football (McCann, 1995, p. 13).

Men's Titles Respond

Just two years after the launch of *Maxim*'s U.S. edition, *Adweek* in 1999 named the editor Mark Golin as Magazine Editor of the Year (Newman, 1999). Early in 1999, magazine observers took note of *Maxim*'s influence on its competitors, especially when both *Details* and *Esquire* joined *Maxim* in using the cover formula in February 1999. With three similar covers at the newsstand that month, a *Newsweek* writer observed, quite presciently, that "[m]en's magazines today practically have to come in a plain brown wrapper" (Turner, 1999, p. 52). Golin quickly moved on to a *Maxim* competitor, *Details*, as editor-in-chief. But despite *Details'* increased circulation in 1999, when compared to 1995 (see Table 1), the magazine changed directions in early 2000. It fired Golin and remade itself into a men's fashion magazine that resumed publication that fall.

One explanation, given to the news media by *Details'* new editors, was the magazine did not "want the pretense of most celebrity and fashion titles or the guilty–and lusty–pleasure of the lads magazines in gen-

TABLE 1. Magazine Circulation Before and After *Maxim*'s Debut in 1997

	1995	1999	2004
Maxim	--	1,152,725	2,531,768
Details	484,472	559,673	412,634
Esquire	710,555	679,648	717,113
GQ	686,962	707,776	814,113

Note: Average circulation the first six months of each year according to ABC Magazine Publisher Statements.

eral, and *Maxim* in particular" (Walker and Golden, 2001). A better explanation for the change, however, might be *Details'* falling number of advertising pages, which were down more than 22% between January and September 1999 (621 pages), compared to the same period in 1998 (801 pages), according to the Publishers' Information Bureau ("Advertising and PIB," 1999). During the same nine-month period in both 1998 and 1999, *Maxim*'s ad pages were up 60%, *Esquire*'s had risen 19%, while *GQ*'s had dropped 12% ("Advertising and PIB," 1999). During this time period, both *GQ* and *Details* were owned by Conde Nast, and this may be why the latter title was switched to a sister publishing company, Fairchild, for a makeover (both Fairchild and Conde Nast are owned by Advance Publications Inc.).

Around the time of *Details'* own failure to use the *Maxim* formula successfully, Golin was asked about his predictions for U.S.-based men's publications, since the formula was losing its luster in the U.K. ("The joy of sex," March 6, 2000). Golin responded "there is going to be saturation. I think it's going to get to the point where the word sex or sexiest on a cover makes your eyes glaze over" (p. M82). Since that time, however, *Maxim*'s success has continued and direct imitators such as *FHM*, owned by U.K.-based Emap, and *Stuff*, owned by Dennis Publishing, have successfully entered the men's lifestyle market with an identical cover formula.

Cover Strategies

Covers are typically produced by a team effort of art, editorial, and circulation departments, and as a rule, the editor-in-chief has final say regarding cover design (Beam, 1998). According to *Wired* magazine's editor-in-chief Kevin Kelly, however, "there is absolutely no good theory as to what makes a cover sell" (Beam, 1998, p. 50). Similarly, Mike McGrath, editor-in-chief at Rodale Press, claims only a fool would try to predict with certainty that a particular cover will sell (Beam, 1998, p. 50). Despite this professional uncertainty, the decision to place sexy images on magazine covers seems commonplace in the current men's magazine market. One instance beyond *Maxim* of this strategy's success is *Rolling Stone*'s cover image of a sexualized Britney Spears, which resulted in more than 230,000 newsstand copies sold and which became that magazine's biggest seller for 1999 ("Best and Worst," 1999).

Former *Maxim* and *Details* editor Golin seems to rely on the "sex sells" mantra wherever he works in the industry, saying that "as an editor, I turned out sex articles at *Cosmo*, I did it at *Maxim*, I even did it back at *Prevention* magazine at Rodale and so on" (M82). Since the "cover of any successful magazine is a shrewd advertisement for what lies inside" (Handy, 1999, p. 75), then consumers are instantly informed about content. This could be one reason why *Details* could not compete using *Maxim*'s cover formula, because its editorial content was not consistent with what its cover advertised, and therefore, it could not attract advertisers who would rather be connected to *Maxim*'s brand; this theory is discussed further in the results section of this case study. At *Rolling Stone*, some readers in their letters to the editor have consistently complained about the use of Spears and other sexualized musicians and actresses on its cover (Lambiase, 2005).

While there may not be consistent empirical evidence for connecting cover design with sales, at least one theory affirms *Maxim*'s strategy. The sexual behavior sequence, a model developed in social psychology, explains responses to stimuli such as sexual arousal, thoughts, emotions, and actions (Byrne, 1982; Fisher, 1986; also see Gould's [2003] adaptation of love maps to consumer behavior). In addition, one academic study shows a link between sexual covers and outcomes. Specifically, Reichert (2005) found that sexual responses to cover models enhanced attention to, and interest in, the magazines they appeared on.

Covers, then, are directly connected to consumer expectations about content, and a sexy cover provides clues about more sexual stimuli inside the magazine. In a content analysis of editorial content in *Maxim* and *Stuff*, both owned by Dennis Publishing, Krassas et al. (2003) found 10 themes that support the sensibilities of a rampant macho culture. These themes include: "the more sex and sexual partners a man has, the better"; "intoxication makes sexual conquest better"; "vulnerable women are easier targets"; "sexual entertainment (is an) important cultural phenomena in which to participate"; and "heterosexuality is the norm men should adhere to" (p. 114). Taylor (2005) reported little difference in sexual content among *Maxim*, *Stuff*, or *FHM*, with most articles focused on improving one's sex life and with most sexual themes consistent with traditional masculine norms.

METHOD

This exploratory case study compares the cover formula of *Maxim* with three older competitors–*Esquire*, *GQ*, and *Details*–during three time periods: in 1995, which was two years before *Maxim* was published; in 1999, which was two years after its debut; and five years later in 2004. Since *Maxim* exclusively featured young, female B-list actresses on its cover, always suggestively dressed, scantily clad, or nude (categories from Soley and Reid, 1988), then a cover was considered to use *Maxim*'s cover formula when a woman appeared who was not demurely dressed. Data used to bolster this case study were gathered in a content analysis of covers of *Maxim* and other men's magazines (Lambiase and Reichert, 2006). Beyond these simple numbers, covers were analyzed qualitatively for the rhetoric of both their text and language, as designers of these covers used different strategies to persuade readers to buy the magazine at the newsstand. Since *Maxim* overtly sold itself as a "safe place for guys to be guys," this case study's descriptive analysis will look for signs of the same macho rhetoric on the covers of competing magazines in 1999 and 2004, after *Maxim*'s debut, compared to 1995, before its debut. Findings based on magazine cover strategies will be linked to circulation data and advertising revenue and total advertising pages. Beyond comparison with older men's lifestyle magazines, the use of *Maxim*'s cover formula and style for newer magazines such as *Stuff* and *FHM* will also be discussed.

RESULTS

Each and every month of its own existence since 1997, the *Maxim* cover presents a three-quarter shot (or sometimes an upper-body shot) of a nearly nude or suggestively dressed and posed female model or models, usually an up-and-coming actress in her 20s. The magazine's cover format is so rigid that its content seems too obvious to bother measuring; however, this consistency has ensured the success of its branding with readers.

Three covers from 1999 and three covers from 2004 reveal the cover's consistency across time. In the October, November, and December 1999 issues of *Maxim*, all three cover models look directly at the camera and none is smiling. They are deadly serious. Only the October model, Melissa Joan Hart, has a slight suggestion of amusement about her lips, or it could be simple self-satisfaction. On covers for the same issues in 2004, the models are again serious. Like 1999, one cover in 2004 features a young woman transitioning from teen star to adult status (Melissa Joan Hart, October 1999; Avril Lavigne, October 2004). In December 2004, the cover format changes slightly by featuring two women in a three-quarter shot, the "girls" of Donald Trump's television reality show *The Apprentice*.

In issues from both 1999 and 2004, sexualized female bodies are surrounded by words, as artificial as the photographer's backdrop and other stylized elements in these mediated scenes. The headlines stand in contrast to these images, the serious and sexy shot matched with the ludicrous and sexy words, the silent feminine image against the playful masculine voice. Declaring the obvious, these teasers rely on pathos to promote this monthly product:

> "Expert sex! Order that replacement headboard today!" (October 1999),
> "Clothes she'll rip off you—with her teeth" (November 1999),
> "Annual lingerie spectacular" (December 1999).

Also similar to 1999 are the teasing headlines from 2004:

> "Groupie sex confessions" (October 2004),
> "College girls tell all" (November 2004),
> "Hometown Hotties" (December 2004).

An overarching headline appears on every *Maxim* issue. One rendition from 1999 is "Sex, Sports, Beer, Gadgets, Clothes, Fitness" (October 1999); another from 2004 reads "Girls, Sports, Beer, Gear, Cherries" (July 2004). This frames a bandwagon enticement crafted for an idealized kind of male audience, to make devoted readers feel at home in this space and to give them ownership beyond the body they wish to buy, hug, and thumb, in McLuhan's words.

Details

During 1999, less than two years after *Maxim*'s debut, at least one competing men's magazine, *Details*, completely abandoned its prior cover formula and adopted the *Maxim* formula almost wholesale (see Table 2). The magazine featured scantily clad actresses and models on 11 of its covers in 1999. Yet in 1995, *Details* used only two images of sexy women, although a third cover featuring Stephen Dorff called the "Road Issue" touts a special report covering "sex, love . . . nipple rings" and also an article on "Sex Drive '95: Guy with Porshe seeks girl." One of the two covers featuring women in 1995 was *Details'* third annual "Sex Issue," with other teasers such as "Sex USA:

TABLE 2. Number of Covers Featuring Female Models in *Maxim*'s Sex-Tinged Style, by Year

	1995	1999	2004
Maxim	Not published	11 of 11 issues	12 of 12 issues
Details	2 of 12 issues	11 of 12 issues	0 of 12 issues
Esquire	3 of 12 issues	6 of 12 issues	4 of 12 issues
GQ	2 of 12 issues	2 of 12 issues	4 of 12 issues

A 20-city guide" and "Are you man enough?" At that time before *Maxim*, *Details* used sexy covers but may be said to have compartmentalized this appeal, by limiting cover hype to one-fourth of its issues. In other words, sex was a frequent topic but not the overarching theme.

By 1999, the magazine's cover transformation into a near clone of *Maxim* had occurred. Indeed, *Details* used four women on the cover in 1999 who had previously appeared on *Maxim*'s covers in 1998; they include Rebecca Romijn, Alyssa Milano, Catherine Zeta Jones, and Rebecca Gayheart. Yet, the cloning experiment did not work for *Details*, as described in the background section of this study. Circulation did increase, but advertising revenue and pages dropped dramatically, while *Maxim*'s circulation, revenue and ad pages all climbed magnificently. Industry watchers called *Details*' incarnation as a lad magazine "disastrous" (Bercovici, 2003). In 2000 its editor, formerly of *Maxim*, was fired and its identity was changed. Described in 2001 as "still-finding-itself" and seeking "its editorial stride" as a men's fashion magazine (Mnookin, 2001), more recently *Details* has been used by at least one magazine, *Gear*, as a model of how to reposition itself in a *Maxim*-influenced world (Bercovici, 2003). Indeed, ad pages for *Details* were up almost 14% in 2004 when compared to 2003, with revenue up for the same period by more than $10 million ("Advertising and PIB revenue," 2005), even though circulation was below its level for 1999 (see Table 1). In 2004, not one cover on *Details* featured the *Maxim* formula (see Table 2).

Esquire *and* GQ

During the time of *Maxim*'s debut and rise, *Esquire* and *GQ* may be seen as using *Maxim*'s cover formula more frequently than they did in 1995 (see Table 2), but both titles never let the formula totally overcome their long-standing identities, as may be seen with *Details* in 1999. *Esquire* continued its emphasis on "man at his best" with trend reporting and investigative journalism, and *GQ*'s focused on fashion and celebrity culture, with both magazine's still working most of the time within a framework of more sophisticated lifestyle themes, rather than bad-boy irony and eye-candy in *Maxim*'s style.

Both magazines, however, used the formula, with *Esquire* adopting it on half its covers in 1999. *Esquire* featured Pamela Anderson wearing men's underwear on its February 1999 cover, with teaser headlines touting "The triumph of cleavage culture" and the "77 things men should know about women." While half of the covers featured male actors and celebrities that year, even those issues used teasing and/or macho headlines: "manhood test" (September 1999), "the clothes come off" (May 1999), and "the four sexiest women on TV" (October 1999). Of the six covers featuring women, three are classified as nude, and three as partially clad in three-quarter or full-body shots. Although these women may be dressed or undressed in styles like *Maxim*'s, *Esquire* covers featured more A-list actresses such as Sharon Stone, Charlize Theron, and Nicole Kidman. All men appearing on covers that year are dressed demurely, with three covers of men primarily focusing on their faces.

GQ in 1999 seemed to stay true to its own identity, featuring the same number of women as it did in 1995, prior to *Maxim*'s debut. In 1995, the magazine featured Uma Thurman dressed suggestively (February 1995) and Sharon Stone nude (November 1995) on its covers; in 1999, Heidi Klum (January 1999) and Ashley Judd (October 1999) appeared partially clad. Again, B-list actresses are in much shorter supply than in *Maxim*.

DISCUSSION

In terms of branding itself, *Maxim* has successfully coupled brand identity–or the promises and values it displays to viewers/readers through its cover–with its brand image, which is the experience of consuming the magazine (Temporal, 2002). Other men's magazines, such as *Details*, could not successfully match brand identity and image. One theory about this formula provides a perspective about the powerful ways that women's bodies attract readership (or viewership) to men's magazines, as part of an economic exchange serving not just an audience's desires but marketing culture as well. Twitchell (1996) describes this exchange in terms of cost externalization. He suggests (p. 10) that:

> just as the 'work' you do at the self-service gas station lowers the price of gas, so consuming ads is the 'work' you do that lowers the price of this entertainment. . . . It is the basis of the fast-food industry. You order. You carry your food to the table. You clean up. You pay less. In Adcult, matters are more complex. True, you are entertained for less cost, but you are also encultured in the process.

These drive-by, consumable images on covers, then, serve as objects or effects of desire, not only to sell magazines but to sell experiences through the branding exchange. And these images both reflect and change the dream of a macho culture looking for an economical way—both in monetary and emotional costs—to feed its fantasies. Much may be learned about macho culture from its objects of desire, namely that images of airbrushed, computer-enhanced women both pander to a supposed need for escape and provide escape. Twitchell's assertion about enculturation means that readers of these magazines are socialized into a desiring and consumption cycle focused on objectified female bodies that are surrounded and codified by a hypersexual environment.

One model and actress who has benefited from exploiting her own eroticized image on more than 300 magazine covers, Cindy Crawford, uses Twitchell's own terms for her work life. She calls the part of herself that is a product "fast food," since much of her fame "comes from disposable pop culture. Literally disposable. You throw magazines away after a week or a month" (1995, Rensin, p. 51). Her repetitive images symbolize a "male-defined ideal" that is depersonalized through its consumption, even though that same action of consumption may seem to enhance a model's power (Dickey, 1987, p. 75).

One finding of this descriptive case analysis was the models' relative "silence" on covers, as the headlines act as textual representations of a macho, masculine voice in relation to the silent feminine image. Since models are willing to be part of this consumption cycle–and are paid well for their participation–their compliance would seem to make them powerful, rather than powerless. In fact, *Maxim* does include interviews with its cover models, perhaps giving them a voice, but interviews focus mostly on their bodies, sexuality, and sexual practices. Bartky (1988) claims this willing participation of women provides an economy for patriarchal culture, since it cannot be blamed for these ideal sexualized constructions of women. In this view, then, the magazines' publishers are less likely to be blamed for creating macho culture, or "a safe place for guys to be guys" (Blanchard, March 1998, p. 14), because women will be seen as helping them create that environment.

CONCLUSIONS

For many new and existing men's titles, covers and the interchangeable sexualized models featured on them must continue to generate not only circulation, but also advertising pages and revenue, or the formula will change. While *Details* dropped from the competition, the history of women's bodies objectified for consumption suggests that this formula continues to be stable, especially because of the U.S. debut of *FHM* by Emap in 2000 and *Stuff* by Dennis Publishing in 2001. Both successful titles experienced quick circulation growth in a slow market (Fine, 2001), plus double-digit percentage gains in advertising revenue during the first two years of existence ("Advertising and PIB revenue," 2002).

Yet the predictable formula also presented complex challenges for men's titles, in terms of creating brand identities, building circulation, and maintaining advertising revenue. One would-be competitor–*Gear*–tried to have it both ways after its 1998 debut. It adopted the look of a lad-mag title like *Maxim* but still published long-form journalism like *Esquire* and *GQ* (Bercovici, 2003). The magazine suspended publication in 2003, and the publisher sought to reposition the title later that year without again succumbing to the degrading "orbit" created by *Maxim* and *FHM*, according to *Gear* publisher Bob Guccione, Jr. (Bercovici, 2003). The biggest problem *Gear* faced, the publisher said, was distinguishing the product for advertisers.

The larger problem faced by *Maxim*'s direct competitors, men's magazines, and the industry in general is the slowly dwindling number of people subscribing to magazines since 1990 (Weaver, 2004); even the most recent magazine circulation results are mixed for the titles discussed in this study and beyond, with *Maxim*'s own circulation flat at 2.5 million, making it a product open to new ownership (Itzkoff, 2007; Reuters, 2007). Instead of launching magazines with fresh ideas to attract more readers, the publishing industry has been content to "follow each other like lemmings" (Weaver, 2004). *Maxim*'s formula may be one example of this trend, in which men's magazines, especially the lad mags, have been taking readership from each other by using provocative images.

Although there are many real consumers for these magazines, the audience is narrowly constructed and idealized as part of a growing macho culture that has arisen in Westernized countries and is consumed worldwide through magazines, music, movies, and television programming (Gauntlett, 2002; "Macho culture," 2000). The magazine covers are simply one effect of that macho culture's reach and influence, so much so that media are branding themselves as the vanguard of that culture. In terms of magazine sales and influence, *Maxim*'s covers represent success for this macho culture at the newsstand; in terms of branding, these covers are the perfect intersection of a brand's identity or its visual presence (sexy cover model who promises more benefits) with brand image (the experience of consuming culture from the magazine behind the cover).

REFERENCES

Advertising and PIB revenue and pages: Jan.-Sept. 1999 vs. 1998. (1999). *Magazine Publishers of America*. Retrieved in January 20, 2005 from http://www.magazine. org/Advertising_and_PIB/PIB_Revenue_and_Pages.

Advertising and PIB revenue and pages: Jan.-Dec. 2002 vs. 2001. (2002). *Magazine Publishers of America*. Retrieved on January 20, 2005 from http://www.magazine. org/Advertising_and_PIB/PIB_Revenue_and_Pages/Revenue___Pages_by_Magazine_ Titles__YTD_/729.cfm.

Advertising and PIB revenue and pages: Jan.-Dec. 2004 vs. 2003. (2005). *Magazine Publishers of America*. Retrieved on January 20, 2005 from http://www.magazine. org/Advertising_and_PIB/PIB_Revenue_and_Pages.

Bartky, S. L. (1988). Foucault, femininity, and the modernization of patriarchal power. In I. Diamond and L. Quinby (eds.), *Feminism and Foucault: Reflections on Resistance* (pp. 61-86). Boston: Northeastern University.

Beam, C. (1998, January 1). A tale of five covers. *Folio*, 50-53.

Bercovici, J. (2003, April 8). Bob G. Jr. on what did in *Gear*: Sucked in, then spit out, of the lads wind tunnel. *Media Life Magazine*. Retrieved on January 21, 2005 from http://www.medialifemagazine.com/news2003/apr03/apr07/2_tues/news3tuesday1. html.

Best and worst sellers of '99 (2000, March 6). *Consumer Magazines* (in *Adweek*), M84.

Blanchard, K. (1998, March). Editor's letter. *Maxim*, p. 14.

Byrne, D. (1982). Predicting human sexual behavior. In A. G. Kraut (ed.), *The G. Stanley Hall Lecture Series* (pp. 207-254). Washington, DC: American Psychological Association.

Cyr, D. (2003, March 15). Boys will be boys. *Direct*. Retrieved on February 15, 2007, from http://directmag.com/casehistories/b2c/marketing_boys_boys/.

Dickey, J. (1987). Women for sale: The construction of advertising images. In K. Davies, J. Dickey, and T. Stratford (eds.), *Out of Focus: Writings on Women and the Media* (pp. 74-77). London: The Women's Press.

Fine, J. (2001, February 19). Circulation still slow for magazines. *Advertising Age*, 12.

Fisher, W.A. (1986). A psychological approach to human sexuality: The sexual behavior sequence. In D. Byrne and K. Kelley (eds.), *Alternative Approaches to the Study of Sexual Behavior* (pp. 131-171). Hillsdale, NJ: Lawrence Erlbaum Associates.

Gauntlett, D. (2002). *Media, Gender, and Identity: An Introduction*. New York: Routledge.

Gremillion, J. (1997, November 1). What men really want. *Mediaweek*, 28.

Gould, S. J. (2003). Toward a theory of advertising lovemaps in marketing communications: Overdetermination, postmodern thought and the advertising hermeneutic circle. In T. Reichert and J. Lambiase (eds.), *Sex in Advertising: Perspectives on the Erotic Appeal* (pp. 151-170). Mahwah, NJ: Lawrence Erlbaum Associates.

Handy, B. (1999, February 15). Bosom buddies. *Time*, 75.

Itzkoff, D. (2007). Lad no more. My escape from *Maxim. New York Press*. Retrieved on February 22, 2007 from http://www.nypress.com/15/23/news&columns/feature.cfm.

Johnson, S. (2002). The art and science of magazine cover research. *Journal of Magazine and New Media Research*, 5(1). Retrieved on January 31, 2007 from http://www.bsu.edu/web/aejmcmagazine/journal/archive/Fall_2002/Sjohnson1.htm.

The joy of sex (2000, March 6). *Consumer Magazines* (in *AdWeek*), M78-M83.

Kitch, C. (2001). *The Girl on the Magazine Cover: The Origins of Visual Stereotypes in American Mass Media*. Chapel Hill, NC: The University of North Carolina Press.

Krassas, N. R., Blauwkamp, J. M., and Wesselink, P. (2003). "Master your Johnson": Sexual rhetoric in *Maxim* and *Stuff* magazines. *Sexuality and Culture*, 7(3), 98-119.

Lambiase, J. (2005). Impressing the editor: *Rolling Stone* letter writers and their rhetorical strategies for getting published. *Journal of Magazine and New Media Research*, 7(2), 1-14.

Lambiase, J., and Reichert, T. (2006). Sex and the marketing of contemporary consumer magazines: How men's magazines sexualized their covers to compete with *Maxim*. In T. Reichert and J. Lambiase (eds.), *Sex in Consumer Culture: The Erotic Content of Media and Marketing* (pp. 67-86). Mahwah, NJ: Lawrence Erlbaum Associates.

Macho culture (2000, January 10). *Talk of the Nation*. New York: National Public Radio.

Malkin, A. R., Wornian, K., and Chrisler, J. C. (1999). Women and weight: Gendered messages on magazine covers. *Sex Roles, 40*(7/8), 647-655.

Maxim continues its reign over men: #1 men's lifestyle mag reaches 10 million men, according to 2004 MRI spring research (2004, June 2). Retrieved on January 13, 2005 from http://www.maximonline.com/press_room/20040106_mri_spring.asp.

McCann, P. (1995, August 18). *Loaded* leads men's title pack. *Marketing Week*, 13.

McLuhan, M. (1964). *Understanding Media: The Extensions of Man*. New York: Signet Books.

Mnookin, S. (2001, August 20). Breaking the last taboo: *Details* takes it all off in Puff Daddy photo spread. *Inside.com.* Retrieved on July 24, 2002 from http://www.inside.com.

Newman, J. (1999, March 8). Men will be boys. *Consumer Magazines* (in *Adweek*), 45-49.

Reichert, T. (2005). Do sexy cover models increase magazine sales? Investigating the effects of sexual response on magazine interest and purchase intention. *Journal of Promotion Management, 11*(2/3), 113-130.

Rensin, D. (1995, September). Playboy interview: Cindy Crawford. *Playboy*, 51 + .

Reuters (2007, February 16). Maxim magazine publisher to explore sale. Syndicated news story. Retrieved on February 22, 2007 from http://www.allmedianews.com/Entertainment/id_50808/.

Soley, L., and Reid, L. (1998). Taking it off: Are models in magazine ads wearing less? *Journalism and Mass Communication Quarterly, 65*(4), 960-966.

Special section: The 50 most beautiful people in the world (1996, May 6). *People Magazine*, 68 + .

Taylor, L. D. (2005). All for him: Articles about sex in American lad magazines. *Sex Roles, 52*(3/4), 153-163.

Temporal, P. (2002). *Advanced Brand Management: From Vision to Valuation*. Hoboken, NJ: Wiley and Sons.

Turner, R. (1999, February 1). Finding the inner swine. *Newsweek*, 52-53.

Twitchell, J. B. (1996). *Adcult USA: The Triumph of Advertising in American Culture*. New York: Columbia University.

Upstarts (2000, March 6). *Consumer Magazines* (in *Adweek*), M47.

Weaver, M. (2004, Dec. 30). Magazine readership hitting a brick wall. *DM News: The Online Newspaper of Record for Direct Marketers*. Retrieved on January 21, 2005 from http://dmnews.com/cgi-bin/artprovbot.cgi?article_id=31400.

doi:10.1300/J057v13n01_08

Consumer Responses
to Sexual Magazine Covers
on a Men's Magazine

Tom Reichert
Shuhua Zhou

SUMMARY. Competing men's magazines often use sexually attractive cover models to enhance circulation. This investigation tested the efficacy of sexual cover models on consumer outcome variables including magazine interest and purchase intention, as well as on psychological variables such as sexual arousal and social comparison. Overall, magazine interest-value and purchase intention were significantly higher in the sexual condition, as were sexual arousal and tendency for upward social comparison. Discussions on sexual information processing and implications for management and future research are offered. doi:10.1300/J057v13n01_09 *[Article copies available for a fee from The Haworth Document Delivery Service: 1-800-HAWORTH. E-mail address: <docdelivery@haworthpress.com> Website: <http://www.HaworthPress.com> © 2007 by The Haworth Press, Inc. All rights reserved.]*

Tom Reichert (PhD, University of Arizona) is Associate Professor, Grady College of Journalism and Mass Communication, University of Georgia, Athens, GA 30602 (E-mail: reichert@uga.edu). Shuhua Zhou (PhD, Indiana University) is Associate Professor, Department of Telecommunication and Film, College of Communication and Information Sciences, University of Alabama, Tuscaloosa, AL 35487-0152 (E-mail: szhou@bama.ua.edu).

[Haworth co-indexing entry note]: "Consumer Responses to Sexual Magazine Covers on a Men's Magazine." Reichert, Tom and Shuhua Zhou. Co-published simultaneously in *Journal of Promotion Management* (Best Business Books, an imprint of The Haworth Press, Inc.) Vol. 13, No. 1/2, 2007, pp. 127-144; and: *Investigating the Use of Sex in Media Promotion and Advertising* (ed: Tom Reichert) Best Business Books, an imprint of The Haworth Press, Inc., 2007, pp. 127-144. Single or multiple copies of this article are available for a fee from The Haworth Document Delivery Service [1-800-HAWORTH, 9:00 a.m. - 5:00 p.m. (EST). E-mail address: docdelivery@haworthpress.com].

KEYWORDS. Advertising, arousal, consumer response, information processing theory, magazine, purchase intention, persuasion, sex

INTRODUCTION

Introduced to American readers in April 1997, *Maxim*, a self-described "Cosmo for men," quickly outpaced the circulation of other men's lifestyle titles (see Lambiase, 2007 in this volume). As important was its effect on the outward appearance of competitive magazines. *Maxim*'s rapid circulation and revenue gains prompted competing titles to partially adopt its cover formula–a dominant image of a physically attractive and provocatively attired cover-woman (Handy, 1999; Lambiase and Reichert, 2006). To quote one observer, "Men's magazines today practically have to come in a plain brown wrapper" (Turner, 1999, p. 52).

Building on the relative lack of quantitative academic research into magazine cover effects, the present study utilizes the same data used in a previously published report (Reichert, 2005). In the current study, however, the data are examined through a new theoretical lens (i.e., dual information-processing model; Moskowitz et al., 1999) and a more appropriate analysis strategy (i.e., within-subject design).[1] The new analysis provides additional insights on several fronts including level of sexual appeal and design value and their effects on magazine interest, purchase intention, and sexual arousal, in addition to the contribution of personality variables such as social comparison and predispositions toward sexual information.

LITERATURE REVIEW

Magazine Covers

Sexualized images of women on the covers of men's magazines are hardly a new phenomenon (see Kitch, 2001). In the 1940s, for instance, George Petty and Alberto Vargas illustrations of pin-up girls were a staple on and within *Esquire* (Howd, 1990). Since *Playboy*'s introduction in 1953, its covers and those of its competitors have regularly featured scantily clad "playmates" (Tate, 1990). Alternately, however, in the last two decades of the 20th century men's magazines such as *GQ* and *Esquire* were more apt to feature notable men on their covers–actors, athletes, celebrities, musicians, and politicians–than women (Lambiase and Reichert, 2006). That trend changed soon after *Maxim*'s introduction.

Popular with men in the United Kingdom (hence the term "laddie" magazine), a similar version of Dennis Publishing's *Maxim* was introduced to America. Invariably the magazine features sexualized editorial content as well as "photo essays" of B-rated female actors and models (Gremillion, 1997; Krassas et al., 2003; Lambiase, 2007 in this volume; Taylor, 2005). Within two years, Maxim's circulation increased to 2.5 million and its editor, Mark Golin, was named *Adweek*'s Editor of the Year. Promptly, two analogous books–*Stuff* and *FHM*–were introduced with similar success. In addition, established men's titles began featuring scantily clad females on their covers with increased frequency. According to one analysis, 72% of *GQ, Details, Esquire*, and *Rolling Stone* covers featured men the 2 1/2 years before April 1997 (*Maxim*'s US debut) compared to 55% in the 2 1/2 years afterward (Lambiase and Reichert, 2006). Images of women constituted the difference with 96% of all women featured as sexually portrayed compared to only 20% of all men: A finding confirmed by related analyses of similar magazines (Brinkley and Fowler, 2001; Malkin et al., 1999).

As previously mentioned, conventional wisdom within the industry and among industry observers was that competing men's magazines placed sexualized women on their covers to stave off *Maxim*'s threat to circulation. Despite a lack of academic literature on the effects of cover content, the publishers' strategy to feature women on the covers is not unfounded due to the importance of covers on single-copy sales. As magazine historians Trebbel and Waller-Zuckerman (1991) note, "The paramount importance of covers continues. Publishers seek headlines, graphics, and logos likely to catch the eye on crowded newsstands. Circulation directors are often involved in the decision process, deciding which covers will most attract buyers" (p. 363). Given the provocative nature of sexual information, covers with barely clad women should enhance the likelihood of attracting attention. Considering that magazines are a branded product, advertising research may provide appropriate conceptual grounding.

Sex in Advertising and Information Processing

Despite anecdotal and proprietary research, there is academic research to suggest that sex can motivate action in a consumer context, especially for impulse and low-risk purchases such as magazine subscriptions. Much of the advertising research has focused on the influence of sexual content on information processing (e.g., brand-name recall) and attitudes (e.g., attitudes-toward-the-ad; for review, see Percy and Rossiter, 1992; Reichert, 2002). Depending on audience and contextual factors, findings indicate that moderate levels of sexual content is rated by viewers as attention-getting, engaging, appealing, and interesting (Belch et al., 1981; LaTour, 1990). Findings also are such that consumers' processing resources are directed toward the sexual image, but with no corresponding brand-recall advantage (Reid and Soley, 1983).

Regarding consumption outcomes, several studies report that sex can positively affect purchase intention and persuasion (Dudley, 1999; Grazer and Keesling, 1995; Reichert et al., 2001; Severn et al., 1990). For example, Dudley (1999) reported that respondents were more likely to try a suntan lotion featured in sexy ads compared to suntan lotion featured in a control ad. Similarly, Grazer and Keesling (1995) reported a purchase intention advantage for moderately sexual jeans and liquor ads compared to those in the high, low, and non-sexual ad conditions. Although there are exceptions to these findings (see Bello et al., 1983; Caballero and Solomon, 1984), the pattern of results indicate that sexual information can influence consumers' intentions to purchase products, albeit low-risk or sexually-relevant products such as jeans, suntan oil, athletic shoes, and fragrances.

These findings as well as the magazine industry's conjecture regarding sexualized covers can be theoretically explained by information-processing theory. For example, cognitive and social psychologists have proposed a dual process model by conceiving of information processing as occurring along a continuum (Moskowitz et al., 1999). On one end of the continuum individuals utilize minimal cognitive effort, elaboration, or capacity when considering information such as that presented on magazine covers in low-risk situations. Consumers may use prior knowledge, heuristics, or expectancies to determine their responses. In these instances preconception, rather than effortful cognitive processing, plays a key role in the integration of new information (top-down approach). On the other hand, people can expend a great deal of time, effort, and mental energy to examine information when systematically forming perceptions and building decisions (bottom-up approach; Moskowitz et al., 1999).

The pattern of advertising findings can be further explained by the affect-evoking nature of sexual stimuli and its effect on consumer response. For one, sexual information, by its very nature, is motivating to humans. Work in social psychology (Byrne, 1976, 1982), later adapted to consumer behavior (Gould, 2003), provides insight into how sexual information can motivate behavior. According to this work, once a stimulus is recognized and interpreted as sexual, a response is evoked within the viewer that consists of sexual feelings, thoughts, and arousal (Fisher, 1986); responses that encourage movement toward the stimulus. For example, sexual images result in increased gazing and interest toward the erotic content. In addition, sexual images can offer the implicit promise of additional or continued exposure to sexualized content within the magazine. This leads to the first hypothesis:

> H1: Sexually attractive cover models will result in more interest in the magazine.

On the other hand, the affective response elicited by sexual content can inhibit viewers' ability to carefully consider the persuasive message or engage in rational processing as delineated in the dual processing model. In low-risk situations, consumers are less apt to deeply consider purchases and more apt to be influenced by peripheral cues such as sexual content. In a sense, viewers' normal self-dialogue which typically contains support and counterarguments is inhibited, making the consumer more susceptible to the motivating nature of sexual content. This effect is supported by ad research demonstrating that sexual content reduces product/message thoughts but increases attitudes about the ad and purchase intention (Reichert et al., 2001; Severn et al., 1990). Therefore,

> H2: Sexually attractive magazine cover models will result in higher purchase intention.

A long history of psychological research identifies two primary factors pertinent to all affective experience as valence polarization–how positive or negative the experience is–and arousal level, or how much the affective system is activated by the experience (Bradley, 1994). Because sexual information is generally positive (Fisher, 1986; P. J. Lang et al., 1993), the concern here is not valence but how arousal affects cognition and decision making. When investigating attention and arousal for still pictures shown to experimental participants for six seconds, P. J. Lang and colleagues have consistently found that participants paid greater attention to arousing messages as opposed to calm ones and participants registered higher self-reported or physiological arousal as well (P. J. Lang et al., 1993). This finding was replicated in the realm of television messages by A. Lang et al. (1999). Therefore,

H3: Sexually attractive cover models will result in higher self-reported sexual arousal.

Other than sexual arousal, social comparison is another psychological variable of interest. Festinger (1954) proposed the concept to argue that human beings, as social animals, have a drive to evaluate themselves in comparison to others, often unknowingly (Wood, 1989). Whereas much comparison occurs interpersonally, the process can occur in response to mediated images of others in television, film, advertising, or in magazines (Martin and Gentry, 1997; Richins, 1991, 1995; Sirgy et al., 1998). There are two types of comparisons: Downward comparison occurs when a person compares him/herself with others who are less successful on one or more dimensions; Upward comparisons, on the other hand, occur when others are perceived as superior on a relevant dimension (Lyubomirsky and Ross, 1997). Upon seeing sexually arousing models, readers are likely to engage in upward comparison by aspiring to be more like the cover-person (Zhou et al., 2002). Therefore,

H4: Sexually attractive cover models will result in upward appearance comparison.

Other than our main focus on cover models, magazine covers also include other elements designed to attract a reader's attention such as positioning of the model, use of color, dimensional projection, and graphic manipulation. The design of the cover can serve to engage a reader's automatic attention by causing the reader to redirect perceptual processes (Geiger and Reeves, 1993). Creative cover design therefore implies effective psychological targeting; tight artistic control of elements to engage an otherwise uninterested consumer. In psychology and communication research, considerable work has shown that structural features (the way information is positioned and presented) can influence perception, attention, and memory (Eysenck, 2001; Grabe et al., 2000). Gestalt theorists have long established that the arrangement of visual elements has a direct effect on human perception because the eye, unlike the camera, engages in a complex process to detect change, form and features, and selectively prepares data for the brain to interpret (Barry, 1997). The following research question is therefore proposed:

RQ: How does cover design affect reported magazine interest and purchase attention?

Note that this research question, unlike previous hypotheses, does not include the dependent variables of sexual arousal and social comparison, as these are human interest variables not directly related to design.

METHOD

Preliminary Research

Given the lack of academic research on magazine purchase consideration, several exploratory focus groups of college-aged participants were asked why they buy and/or read certain magazines. Overall the six focus groups (four all-female groups and two all-male groups, 4-6 students per group) each lasted approximately 20-30 minutes. Students were also asked to rank-order the determinants of why they buy certain magazines.

The most common reason reported by women was the person on the cover. Second was stories or article headlines. Status, fashion, attractiveness, and interest value of the cover model were other reasons that could be grouped to include "person on the cover." Men listed headlines, the magazine's content, and good-looking "girls" on the cover as top reasons they purchase magazines. The insights regarding the importance of the "person on the cover" on magazine purchases, in addition to the work on sex in advertising, led to the following study.

Experiment

An experiment was conducted in the form of a fractionally factorial 2 (Sexual Attractiveness) × 2 (Design Appeal) × 8 (Cover) design. Unlike Reichert's (2005) design, all three factors were within-subject factors. However, only the first two were variables of interest whereas the third factor (Cover) was used as a repeated measure to reduce random variance introduced by any uninteresting features of a particular cover (Jackson and Jacobs, 1983). All participants viewed all the covers and all levels of each factor.

Participants. Undergraduate students enrolled in an introductory mass media course at a large state university were recruited to participate for extra credit ($N = 87$). Ages ranged from 18-26 years of age ($M = 20.40$ years, $SD = 2.09$). Females (65%) represented a larger proportion of the sample than males and most participants were white (86%).

Stimuli. To control for uninteresting factors such as type of magazine, gender of cover person, and the number of persons on the cover, 11 covers of *Details* magazine published from August 1997 to June 1998 were selected for evaluation.[2] Past issues were chosen so that participants were oblivious to these covers. For the purposes of the present analysis, eight issues represented the manipulation and three issues served as distracters. *Details* was chosen because it is a nationally distributed general-interest magazine written for young men that appeals to both genders. In addition to participant relevance, *Details* offered variability of cover-person gender. For instance, of the treatment ads four issues featured female models and four issues featured male models.

Experimental Procedure

The study took place over a one-week period. Respondents signed-up for the study and participated individually. After providing consent, participants were given a booklet containing instructions and measures for evaluating each cover. Respondents were told that editors and publishers were interested in how consumers evaluate magazines on the newsstand. To reduce order effects, each respondent was randomly assigned to one of the 11 issues.

A full-size, color copy of each cover was placed in order of publication along a long row of tables. Once the respondent finished evaluating the initial issue, he/she evaluated each issue in order through June 1998. They then moved to the first issue on the table (August 1997) and evaluated issues up to the one they began with. The covers were spaced approximately two feet from one another. Time taken to complete the study ranged from 20 to 30 minutes. Participants were quiet throughout the procedure and no interaction occurred.

Variables

Sexual Attractiveness (IV). This independent variable was manipulated by selecting four highly attractive models and four average models, with male and female models equally distributed. As a manipulation check, respondents also rated each cover-person on a seven-point sexy scale using two items (sexy/not sexy; sexually desirable/sexually undesirable; LaTour and Henthorne, 1993). Respondents' ratings confirmed that the manipulation was successful ($M = 4.45$, sexy; $M = 3.10$, less sexy; $t (1, 86) = 37.69, p < .01$).

Design Value (IV). Superior design has a mercurial nature that depends on a shared understanding among design professionals and readers (Wilson, 2003). Because of the non-definitive nature of this variable, three items were used to assess the cover design (without the cover model; unless otherwise noted, all items were measured on a 7-point Likert-type scale). These items were adapted from Wells' (1964) Reaction Profile for advertising evaluation (appealing/unappealing, attractive/unattractive, exciting/unexciting). Items were summed to form a scale ($\alpha = .86$) and a median split procedure was performed. The resulting high and low conditions for this independent variable were used for data analysis.

Magazine Interest (DV). Three items were created to measure interest in the magazine issue generated by the cover. Participants were asked to rate the likelihood of three statements (anchored by "Not at all likely/Very Likely), e.g., "How likely are you to look at the cover of this issue on the newsstand, the doctor's office or a friend's house?" Responses were summed and divided by three to create a mean response for each participant ($\alpha = .85$).

Purchase Intention (DV). Two items measured the likelihood of buying each issue. Respondents were asked how likely they were to agree with the following two statements (anchored by "Not at all likely/Very likely"), "How likely are you to buy this issue of this magazine?" and "Overall, how likely are you to strongly consider purchasing this magazine?" ($\alpha = .96$).

Sexual Arousal (DV). Respondents' subjective sexual arousal evoked by the cover-person was measured with three items adapted from a sexual arousal scale created by Mosher, Barton-Henry, and Green (1988). Respondents rated how they felt while viewing the person on the cover (extremely sexually aroused/no sexual arousal at all, extreme sexual absorption/no sexual absorption at all, extreme sexual warmth/no sexual warmth at all; $\alpha = .97$). The scale correlates with other measures of sexual arousal and demonstrates high reliability.

Social Comparison (DV). Two items measured the likelihood of respondents' social comparison to the cover-model. Respondents were asked how likely they were to agree with the following two statements (anchored by "Not at all likely/Very likely"), "How likely are you to want to look like the person(s) on the cover? . . . be more like the person(s) on the cover?" ($\alpha = .87$).

Sexual Opinion Survey. Erotophobia/Erotophilia is a personality construct that measures a person's disposition to respond to sexual information along a single positive-negative affective dimension. It is measured with the shortened version of the Sexual Opinion Survey (SOS; Fisher et al., 1988). This variable was only used to check for variability among participants in the various conditions. Distribution was normal in this experiment.

RESULTS

A series of repeated-measure ANOVAs using sexual attractiveness, design value, and cover were conducted to test the proposed hypotheses and research questions. Cover was not a significant factor in all analyses, indicating that no particular cover among the eight used in the experiment significantly affected the dependent variables.

Hypothesis one predicted that sexually attractive magazine cover models would result in more interest in the magazine. The main effect for this factor was significant, $F (1, 692) = 10.39, p < .01, \eta^2 = .11$. Participants reported higher interest in the magazine in response to sexually attractive cover models than to less sexually attractive cover models ($M = 4.45, SD = 1.87$ vs. $M = 4.07, SD = 1.92$). There also was a significant interaction between sexual attractiveness and design, $F (1, 692) = 6.11$, $p < .05, \eta^2 = .07$, indicating that the effect of sexual attractiveness was most prominent when the design was superior. When design was inferior, the effect of sexual attractiveness was partially offset (see Figure 1).

Hypothesis two predicted that sexually attractive magazine cover models would result in higher purchase intention. The main effect for sexual attractiveness was significant, $F (1, 692) = 12.25, p < .01, \eta^2 = .13$. Participants reported higher purchase intention in response to sexually attractive cover models than to less sexually attractive cover models ($M = 3.05, SD = 1.69$ vs. $M = 2.66, SD = 1.94$). No significant interaction between this variable and design was found.

Hypothesis three predicted that sexually attractive magazine cover models would result in higher self-reported sexual arousal. The main effect for this factor was significant, $F (1, 692) = 23.04, p < .01, \eta^2 = .15$. Participants reported higher sexual arousal in response to the sexually attractive cover models than to the less sexually attractive cover models ($M = 2.99, SD = 1.79$ vs. $M = 2.43, SD = 1.82$). There was no significant interaction between this variable and design.

FIGURE 1. Magazine Interest as a Function of Sexual Attractiveness and Design Evaluation

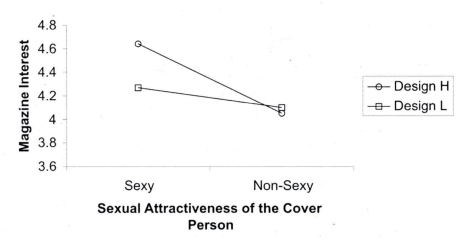

Hypothesis four predicted that sexually attractive magazine cover models would result in upward comparison. The main effect for this factor was significant, $F(1, 692) = 10.82$, $p < .01$, $\eta^2 = .16$. Participants indicated that, in terms of appearance, they would prefer to be more like the sexually attractive cover models than the less sexually attractive models ($M = 2.90$, $SD = 1.69$ vs. $M = 2.34$, $SD = 1.98$). There was no interaction between this variable and design.

The research question (RQ) concerning design and its effect on magazine interest and purchase intention also was tested using the same statistical analysis. No significant effect was found on either dependent variable.

DISCUSSION

This study was designed to test the efficacy of sexual cover models on consumer outcome variables such as magazine interest and purchase intention. Overall, the predictions that more sexualized covers would result in positive consumer responses are supported. In addition, respondents were expected to experience more sexual arousal and positive social comparison effects as a result of viewing the sexual covers. These predictions also are supported. Last, cover design was found to have no influence on the dependent variables except through an interaction with the sexuality of the cover model. These findings are discussed in the following section.

Consumer Outcomes

As stated, the prediction that sexually attractive cover models stimulate higher consumer interest is confirmed. This finding is in line with the previous advertising research showing that sexual messages are generally more intriguing, engaging, and interesting than their nonsexual counterparts (Dudley, 1999; Judd and Alexander, 1983; Reichert et al., 2001). This effect should influence newsstand or single-copy sales when magazines are an impulse purchase or they are perceived as indistinguishable (parity) from each other. According to the findings, magazines with sexual covers are more likely to be noticed, picked up, and looked through.

Interest in the magazine is affected, however, by the interaction between design value and sexual attractiveness. It appears that superior design bolsters the effect of sex whereas inferior design diminishes the effect (see Figure 1). In other words, when sexual attractiveness is low, design value seems to matter little. Design works in tandem with sexually attractiveness to spur magazine interest but the extent of the design effect appears to end there, as purchase intention, a variable more akin to behavior than magazine interest, is not affected by design.

The prediction that sexually attractive cover models influence purchase intention also is confirmed. At the theoretical level sexual information enhances affect, which, in turn, directs perceptual processes toward the heuristic processing system rather than the rational system. As a result, the response generated by the hedonically pleasing image overrides capacity for systemic thought such as support- and counterarguments. This effect is similar to that in advertising in which consumers are more likely to report more positive attitudes and behavioral intentions in response to sexual ads than to nonsexual ads (e.g., LaTour and Henthorne, 1994; Severn et al., 1990).

Psychological Variables

In addition to outcome variables, sexual arousal and social comparison are assessed in this investigation. As predicted, both variables are influenced by sexually-attractive cover models. Regarding arousal, respondents reported being more sexually aroused by the sexually attractive cover models. Far from being an obvious prediction, the inclusion of sexual arousal contributes to the theoretical significance of the study. As previously argued, sex is a positive construct (e.g., considering prevailing tone, etc.; Fisher, 1986; Harris, 1994). As such, the burden of proof in the role sex plays in human affect and subsequent information processing lies in the arousal dimension. An interesting question for future research, for example, is the amount of variance that sexual arousal explains in the overall arousal construct when participants encounter sexual stimuli. In the event that sexual arousal is the equivalent of overall arousal, attention can be focused on the types of stimuli that instigate sexual arousal. If, however, sexual arousal only explains a minimum amount of variance in overall arousal, then attention should be given to the types of stimuli that produce arousal.

Last, the prediction that upward social comparison is influenced by sexually attractive cover models is confirmed. The inclusion of social comparison offers several opportunities for additional research. If sex does indeed sell, as this study indicates, is it because the consumer is only affected in the way they process information or are additional mechanisms involved? All too often, comparisons explain why consumers make superfluous purchases. In this study, sexually attractive cover models encourage upward comparison. However, upward comparisons are often associated with detrimental effects such as lower self-esteem and life-satisfaction (Zhou et al., 2002). Future research should explore if upward comparison directly links to magazine interest and purchase intention or if the desire to repair self-esteem results in more interest in the magazine. As these specific mechanisms have yet to be fully analyzed, future research may enlighten the process.

Implications

The present research offers both professional and theoretical implications. In the magazine profession, covers are typically chosen by a team that includes members of the art, editorial, and circulation departments. The editor in chief, however, usually has the final say on which shot makes the cover. The present findings support some of the decisions made by industry professionals of men's magazines regarding strategic cover decisions.

However, the results can only be generalized to short-term purchase decisions, and nothing can be said about the moderate to long-term effects on circulation. As the findings suggest, sexualized cover models influence interest in the magazine as well as intentions to purchase. If the editorial content is inadequate or fails to match the implicit promise of "seeing more" of what's on the cover, consumers may feel duped and reject the magazine from future consideration.

As Lambiase and Reichert (2006) point out in their analysis of men's consumer magazines before and after *Maxim*'s introduction, some titles met with mixed success when adopting *Maxim*'s cover formula. They concluded that a magazine can be considered a brand (i.e., a known quantity) and that altering its editorial formula to attract new readers can disgruntle current (i.e., brand loyal) readers because the brand ceases to be familiar (Lambiase, 2005). As such, editorial teams should treat the present study's results within the context of long-term strategic branding decisions in addition to short-term circulation generation.

Additionally, this study has implications for theory when investigating the effects of sexual marketing information. The industry's maxim that "sex sells" implies that sex directly affects behavior. This study and the theories outlined, pertain more to human information processing and thoughts than behavior. Emotional responses, such as the affect evoked by sexual imagery, appear to influence the route individuals take when processing information. Anecdotal evidence often points to the irrational behaviors of seemingly rational people because of sexual allurement. Sexual information is associated with affective response which–because of its instinctual nature–can override the tendency for rational processing. As a result, one can explain the pattern of findings in sex in advertising research that show an inverse relationship between outcomes and processing. Sexual images on the covers of magazines appear to exhibit this pattern of effects. The actual translation between magazine interest and purchase intention into actual sales, while beyond the scope of this investigation, remains a fertile area for marketing and mass communication research. For instance, future research can incorporate personality variables such as impulsive consumption and sex-related personality variables to test the effects of sexual cover models and the reactions of different personality groups.

Last, in order to investigate the robustness of sexual covers, this study purposely incorporated male and female cover models as well as male and female participants without distinguishing gender. Given that most of the participants were female and the effects of sexually attractive cover models were statistically significant, one is inclined to believe that a pool of male participants responding to sexually attractive female cover models would produce more pronounced effects. Because of the desire to control for the effect of magazine, this study did not test various men's and women's magazines. For ecological reasons *Details* was chosen because it is accessible for both sexes, and because it featured both male and female cover models, it was deemed appropriate to test male and female respondents. It is advisable, however, that future research integrate gender into the investigation.

CONCLUSIONS

Does "sex sell"? The purpose of this study was to shed light on this process by analyzing how the phenomenon of sexy cover models influence magazine purchases. Overall, the findings indicate that sexual attractiveness does positively influence both interest and purchase intention for a general-interest consumer magazine. In addition, analysis of sexual arousal generated by the cover models lends speculative support to the dual information processing theory with regard to the influence of sexual information such that positively-valenced arousal leads to peripheral-style processing. For impulse purchases such as magazines, this study indicates that affectively oriented cover images such as those of sexy celebrities, rock stars, and actors not only grab attention, but provide motivation to purchase the magazine. Such a formula has been especially effective for *Maxim* and related titles. For competing titles with established nonsexual brand identities (e.g., *GQ, Esquire, Details*), the long-term effects of partially adopting the *Maxim* cover formula remain to be seen.

NOTES

1. Additional variables such as Erotophobia/erotophilia and social comparison are included in the present analysis as well. Because the within-subjects analysis is more appropriate than the analysis plan employed by Reichert (2005), findings from the previous study are not discussed.

2. Responses to only 10 of the 11 issues were reported in the previous report. For additional information on *Details*, see Reichert (2005).

REFERENCES

Barry, A. M. S. (1997). *Visual Intelligence, Perception, Image, and Manipulation in Visual Communication*. New York: University of New York Press.

Belch, M., Holgerson, B., Belch, G., and Koppman, J. (1981). Psychophysical and cognitive responses to sex in advertising. In A. Mitchell (ed.), *Advances in Consumer Research* (pp. 424-427). Ann Arbor, MI: Association for Consumer Research.

Bello, D. C., Pitts, P. E., and Etzel, M. J. (1983). The communication effects of controversial sexual content in television programs and commercials. *Journal of Advertising*, 12(3), 32-42.

Bradley, M. M. (1994). Emotional memory: A dimensional analysis. In S. Goozen, N. Ven de Poll and J. A. Sergeant (eds.), *Emotions: Essays on Emotion Theory* (pp. 97-134). Hillsdale, NJ: Lawrence Erlbaum Associates.

Brinkley, A., and Fowler, G. (2001, November). *The politics of aesthetics: A comparison of appearance-driven messages on men's and women's magazine covers.* Paper presented at the annual meeting of the Southwest Education Council for Journalism and Mass Communication, Tulsa, OK.

Byrne, D. (1976). Social psychology and the study of sexual behavior. *Personality and Social Psychology Bulletin*, 3(1), 3-30.

Byrne, D. (1982). Predicting human sexual behavior. In A. Kraut (ed.), *The G. Stanley Hall Lecture Series* (pp. 207-254). Washington, DC: American Psychological Association.

Caballero, M., and Solomon, P. J. (1984). Effects of model attractiveness on sales response. *Journal of Advertising*, 13(1), 17-33.

Dudley, S. C. (1999). Consumer attitudes toward nudity in advertising. *Journal of Marketing Theory and Practice*, 7(4), 89-96.

Eysenck, M. W. (2001). *Principles of Cognitive Psychology*, 2nd ed. East Sussex, UK: Psychology Press.

Festinger, L. (1954). A theory of social comparison processes. *Human Relations*, 7(2), 117-140.

Fisher, W. A. (1986). A psychological approach to human sexuality: The sexual behavior sequence. In D. Byrne and K. Kelley (eds.), *Alternative Approaches to the Study of Sexual Behavior* (pp. 131-171). Hillsdale, NJ: Lawrence Erlbaum Associates.

Fisher, W. A., Byrne, D., White, L., and Kelley, K. (1988). Erotophobia-Erotophilia as a dimension of personality. *Journal of Sex Research*, 25(1), 123-151.

Forest, B. (1999, October 15). Taking cover. *Consumer Magazines* (in *Adweek*), 46.

Geiger, S., and Reeves, B. (1993). The effects of scene changes and semantic relatedness on attention to television. *Communication Research*, 20(2), 155-175.

Gould, S. J. (2003). Toward a theory of advertising lovemaps in marketing communications: overdetermination, postmodern thought and the advertising hermeneutic circle. In T. Reichert and J. Lambiase (eds.), *Sex in Advertising: Perspectives on the Erotic Appeal* (pp. 151-170). Mahwah, NJ: Lawrence Erlbaum Associates.

Grabe, M. E., Zhou, S., Lang, A., and Bolls, P. D. (2000). Packaging television news: The effects of tabloid on information processing and evaluative responses. *Journal of Broadcasting and Electronic Media*, 44(4), 581-598.

Germillion, J. (1997, November 1). What men really want. *Mediaweek*, 28.

Grazer, W., and Keesling, J. (1995). The effect of print advertising's use of sexual themes on brand recall and purchase intention: A product specific investigation of male responses. *Journal of Applied Business Research*, 11(3), 47-58.

Handy, B. (1999, February 15). Bosom buddies. *Time*, 75.

Harris, R. J. (1994). The impact of sexually explicit media. In J. Bryant and D. Zillmann (eds.), Media Effects (pp. 247-272). Mahwah, NJ: Lawrence Erlbaum Associates.

Howd, D. (1990). Esquire. In A. Nourie and B. Nourie (eds.), *American mass-market magazines* (pp. 108-115). Westport, CT: Greenwood.

Jackson, S., and Jacobs, S. (1983). Generalizing about messages: suggestions for design and analysis of experiments. *Human Communication Research*, 9(2), 169-191.

Judd, B. B., and Alexander, M. W. (1983). On the reduced effectiveness of some sexually suggestive ads. *Journal of the Academy of Marketing Science*, 11(2), 156 168.

Kitch, Carolyn L. (2001). *Girl on the Magazine Cover: The Origins of Visual Stereotypes in American Mass Media*. Chapel Hill: University of North Carolina Press.

Krassas, N. R., Blauwkamp, J. M., and Wesselink, P. (2003). "Master your Johnson": Sexual rhetoric in Maxim and Stuff magazines. *Sexuality and Culture*, 7(3), 98-119.

Lambiase, J. (2005). Impressing the editor: Rolling Stone letter writers and their rhetorical strategies for getting published. *Journal of Magazine and New Media Research*, 7(2), 1-14.

Lambiase, J. (2007). Promoting sexy images: Case study scrutinizes Maxim's cover formula for building quick circulation and challenging competitors. *Journal of Promotion Management*, 13(1/2), 109-123.

Lambiase, J., and Reichert, T. (2006). Sex and the marketing of contemporary consumer magazines: How men's magazines sexualized their covers to compete with Maxim. In T. Reichert and J. Lambiase (eds.), *Sex in Consumer Culture: The Erotic Content of Media and Marketing* (pp. 67-86). Mahwah, NJ: Lawrence Erlbaum Associates.

Lang, A., Bolls, P., Potter, R. F., and Kawahara, K. (1999). The effects of production pacing and arousing content on the information processing of television messages. *Journal of Broadcasting and Electronic Media*, 43(4), 451-475.

Lang, P. J., Greenwald, M., Bradley, M. M., and Hamm, A. O. (1993). Looking at pictures: Affective, facial, visceral and behavioral reactions. Psychophysiology, 30(3), 261-273.

LaTour, M. (1990). Female nudity in print advertising: An analysis of gender differences in arousal and ad response. *Psychology and Marketing*, 7(1), 65-81.

LaTour, M., and Henthorne, T. (1993). Female nudity: Attitudes toward the ad and the brand, and implications for advertising strategy. *Journal of Consumer Marketing*, 10(3), 25-32.

LaTour, M. S., and Henthorne, T. L. (1994). Ethical judgments of sexual appeals in print advertising. *Journal of Advertising*, 23(3), 81-90.

Lyubomirsky, S., and Ross, L. (1997). Hedonic consequences of social comparison: A contrast of happy and unhappy people. *Journal of Personality and Social Psychology*, 73(6), 1141-1157.

Malkin, A. R., Wornian, K., and Chrisler, J. C. (1999). Women and weight: Gendered messages on magazine covers. *Sex Roles*, 40(7/8), 647-655.

Martin, M. C., and Gentry, J. W. (1997). Stuck in the model trap: The effects of beautiful models in ads on female pre-adolescents and adolescents. *Journal of Advertising*, 26(2), 19-33.

Mosher, D., Barton-Henry, M., and Green, S. (1988). Subjective sexual arousal and involvement: Development of multiple indicators. *Journal of Sex Research*, 25(3), 412-425.

Moskowitz, G. B., Skurnik, I., and Galinsky, A. D. (1999). The history of dual-process notions, and the future of preconscious control. In S. Chaiken and Y. Trope (eds.), *Dual-process Theories in Social Psychology* (pp. 12-36). New York: The Guilford Press.

Percy, L., and Rossiter, J. (1992). Advertising stimulus effects: A review. *Journal of Current Issues and Research in Advertising,* 14(1), 75-90.

Reichert, T. (2002). Sex in advertising research: A review of content, effects, and functions of sexual information in consumer advertising. *Annual Review of Sex Research,* 13, 241-273.

Reichert, T. (2005). Do sexy cover models increase magazine sales? Investigating the effects of sexual response on magazine interest and purchase intention. *Journal of Promotion Management,* 11(2/3), 113-130.

Reichert, T., Heckler, S. E., and Jackson, S. (2001). The effects of sexual social marketing appeals on cognitive processing and persuasion. *Journal of Advertising,* 30(1), 13-27.

Reid, L., and Soley, L. (1983). Decorative models and the readership of magazine ads. *Journal of Advertising Research,* 23(2), 27-32.

Richins, M. L. (1991). Social comparison and the idealized images of advertising. *Journal of Consumer Research,* 18(1), 71-83.

Richins, M. L. (1995). Social comparison, advertising, and consumer discontent. *American Behavioral Scientist,* 38(49), 593-607.

Severn, J., Belch, G., and Belch, M. (1990). The effects of sexual and non-sexual advertising appeals and information level on cognitive processing and communication effectiveness. *Journal of Advertising,* 19(1), 14-22.

Sirgy, M. J., Lee, D-Jin, Kosenko, R., Meadow, H. L., Rahtz, D., Cicic, M., Xi Jin, G., Yarsuvat, D., Blenkhorn, D. L., and Wright, N. (1998). Does television viewership play a role in the perception of quality of life? *Journal of Advertising,* 27(1), 125-143.

Tate, V. (1990). Playboy. In A. Nourie and B. Nourie (eds.), *American mass-market magazines* (pp. 367-375). Westport, CT: Greenwood.

Taylor, L. (2005). All for him: Articles about sex in American lad magazines. *Sex Roles,* 52(3/4), 153-163.

Tebbel, J., and Zuckerman, M. (1991). *The Magazine in America: 1741-1990.* NY: Oxford University Press.

Turner, R. (1999, February 1). Finding the inner swine. Newsweek, 52-53.

Wells, W. (1964). EQ, son of EQ, and the reaction profile. *Journal of Marketing,* 28(4), 45-52.

Wilson, L. (2003). Explaining variability in newspaper design: An examination of the role of newsroom subgroups. *Journal and Mass Communication Quarterly,* 80(2), 348-367.

Wood, J. V. (1989). Theory and research concerning social comparisons of personal attributes. *Personality Bulletin,* 106(2), 231-248.

Zhou, S., Xue, F., and Zhou, P. (2002). Self-esteem, life-satisfaction and materialism: Effects of advertising images on Chinese college students. In C. R. Taylor (ed.) *New Directions in International Advertising Research,* Volume 12 (pp. 243-261). Boston: JAI.

doi:10.1300/J057v13n01_09

ADVERTISING

A Cross-Cultural
and Cross-Media Comparison
of Female Nudity in Advertising

Hye-Jin Paek
Michelle R. Nelson

SUMMARY. This study examines to what extent degrees of nudity presented in advertising differ across five countries (Brazil, China, South Korea, Thailand, and the U.S.). Content is examined by media type (TV vs. magazine) and product category (congruent vs. others). Results show that Thai and U.S. ads employ the highest degrees of nudity, whereas Chi-

Hye-Jin Paek (PhD, University of Wisconsin-Madison) is Assistant Professor, Department of Advertising and Public Relations, Grady College of Journalism and Mass Communication, University of Georgia, Athens, GA 30602 (E-mail: hpaek@uga.edu). Michelle R. Nelson (PhD, University of Illinois, Urbana-Champaign) is Associate Professor, Department of Advertising, University of Illinois at Urbana-Champaign, Urbana, IL 61801 (E-mail: nelsonmr@uiuc.edu).

[Haworth co-indexing entry note]: "A Cross-Cultural and Cross-Media Comparison of Female Nudity in Advertising." Paek, Hye-Jin and Michelle R. Nelson. Co-published simultaneously in *Journal of Promotion Management* (Best Business Books, an imprint of The Haworth Press, Inc.) Vol. 13, No. 1/2, 2007, pp. 145-167; and: *Investigating the Use of Sex in Media Promotion and Advertising* (ed: Tom Reichert) Best Business Books, an imprint of The Haworth Press, Inc., 2007, pp. 145-167. Single or multiple copies of this article are available for a fee from The Haworth Document Delivery Service [1-800-HAWORTH, 9:00 a.m. - 5:00 p.m. (EST). E-mail address: docdelivery@haworthpress.com].

nese ads present the lowest degrees. Across all the countries, magazine ads and congruent-product ads employ higher degrees of nudity than TV ads and non-congruent product ads. The effect of product type on degrees of nudity is stronger in TV ads than in magazine ads and the interaction effect between media type and product type also varies across the countries. Our study provides richer and more specific implications for global advertising strategy with respect to representation of models and use of sex appeals. *doi:10.1300/ J057v13n01_10 [Article copies available for a fee from The Haworth Document Delivery Service: 1-800-HAWORTH. E-mail address: <docdelivery@haworthpress. com> Website: <http://www.HaworthPress.com> © 2007 by The Haworth Press, Inc. All rights reserved.]*

KEYWORDS. Advertising, congruence, content analysis, cross-cultural research, female, media, nudity, sex

Advertising, for almost as long as it has existed, has used some sort of sexual sell, sometimes promising seductive capacities, sometimes more simply attracting our attention with sexual stimuli, even if irrelevant to the product or the selling point. (Pollay, 1986, p. 906)

INTRODUCTION

Pollay's quote was exemplified by *GoDaddy.com*, the domain-name company, well known for its racy ad during Super Bowl 2005. The company aired their 14th-edited version of a "much-toned-down" advertisement for Super Bowl 2006 with a parody on censor-ship of sexual content in the wake of Janet Jackson's "wardrobe malfunction" (Gonsalves, 2006). Internet domain names have absolutely nothing to do with sex, and the level of sexuality employed in *GoDaddy.com* ads sparked controversy and criticism related to taste and decency. Nevertheless, the company reported 900,000 unique visitors during the game, up more than 1,000% from a typical Sunday (Mills, 2006). The ensuing controversy also resulted in more than $11 million of publicity for the company (*Adweek*, 2006). It appears that sexual content in advertising continues to attract attention among viewers and newsmakers.

Recent reports indeed indicate that up to 12% of U.S. television spots and 40% of magazine ads contain sexual content (Reichert, 2002).

Within U.S. media, such depictions of male and (particularly) female sexuality are increasing (e.g., Reichert and Carpenter, 2004; Reichert and Lambiase, 2003). Nevertheless, little is known about sexual imagery in non-U.S. advertising content (Reichert, 2002). Given the movement of advertising across national borders, global advertisers should consider the boundaries of sexual imagery. Because advertising must operate within culturally defined and time-bound constraints, including regulations (Boddewyn, 1991), the prevalence and relevance of sexual content are important areas of study. Our study focuses on the prevalence of sexual content in print and television advertising across five countries. To our awareness, no previous study has contrasted sexual content across media in a multi-country study. Thus, we take a teleological approach toward understanding issues related to advertising effectiveness with an assessment of sexual appeals in advertising (Gould, 1994), but do so within a global context.

In the international advertising effectiveness literature, long-standing debates focus on whether or not to standardize (globalize) or localize (customize) international advertising content (for detailed discussions, see Agrawal, 1995; Ryans et al., 2003). But, in reality, most campaigns are not fully standardized or localized, with many ads partially standardized (e.g., Harris and Attour, 2003). It becomes a more important question to ask the extent to which standardization is possible and which execution elements can be most easily adapted to fit foreign markets (Kates and Goh, 2003). In particular, to what extent are sex appeals, as one of the most popular advertising tactics, being used across countries?

The purpose of this study is two-fold: to examine (1) to what extent degrees of sexuality (operationalized as degrees of female model nudity) presented in advertising differ across five countries (Brazil, China, South Korea, Thailand, and the U.S.) and (2) how the degrees of nudity in advertising vary by media type (TV vs. magazine) and product category (congruent vs. others). In addition to investigating cultural differences or similarities, we argue that other factors should be examined at the executional level, including consideration of characteristics of target audiences, products, and media. Our examination and comparison of prime-time television and magazine advertisements across five critical global markets will provide a richer understanding of how global advertising strategy and tactics should be implemented.

LITERATURE REVIEW

Advertising Imagery and Sexuality

Advertising communicates through verbal and non-verbal elements. In recent years, researchers have realized the importance of analyzing the visual nature of advertising (Scott, 1994), particularly as we are now in a new visual century (Kahan, 1992) where media rely on visuals to communicate in the cluttered, global media world. Images of models or spokespersons operate as symbols in a visual grammar that creates meanings understood by members of a culture (Warlaumont, 1993). In fact, these visuals are typically regarded as the most easily standardized element in global advertising because there is no translation of body copy required (de Mooij, 1998).

In examining sexuality in advertising, the visual, especially the state of undress of the model, is the most likely place for sexualized elements to occur (Soley and Kurzbard, 1986). When U.S. consumers were asked "what makes an ad sexual?" they almost unanimously referred to the model's physique and the amount and style of clothing (Reichert and Ramirez, 2000). In a review of past literature on sex in advertising, Reichert (2003) suggested that nearly all researchers examining sex in advertising have considered levels of nudity as a form of sexual content. Nudity here can be defined as and measured by the amount and style of clothing and the amount of skin shown (Reichert, 2003).

Studies conducted within a U.S. context have revealed an increase in visual sexuality in general interest, men's, and women's magazines between 1964 and 1984 (Soley and Kurzbard, 1986; Soley and Reid, 1988). The researchers reported that the increase in sexual dress/undress was found for general interest and men's magazines, but not for women's magazines, although women's magazines contained the greatest proportion of nudity (34.2%). Across both years, women were more likely than men to be shown suggestively or partially clad or in the nude. A content analytic study of 1993 prime-time television commercials showed that most men and women were fully clothed, although women tended to show more nudity than men did (Lin, 1998).

Sexuality in a Global Context

Despite the role of female nudity in advertising, sexuality is regarded differently around the world. In the U.S., for example, some people say they do not like sexy advertisements and will boycott products that feature sexuality in advertisements (Fetto, 2001). However, in continental European countries (e.g., Italy and France), consumers seem more accepting of nudity in ads (Frith and Mueller, 2003; Lass and Hart, 2004). Indeed, it has been observed that "Germans don't perceive female nudity in advertising as an affront or as sexist exploitation. They might see it as nothing more than a cheap advertising trick" (de Mooij, 2004, p. 122). In France, ads are so risqué that they are referred to as "porno-chic" (Mueller, 2004, p. 298), and even French women typically regard female nudity and sexuality as aesthetic rather than sexist (Tissier-Desbordes and Manceau, 2002). In 2001, when France updated its self-regulatory codes related to depictions of women, the regulators insisted that nudity in and of itself was not under attack (Galloni, 2001). Conversely, countries in Asia and the Middle East tend to be more conservative than the U.S. and Europe with respect to nudity (Frith and Mueller, 2003).

Indeed, the prevalence of sexuality and nudity in advertising has been found to vary cross-culturally. For instance, according to a content analysis of Clio-award winning television commercials, nudity was more prevalent in international than in U.S. ads (Reid et al., 1984). In another study, Piron and Young (1996) compared nudity within German and U.S. women's magazine advertising in 1986, 1989, and 1992. They found that degrees of nudity became lower over time with a shift from the use of partially clad (i.e., showing bare body parts) to suggestively clad (e.g., open blouses, tight clothing) women. But these images also seemed to amplify the depiction of women as sex objects. In a comparison of sex appeals in U.S. and French women's magazine ads, it was found that French ads used more sex appeals than American ads did (Biswas et al., 1992). Also, in both countries, women were used for sex appeals more frequently than men. In contrast to these European cases, only a few studies have examined degrees of sexuality presented in Asian countries' ads. In a study of television advertising content in Japan, for example, Arima (2003) reported that women were significantly more likely than men to appear as "attention-getters." In another study, Chinese women were found to wear less sexually suggestive clothing than their U.S. counterparts did (Cheng, 1997).

Despite these studies that examined sexuality cross-culturally, we found only one study that has investigated sexual content in advertising across multiple countries (Nelson and Paek, 2005). These researchers examined levels of female nudity in *Cosmopolitan* magazine ads by comparing the U.S. and six other countries–Brazil, China, France, India, South Korea, and Thailand. The researchers found that nudity differed greatly across national cultures. For example, French and Brazilian ads employed the greatest percentage of women in the highest level of undress (i.e., the display of bare bodies). But when mean levels of nudity were compared, Chinese ads scored significantly lower and Thai ads significantly higher than ads in all the other countries. These findings imply that the East-West cultural distinction may not be the only one that determines degrees of sexuality in ads. Since the scope of these findings and implications were limited to *Cosmopolitan*, we aim to expand the previous study by examining TV commercials across countries and by comparing the differences related to degrees of nudity between TV and magazine ads.

In this study, we examine three different Asian countries (China, South Korea, Thailand) and two North and South American countries (U.S. and Brazil). Informed by the previous studies, we start from the following research question.

> RQ1: Do degrees of sexuality presented in TV and magazine advertisements differ across the five countries?

Determinants of Sexuality in Ads: Media Type and Product Type

Ads in different countries may employ varying degrees of sexuality due to differences of cultures, values, regulations, and people's tastes (Boddewyn, 1991). However, other executional factors may also be relevant for determining degrees of sexuality. In particular, we focus on media type and product type, which are primary considerations for advertising strategy, and examine how these two factors play a role in determining degrees of sexuality in advertisements across the five countries.

Media Type. Media present different target audiences, content and regulations. For example, magazines such as *Cosmopolitan* often reach niche audiences, whereas broadcast television offers a wider audience in age and other demographic characteristics (Zhang and Shavitt, 2003). The differences in target audiences suggest ramifications for content, including sexual content in programming and advertising. Sexuality in prime-time TV commercials may differ from magazine ads due to a heterogeneous broadcast audience, including children, who can easily view the content (Boddewyn 1991), as well as an older audience, who may be less accepting of nudity than younger readers of certain magazines (Johnson and Satow, 1978). In addition, television is often subject to more stringent indecency regulations than are print media (Lin, 1998).

Indeed, although they employ different coding schemes, some content analyses in the U.S. have shown that magazine ads offer more sexual content than do television commercials. For example, women have been portrayed in revealing or little clothing in between 30% and 40% of mainstream magazine ads (Reichert et al., 1999). By contrast, studies of television advertising content over time show much less emphasis on sex than studies of magazine advertising have shown. For example, in 1993 prime-time network ads, 18% of the models were assessed as "very sexy" according to their physical attractiveness and nudity level (Lin, 1998). In 1998, only 12% of women models on prime-time television commercials were dressed sexually (Fullerton and Kendrick, 2001).

Meanwhile, we have not found any studies conducted in countries other than the U.S. that have compared sexual advertising content across media. But, based on the fact that advertising regulations for 'soft' issues such as decency and model portrayals are more likely to occur in broadcast than print (Boddewyn, 1991), and based on the characteristics of the media outlined above, we formulate the following hypothesis.

> H1: Among all the countries, magazine ads will present higher degrees of sexuality than TV ads.

Product Category. The quote introduced in the beginning of this study by Pollay (1986) and the example of *GoDaddy.com* suggest that sexual stimuli are widely adopted, even to promote irrelevant products. While there are certainly examples of sex being used to sell goods that have nothing to do with sex, studies have revealed that sex appeals are more often found in ads that promote products that are relevant to the use of model nudity or sexuality. For example, models exposing their sexuality often appear in ads for fragrances, designer clothing and accessories, and health and beauty products (Reichert, 2002). Further, although the relevance and ethics may be debated, sexuality is often found in ads for tobacco and alcoholic beverages (Kilbourne, 2003). Rarely is sexuality used to sell financial services, medicine, or home computers (Reichert, 2002). Other researchers have also suggested that sexuality or nudity may be regarded as "relevant" or congruent with the attributes of beauty or personal care products, clothing, or alcohol (Peterson and Kerin, 1977; Tinkham and Reid, 1988).

The ramifications of sex-product congruency for advertising effectiveness have also been explored. Superior effects of recall and attitudes for sexual ads that are deemed congruent or appropriate to the product category have been noted in both quantitative (Simpson et al., 1996) and qualitative (Beetles and Harris, 2004) studies. In addition, sexuality present in ads for un-related products (e.g., 'do-it-yourself' tools, electronics) may act as a distractor or may be negatively regarded as sexist (Tuncay et al., 2004). To what extent advertisers are using nudity within congruent or incongruent product categories has not been researched much, especially within an international context (Reichert, 2002). Based on the research conducted in an U.S. context (e.g., Reichert et al., 1999; Reichert and Ramirez, 2000), however, we predict that degrees of sexuality will be higher in ads that promote congruent products irrespective of countries that have different cultural values. Thus, the following hypothesis is formulated.

> H2: Degrees of sexuality will be greater for product ads that are considered more congruent with sex appeals than for other (incongruent) product ads.

Interaction Effects Among Country, Product Type, and Media Type. Research question 1 and the two hypotheses addressed above look at the association between degrees of sexuality and each of the factors (country, media type, and product type) separately. A more intriguing question would be whether or not and to what extent these three factors interact with one another. The answer may provide more specific implications for global advertising strategy and tactics by products and media. Therefore, we address the following research question.

> RQ2: Are there any interactions in degrees of sexuality among the country, product type and media type?

METHOD

Sample

Both magazine and TV ads collected in five countries (Brazil, China, South Korea, Thailand, and the U.S.) were analyzed for cross-cultural and cross-media comparison. The five countries represent vast cultural differences and provide critical international markets for top global brands. According to *Advertising Age* (2004), for example, China and South Korea were ranked as the sixth and seventh largest advertising markets worldwide with a total of USD 7.7 and 6.8 billion in 2003 ad spending, respectively. Thailand is also amongst the leading countries in the Asia Pacific region and recently recorded double-digit ad growth of 15%, ranking number four in 2004 for the ten Asian countries tracked (*AC Nielsen Thailand*, 2005). Brazil set the pace for growth in Latin America with its advertising investments in the first quarter of the 2005 up to R$6.9 billion (Azedo, 2005).

Sampling procedure. Prime-time TV ads were collected during a two- to six-day period in 2002 (10 to 18 hours of advertising). Ads in the U.S were collected during November, while ads in Brazil, China, South Korea, and Thailand were collected between July and August, when there were no national holidays or special events. The ads were taped from the following national TV network channels: Brazil–CH12, 7, 4, and 2; China–CCTV1, 2, and 5; South Korea–MBC, KBS2, and SBS; Thailand–Thai 2, 3, 4, 5, and 9; and the U.S.–ABC and FOX. Considering the different time periods when ads across each country were collected, seasonality and length of each ad were preliminarily examined and found to have no influence on the degrees of sexuality in ads. Substantial differences across TV stations within each country were not found either.

For magazines, three issues of *Cosmopolitan* magazines in 2002-2003 were selected from the five countries. This magazine was selected because of its wide distribution worldwide (110 editions in 28 languages with reach of 36 million women) and its significant market share in each country (Carr, 2002). The magazine was introduced in Brazil, China, South Korea, and Thailand, in the years of 1974, 1998, 1997, and 2000, respectively (Nelson and Paek, 2003). The following issues of *Cosmopolitan* were analyzed: Brazil–January/August 2002, April 2003; China–September 2002, January/June 2003; South Korea–January/July 2002, April 2003; Thailand–January/August 2002, April 2003; U.S.–January/July 2002, April 2003. Systematic differences across magazine issues and by seasonality and advertising sizes were not detected.

The unit of analysis was at least a full-page (for magazine) or a 10-second commercial (for TV), which contained female human models. Local or retail ads were excluded, while redundant ads were included in order to consider the number of times consumers were actually exposed to such ads.

To assess degrees of female nudity as an indication of sexuality in advertising, ads that did not present any human models were eliminated.

As a result, overall 1,703 (989 for TV ads and 732 for magazine ads) out of 2,571 ads (1,570 for TV and 1,001 for magazine) remained with 33.8 % of the total ads excluded. The final number of ads analyzed in the study is as follows: TV ads, Brazil = 112, China = 213, South Korea = 358, Thailand = 219, and the U.S. = 87; magazine ads, Brazil = 71, China = 212, South Korea = 191, Thailand = 82, and the U.S. = 235.

Coding Procedures

More than ten coders were recruited from a large Midwestern university in the U.S. At least two native coders independently coded the TV and magazine ads for their respective country so as to calculate inter-coder reliability. All the coders were trained through multiple sessions and group discussions, where each coder shared meanings and nuances about the variables to code. They received monetary compensation for their work.

For inter-coder reliability computation, we adopted Perreault and Leigh's (1989) Index (P/L Index) for nominal variables and Krippendorff's alpha for the ordinal variables. Both reliability formulas are known to be relatively rigorous and to take chance agreements into account (see Krippendorff, 2004, for detailed reviews of intercoder reliability). All reliability coefficients exceeded the rule-of-thumb coefficient size, .70 (Rust and Cooil, 1994), ranging from .75 (female nudity in Brazil and Thai ads) to 1.00 (length of ads in U.S. TV ads).

Criterion Variable

Sexuality. Our operationalization of sexuality is degrees of female nudity. We employed an etic (standard) measure of nudity to compare ads along the same objective criteria across countries (Triandis, 1995). The nudity scale was developed in the U.S. but was also applied previously in Germany (Piron and Young, 1996) and in each of the countries studied here (Nelson and Paek, 2005). This scale examines degrees of nudity measured with the following 5-point ordinal scale: Level "0" = no sexual appeal, fully clothed; level "1" = sexy lips, subtle sexual nuance; level "2" = suggestively clad, wearing open blouses, full-length lingerie, muscle shirts, mini-skirts; level "3" = partially clad, showing under apparel, three-quarter length or shorter lingerie, bikinis; level "4" = nudity, bare bodies, wearing translucent under-apparel or lingerie.

Predictor Variables

Media type and product type served as predictor variables to examine main and interaction effects on degrees of sexuality in ads across the five countries. Media type is a binary variable that codes magazine as "1" and TV as "2." For product category, twenty-two initial product categories were grouped into two types of products based on previous studies on the association between product categories and sexuality (e.g., Reichert, 2002): congruent products versus others. *Congruent product* is a binary variable with a summation of the product categories including alcohol, personal care, cosmetics, and fashion being "1" ($n = 722$) and other categories being "0" ($n = 981$). Products in the other category include the other 18 product categories such as food, automobiles, home appliances, business/finances, and furniture.

RESULTS

Mean Differences of Degrees of Nudity by Country

RQ1 asked whether there is any difference in terms of degrees of nudity presented in TV and magazine advertisements across the countries. A one-way ANOVA test using pooled-sample ads (TV and magazine ads combined) across the countries reveals a statistically significant difference across the five countries ($F_{(4,1698)} = 13.24$, $p < .001$). Table 1 reports mean and standard deviation of degrees of nudity in ads across the five countries. Post-hoc multiple comparison tests indicate that the Thai and the U.S. ads present the greatest degrees of female nudity among the five countries at the mean score level. Both countries' ads had a significantly higher mean value of nudity than the other three country ads, while there was no difference with regard to degrees of nudity between the two country ads. By contrast, South Korean and Chinese ads presented the least degrees of female nudity among the countries.

Further, it was predicted that the degrees of nudity would be higher in magazine ads than in TV ads (H1) and in congruent product ads than in non-congruent product ads (H2) among all the countries. Table 2 presents the findings of the analyses. Figures 1 and 2 illustrate the mean differences in degrees of nudity across the five countries by media type and by product type.

TABLE 1. Mean and Standard Deviation of Degrees of Sexuality Across the Five Countries

Country	Sample (N)	N	Mean	SD	t-value (df) [a]
Brazil	TV	112	.26	.81	-4.68 $_{(91.20)}$ ***
	Magazine	67	1.16	1.45	
	Pooled	179	.60	1.18	
China	TV	210	.24	.65	-5.64 $_{(255.12)}$ ***
	Magazine	166	.78	1.09	
	Pooled	376	.48	.91	
South Korea	TV	351	.15	.40	-11.73 $_{(215.28)}$ ***
	Magazine	189	1.11	1.11	
	Pooled	540	.48	.86	
Thailand	TV	211	.60	.99	-6.58 $_{(111.36)}$ ***
	Magazine	77	1.66	1.27	
	Pooled	288	.89	1.17	
U.S.	TV	87	.14	.51	-9.81 $_{(317.52)}$ ***
	Magazine	233	1.14	1.31	
	Pooled	320	.87	1.23	
Total	TV	971	.28	.70	-16.23 $_{(1078.83)}$ ***
	Magazine	732	1.11	1.24	
	Pooled	1703	.64	1.05	

[a]Independent-samples *t*-tests between TV and Magazine ads within each country; because *F* was significant in Levene's test for equality of variances ($p < .05$), equal variances were not assumed.
* $p < .05$, ** $p < .01$, *** $p < .001$

First, a univariate Analysis of Variance (ANOVA) through the GLM procedure reports that media type had significant main effects on degrees of nudity presented in ads ($F_{(1, 1683)} = 125.52$, $p < .001$, partial $\eta = .069$). That is to say, the magazine ads had significantly higher de-

TABLE 2. Analysis of Variance for Sexuality in Advertising (Main and Interaction Effects of Country, Media, and Product Type)

Independent variable	df	F	Partial Eta-squared
Country	4	17.22***	.04
Media type	1	125.52***	.07
Product type	1	18.97***	.01
Country x Media	4	1.36	.00
Country x Product	4	1.97	.01
Media x Product	1	8.28**	.01
Country x Media x Product	4	2.73*	.01
Error	1683		
R^2	.22		

* $p < .05$, ** $p < .01$, *** $p < .001$

FIGURE 1. Degrees of Sexuality by Product Type Across the Five Countries (TV Ads)

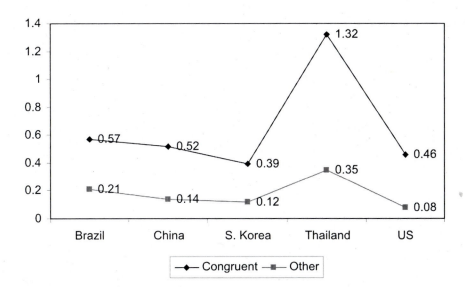

FIGURE 2. Degrees of Sexuality by Product Type Across the Five Countries (Magazine Ads)

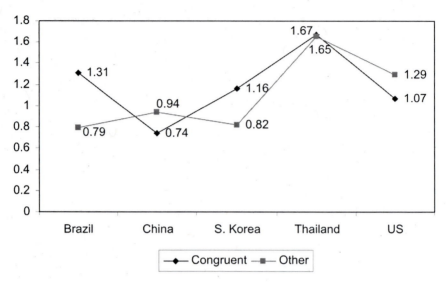

grees of nudity than TV ads. In addition, independent samples t-tests conducted within each country also indicated that magazine ads presented significantly higher degrees of nudity than TV ads in all the five countries (see within-country t-test results in Table 1). This finding supports H1.

Ads promoting congruent products such as fashion goods, cosmetics, alcohol, and personal care goods presented higher degrees of nudity than those promoting non-congruent products such as food, automobiles, and computers. As shown in Table 2, there were significant main effects of product type on degrees of nudity ($F_{(1,1683)} = 18.97, p < .001$, partial $\eta = .01$). Thus, H2 was also supported. Furthermore, independent samples t-tests within each country indicated that congruent product ads present statistically higher degrees of nudity than non-congruent product ads for all five countries.

But, when TV and magazine ads were examined separately, each country shows variability with regards to degrees of nudity presented in its own ads. In Brazil and the U.S., significant differences of degrees of nudity were not found between congruent and non-congruent product ads delivered by TV or magazines. By contrast, in the other countries (China, South Korea, and Thailand) significant differences of degrees of nudity were detected by product type in TV ads, but not in magazine ads (Figures 1 and 2).

Lastly, RQ2 sought to investigate any interaction effects between the three variables–media type, product type, and countries–on degrees of nudity presented in ads. As shown in Table 2, a two-way interaction between media type and product type and a three-way interaction among media type, product type, and country variables were found. The two-way interaction suggests that the effect of product type on degrees of nudity is stronger in TV ads than in magazine ads ($F_{(1,1683)} = 8.28, p < .01$, partial $\eta = .01$). In other words, whether ads promote congruent products or non-congruent products matter more in TV ads than in magazine ads for determining degrees of nudity. Figure 3 illustrates the interaction between the media type and product type variables. In a similar fashion, the three-way interaction shows that the interaction between media type and product type varies across the five countries ($F_{(4,1683)} = 2.73, p < .05$, partial $\eta = .01$). This finding implies that the interaction effect became larger in some country ads (seemingly Thai ads) than in the other country ads. Overall, the univariate ANOVA model explains 22% of total variance in degrees of nudity.

FIGURE 3. Interaction Effects on Degrees of Sexuality Between Media Type and Product Type

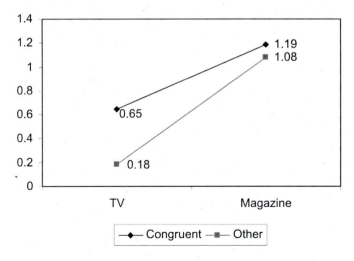

DISCUSSION

Advertising Week, one of the major trade journals in advertising industry, sponsored a full-page print ad that featured a close-up of a women's chest, with the slogan: "Advertising: We All Do It" (printed in *Advertising Week*, July 18, 2005, p. 19) The advertisement attracted attention but the assumption may be that all advertising professionals 'do' sexual advertising. While studies over time show an increasing number of sex appeals in the U.S., little is known about sexuality in advertising in a global context. The handful of studies that have examined sexual content across cultures mainly compared the U.S. and a European country (e.g., Biswas et al., 1992; Piron and Young, 1996). Cross-cultural studies that involve a wider array of multiple countries are even scarcer (for exception, see Nelson and Paek, 2005). Based on the results of our five-country study, it appears that 'we' do not all use sexual appeals to the same extent. In fact, the use of female nudity varied widely across our countries, which suggests that the use of sexuality may not be an accepted tactic in certain cultures (e.g., China) but is quite 'normal' in others (e.g., Thailand). We hope this examination provides implications for global advertising strategy and tactics, particularly related to the use of female nudity or sex appeals within ads.

Degrees of Female Nudity by Country

Media in general and advertising in particular are often cited as major forces shaping the drive toward globalization and creating a shared set of values (Appadurai, 1990; Paek and Pan, 2004). In a cyclical fashion, globalization is meant to allow standardized advertising appeals to be easily exported and transported across the global village, or at least across regions. Our content-analytic study of both TV and magazine ads suggests that these assumptions may not be entirely true. For example, in Asia, Thai ads were found to employ the highest degrees of female nudity, which were delivered via both TV and magazine, whereas China and South Korea were found to employ very low levels of nudity. Surprisingly, Brazil, which is generally regarded as a sexually liberal country, actually showed relatively lower degrees of nudity in their ads compared with the other countries. This finding also implies that deep-rooted, traditional assumptions between Western and Eastern values may no longer hold in this fast moving globalization era.

Of course, the pooled-sample comparison of ads across the five countries does not tell the entire story. While country or culture difference may operate at a higher level, more closely, advertising executions may be determined by other strategic considerations including positioning and media strategy (Wells et al., 2003). In other words, product type and media type are also closely related to the types of creative strategy and tactics that should be employed. Indeed, our findings show that the degrees of female nudity varied by media type and product type.

Degrees of Female Nudity by Media Type

In general, magazine ads presented higher degrees of nudity than TV ads across all the five countries. These results have been discussed and demonstrated within the U.S. (see Reichert, 2002) but never within other country contexts. There are several explanations for the varying degrees of nudity by media type. First, the difference is likely due to more stringent regulations or censorship of broadcast content of 'soft' issues such as sexuality or decency than for magazines. Not empirically tested here, some ad-hoc secondary research shows that, in each country, advertising regulation is more strictly applied to TV advertising than magazine advertising (Nelson and Paek, 2006). In addition, the three Asian countries examined in this study have governmental pre-clearance (or censorship) for TV commercials, while Brazil and the U.S. do not. However, this additional consideration of advertising regulation explains our findings only partially, given that Thailand presented the highest degrees of nudity presented in both TV and magazine ads. Perhaps the pre-clearance standards vary among the three Asian countries. For example, *Cosmopolitan* was one of the few Western publications to win the Chinese government's approval, albeit under restrictions related to sexual editorial content (Reilly, 1998). Such restrictions may also be applied to advertising codes in China, for our findings also indicated Chinese ads in both TV and magazine showed the lowest degrees of nudity across all countries. Closely related, fear of broadcast censorship is reported to cause some advertisers in Asia to avoid using sexual content (Prystay, 2004).

Second, the difference can be related to the difference in target audiences across TV and magazines in general (Wells et al., 2003) and to the particular magazine examined here. *Cosmopolitan* magazine is targeted at young women who may be more accepting of female nudity than the broad audience for prime-time network television. Empirical evidence shows that the link between the sexual editorial content of *Cosmopolitan* and the advertising content appears to be quite closely matched (Nelson and Paek, 2003). Some studies (e.g., Kacen and Nelson, 2002) have also demonstrated that the sexist portrayals of women vary widely by magazine, with general news magazines (e.g., *Time*) showing significantly fewer sexist portrayals than niche men's magazines (e.g., *Playboy*). Future research might examine the sexual content of other magazines, including those targeted at older audiences or for a wider audience. In addition, television content directed to particular niche audiences that match the demographics of *Cosmopolitan* may also reveal higher sexual content in ads.

Degrees of Female Nudity by Product Type

Our findings also reveal that the type of product being advertised related to the degree of nudity that was depicted by the model in the ad. We found that, in general, congruent product ads employed higher degrees of nudity than non-congruent products. This pattern of results was found to be consistent for all countries when pooled-sample ads were examined. But the level of nudity by media type varied across the countries. In most countries (except for Brazil and the U.S.), it mattered whether or not the advertised products were congruent with sexual content in the TV ads, but product type did not matter as much in the magazine ads. These findings highlight several implications. First, Pollay's argument (1986) that sex sells regardless of its relevancy to the product may only work for Brazil and U.S. ads, but may not be generalizable across the countries. His argument may also be much more applicable to a certain magazine's ads, but not TV ads. Second, by contrast, the match-up between sex appeals and product type may vary not only by media that deliver the ads, but also depending on the country in which the ads are executed. These arguments are also supported by our findings on the two-way interaction between media type and product type and on the three-way interaction among media type, product type, and country.

CONCLUSIONS

Implications

Taken together, our findings provide insight into the prevalence of sexual appeals across media and countries. Based on our results, we suggest several implications for global advertising and marketing professionals. First, they should pay attention to the cultural values and tastes within each country, which suggests a localized approach to sexuality. Second, there may be an opportunity for applying similar strategic decisions for advertising creative strategy and tactics, at least with regards to media and brand/product strategy. That is to say, if advertising professionals wish to use sex appeals as a part of global advertising tactics, it may be more appropriate for congruent product categories (e.g., personal care) that are delivered by female fashion magazines. This suggestion is based on our findings that all the countries in our study employed some level of nudity for relevant products. Third, rather than attempting to categorize by regions (e.g., Asia, Europe, and America), practitioners should look at each country more closely to discern how the cultural factors and executional factors operate together.

Limitations

We believe that our study provides a richer understanding of considerations for global advertising and marketing professionals with respect to representation of models and the use of sex appeals. Our study advances previous cross-cultural studies that often remained at the cultural level with a two-country examination, by examining also at the executional level of TV and magazine ads across multiple countries (e.g., medium, product). That said, we do not mean to generalize our findings across all TV or magazine ads or to other countries due to several limitations.

First, this study used an etic or standard measure of nudity across five different countries. Although a standardized scale allows researchers to compare easily, and although we employed local coders, the meanings or nuances related to various states of undress may not be captured by applying the same scale across five very different countries. Indeed, the relationship between sex and nudity may not be standard across cultures. For example, de Mooij (2004) cautions that "in some cultures nudity is related to sex, whereas in others nudity symbolizes purity or beauty" (p. 122). For example, nudity is common in Germany, but "it is unthinkable in the United States, where people are extremely sensitive to nudity, which tends to be confused with sex" (de Mooij, 2004, p. 122).

Second, as previously discussed in detail, TV and magazine ads analyzed in this study were not collected through a random sampling procedure. The convenience or purposive sampling procedure is common in cross-cultural advertising studies, given the difficulty of content analysis procedures where researchers have to deal with multi-layered barriers such as different languages, technological systems, media systems, and seasonality. Nevertheless, future cross-cultural studies should strive for more systematic procedures.

Lastly, our operationalization of sexuality with degrees of female nudity may be limited because it captures only one dimension of sex appeals in advertising executions. Considering various ways of creating sex appeals in advertising executions, future studies should examine advertising content that employs other indicators of sexuality, including male nudity, intimacy between male and female models, and gaze. In addition, different methodology should be employed for cross-cultural studies, in order to examine causal effects or consumer responses regarding sexuality presented in advertising.

REFERENCES

AC Nielsen Thailand (2005). Thailand enjoys double digit growth in advertising spend. Retrieved on June 22, 2005 from http://64.233.167.104/search?q=cache: kW10UeeKSeQJ: www.acnielsen.co.th/news.asp%3FnewsID%3D69+thailand+advertising+spending&hl = ko.

Advertising Age (2004). 2005 quick reference synopsis of the year's marketing and advertising data. Retrieved on March 15, 2005 from http://www.adage.com/news.cms?newsId=44274.

Adweek (February 2, 2006). ABC approves GoDaddy spot. Retrieved on June 11, 2006 from http://www.adweek.com/aw/national/article_display.jsp?vnu_ content_id=1001956657.

Agrawal, M. (1995). Review of a 40-year debate in international advertising: Practitioner and academician perspectives to the standardization/adaptation issue. *International Marketing Review, 12*(1), 26-48.

Appadurai, A. (1990). Disjuncture and difference in the global cultural economy. *Public Culture, 2*(2), 1-24.

Arima, A. N. (2003). Gender stereotypes in Japanese television advertisements. *Sex Roles, 49*(1/2), 81-90.

Azedo, S. (2005, April 20). Advertising spending increases by 23% in the first quarter in Brazil. *Gazeta Mercantil.* Retrieved on June 22, 2005 from LexisNexis.

Beetles, A., and Harris, L. C. (2004, June). Female nudity in advertising: An exploratory study. Paper presented to the ACR Conference on Gender, Marketing and Consumer Behavior, Madison, Wisconsin.

Biswas, A., Olson, J. E., and Carlet, V. (1992). A comparison of print advertisements from the United States and France. *Journal of Advertising, 21*(4), 73-82.

Boddewyn, J. J. (1991). Controlling sex and decency in advertising around the world. *Journal of Advertising, 20*(4), 25-35.

Carr, D. (2002, May 26). Romance, in Cosmo's world, is translated in many ways. *New York Times,* sect. 1, 1.

Cheng, H. (1997). Holding up half of the sky? A socio-cultural comparison of gender-role portrayals in Chinese and U.S. advertising. *International Journal of Advertising, 16*(4), 259-319.

de Mooij, M. (1998). *Global Marketing and Advertising: Understanding Cultural Paradoxes.* Thousand Oaks, CA: Sage.

de Mooij, M. (2004). *Consumer Behavior and Culture: Consequences for Global Marketing and Advertising.* Thousand Oaks, CA: Sage.

Fetto, J. (2001). Where's the lovin'? *American Demographics, 23*(2), 10-11.

Frith, K. T., and Mueller, B. (2003). *Advertising and Societies.* New York: Peter Lang.

Fullerton, J., and Kendrick, A. (2001). Comparing content of commercials from general market and Spanish language television. *Southwestern Mass Communication Journal, 17*(1), 53-62.

Galloni, A. (2001, October 25). Clampdown on 'porno-chic' ads is pushed by French authorities. *Wall Street Journal,* B4.

Gonsalves, A. (2006, February 2). Go Daddy gets ok for Super Bowl ad. *TechWeb News.* Retrieved on February 26, 2007 from http://www.informationweek.com/news/showArticle.jhtml?articleID=178601594.

Gould, S. J. (1994). Sexuality and ethics in advertising: A research agenda and policy guideline perspective. *Journal of Advertising, 23*(3), 73-80.

Harris, G., and Attour, S. (2003). The international advertising practices of multinational companies. *European Journal of Marketing, 37*(1/2), 154-168.

Johnson, D. K., and Satow, K. (1978). Consumers' reactions to sex in TV commercials. In H. K. Hunt (ed.), *Advances in Consumer Research, Vol. 5* (pp. 411-414). Ann Arbor, MI: Association for Consumer Research.

Kacen, J. J., and Nelson, M. R. (2002). We've come a long way baby–or have we? Sexism in advertising revisited. In P. Maclaran and E. Tissier-Desbordes (eds.), *Gender, Marketing and Consumer Behavior Sixth Conference Proceedings* (pp. 291-308). Provo, UT: Association for Consumer Research.

Kahan, R. (1992). America in a visual century. *Journalism Quarterly, 69*(2), 262-265.

Kates, S. M., and Goh, C. (2003). Brand morphing: Implications for advertising theory and practice. *Journal of Advertising, 32*(1), 59-69.

Kilbourne, J. (2003). Advertising and disconnection. In T. Reichert and J. Lambiase (eds.), *Sex in Advertising: Perspectives on the Erotic Appeal* (pp. 173-180). Mahwah, NJ: Lawrence Erlbaum Associates.

Krippendorff, K. (2004). Reliability in content analysis: Some common misconceptions and recommendations. *Human Communication Research, 30*(3), 411-433.

Lass, P., and Hart, S. (2004). National cultures, values and lifestyles influencing consumers' perception towards sexual imagery in alcohol advertising: An exploratory study in the UK, Germany and Italy. *Journal of Marketing Management, 20*(5/6), 607-623.

Lin, C. A. (1998). Uses of sex appeals in prime-time television commercials. *Sex Roles, 38*(5/6), 461-475.

Mills, E. (2006, February 6). Viewers of bowl ads rush to internet. *CNET.* Retrieved on February 11, 2007 from http://news.com.com/Viewers+of+Bowl+ads+rush+to+Internet/2100-1024_3-6035820.html?tag=cd.top.

Mueller, B. (2004). *Dynamics of International Advertising: Theoretical and Practical Perspectives.* New York, NY: Peter Lang.

Nelson, M. R., and Paek, H.-J. (2006). Can sex (appeals) be standardized? An analysis of model nudity in prime-time TV advertising across seven countries. Working paper.

Nelson, M., and Paek, H.-J. (2005). Predicting cross-cultural differences in sexual advertising contents in a transnational women's magazine. *Sex Roles, 53*(5/6), 371-383.

Nelson, M. R., and Paek, H.-J. (2003, August). Exporting the "fun, fearless female": *Cosmopolitan* magazine as a case study of a global media brand. Paper presented at Advertising Division, the Association for Education in Journalism and Mass Communication Annual Convention, Kansas City, Missouri.

Paek, H.-J., and Pan, Z. (2004). Spreading the global consumerism? Mass media and consumerist values in China. *Mass Communication and Society, 7*(4), 491-515.

Perreault, W. D., and Leigh, L. E. (1989). Reliability of nominal data based on qualitative judgments. *Journal of Marketing Research, 26*(2), 135-148.

Peterson, R. A., and Kerin, R. A. (1977). The female role in advertisements: Some experimental evidence. *Journal of Marketing, 41*(4), 59-63.

Piron, F., and Young, M. (1996). Consumer advertising in Germany and the United States: A study of sexual explicitness and cross-gender contact. In L. A. Manrai and A. K. Manrai (eds). *Global Perspectives in Cross-cultural and Cross-national Consumer Research* (pp. 211-228). New York: International Business Press.

Pollay, R. W. (1986). The distorted mirror: Reflections on the unintended consequences of Advertising. *Journal of Marketing, 50*(2), 18-36.

Prystay, C. (2004, May 13). Sexing up Asia's ads. *Far Eastern Economic Review*, 167.

Reichert, T. (2002). Sex in advertising research: A review of content, effects, and functions of sexual information in consumer advertising. *Annual Review of Sex Research, 13*, 241-273.

Reichert, T. (2003). What is sex in advertising? Perspectives from consumer behavior and social science research. In T. Reichert and J. Lambiase (eds.) *Sex in Advertising: Perspectives on the Erotic Appeal* (pp. 11-38). Mahwah, NJ: Lawrence Erlbaum Associates.

Reichert, T., and Carpenter, C. (2004). An update on sex in magazine advertising: 1983 to 2003. *Journalism and Mass Communication Quarterly, 81*(4), 823-837.

Reichert, T., and Lambiase, J. (2003). One phenomenon, multiple lenses: bridging perspectives to examine sex in advertising. In T. Reichert and J. Lambiase (eds.) *Sex in Advertising: Perspectives on the Erotic Appeal* (pp. 1-8). Mahwah, NJ: Lawrence Erlbaum Associates.

Reichert, T., Lambiase, J., Morgan, S., Carstarphen, M., and Zavoina, S. (1999). Cheesecake and beefcake: No matter how you slice it, sexual explicitness in advertising continues to increase. *Journalism and Mass Communication Quarterly, 76*(1), 7-20.

Reichert, T., and Ramirez, A. (2000). Defining sexually oriented appeals in advertising: A grounded theory investigation. In S. J. Hoch and R. J. Meyer (eds.), *Advances in Consumer Research, Vol. 27* (pp. 267-273). Provo, UT: Association for Consumer Research.

Reid, L. N., Salmon, C., and Soley, L. (1984). The nature of sexual content in television. In R. W. Belk (eds*). Proceedings of the 1984 American Marketing Association Meeting* (pp. 214-216). Chicago: American Marketing Association.

Reilly, P. M. (1998, April 3). Cosmo to tone down language for version planned for China. *Wall Street Journal* (Eastern Edition), B7.

Rust, R. T., and Cooil, B. (1994). Reliability measures for qualitative data: Theory and implications. *Journal of Marketing Research, 31*(1), 1-14.

Ryans, J. J., Griffith, D. A., and White, S. D. (2003). Standardization/adaptation of international marketing strategy: Necessary conditions for the advancement of knowledge. *International Marketing Review, 20*(6), 588-603.

Scott, L. M. (1994). Images in advertising: The need for a theory of visual rhetoric. *Journal of Consumer Research, 21*(2), 252-273.

Simpson, P. M., Horton, S., and Brown, G. (1996). Male nudity in advertisements: A modified replication and extension of gender and product effects. *Journal of the Academy of Marketing Science, 24*(3), 257-262.

Soley, L. C., and Kurzbard, G. (1986). Sex in advertising: A comparison of 1964 and 1984 magazine advertisements. *Journal of Advertising, 15*(3), 46-54.

Soley, L. C., and Reid, L. N. (1988). Taking it off: Are models in magazine ads wearing less? *Journalism Quarterly, 65*(4), 960-966.

Tinkham, S. F., and Reid, L. N. (1988). Sex appeal in advertising revisited: Validation of a typology. In J. D. Leckenby (ed.), *Proceedings of the 1988 Conference of the American Academy of Advertising* (pp.118-123). Austin, TX: American Academy of Advertising.

Tissier-Desbordes, E., and Manceau, D. (2002). Female nudity in advertising: What do French women think. In P. Maclaren, and E. Tissier-Desbordes (eds.), *Proceedings of the 6th ACR Conference on Gender, Marketing and Consumer Behavior (Dublin, Ireland)* (pp. 85-104). Duluth, MN: Association for Consumer Research; Paris: ESCP-EAP Printing Services.

Triandis, H. (1995). *Individualism and Collectivism.* Boulder, CO: Westview.

Tuncay, L., Nelson, M. R., and Kacen, J. J. (2004, June). What do we really know about sexism in advertising? Shedding new light on consumers' construal of sexism in advertising. Paper presented at the 7th ACR Conference on Gender, Marketing, and Consumer Behavior, Madison, Wisconsin.

Warlaumont, H. G. (1993). Visual grammars of gender: The gaze and psychoanalytic theory in advertisements. *Journal of Communication Inquiry, 17*(1), 25-40.

Wells, W., Burnett, J., and Moriarty, S. (2003). *Advertising: Principles and Practice,* 6th ed. Upper Saddle River, NJ: Prentice Hall.

Zhang, J., and Shavitt, S. (2003). Cultural values in advertisements to the Chinese X-Generation: Promoting modernity and individualism. *Journal of Advertising, 32*(1), 23-33.

doi:10.1300/J057v13n01_10

Selling with Sex in Sin City:
The Case of the Hard Rock Hotel Casino

Erika Engstrom

SUMMARY. The author presents a case study of the sexual appeals used in several billboards for the Hard Rock Hotel Casino in Las Vegas, Nevada. In 2004, the Hard Rock paid a $100,000 settlement with the Nevada Gaming Commission for advertising deemed "inappropriate." The author analyzes the messages concerning female nudity and implied sexual activity contained in two billboards cited in the formal complaint, and another billboard that used female same-sex eroticism to promote the Hard Rock as an entertainment experience. The article concludes with a discussion of the deontological concerns warranted by overtly sexual advertising. doi:10.1300/J057v13n01_11 *[Article copies available for a fee from The Haworth Document Delivery Service: 1-800-HAWORTH. E-mail address: <docdelivery@haworthpress.com> Website: <http://www.HaworthPress. com> © 2007 by The Haworth Press, Inc. All rights reserved.]*

KEYWORDS. Advertising, billboards, branding, case study, casino, Las Vegas, sexual appeals

Erika Engstrom (PhD, University of Florida) is Associate Dean, Greenspun College of Urban Affairs and Associate Professor, Department of Communication Studies, University of Nevada, Las Vegas, Box 454052, 4505 Maryland Parkway, Las Vegas, NV 89154-4052 (E-mail: erika.engstrom@unlv.edu).

The author thanks Geri Kodey of UNLV Photographic Services for her invaluable assistance.

[Haworth co-indexing entry note]: "Selling with Sex in Sin City: The Case of the Hard Rock Hotel Casino." Engstrom, Erika. Co-published simultaneously in *Journal of Promotion Management* (Best Business Books, an imprint of The Haworth Press, Inc.) Vol. 13, No. 1/2, 2007, pp. 169-188; and: *Investigating the Use of Sex in Media Promotion and Advertising* (ed: Tom Reichert) Best Business Books, an imprint of The Haworth Press, Inc., 2007, pp. 169-188. Single or multiple copies of this article are available for a fee from The Haworth Document Delivery Service [1-800-HAWORTH, 9:00 a.m. - 5:00 p.m. (EST). E-mail address: docdelivery@haworthpress.com].

INTRODUCTION

In 2004, the Hard Rock Hotel Casino in Las Vegas, Nevada agreed to pay a $100,000 fine resulting from complaints about its billboard and print advertising (Benston, 2004; Hard Rock Hotel Form 10-K, 2004; Velotta, 2004e). The ads in question not only contained sexual images, but language that implied approval of cheating on one's spouse and the use of illegal drugs. One ad in particular, a billboard proclaiming "We Sell Used Dice," even resulted in a citizen complaint to a local governmental agency. The Hard Rock's use of sexual appeals in its advertising contributed to its troubles with both state gaming regulators and concerned citizens who found that the edgy ads crossed the line, even in a town infamously referred to as "Sin City."

Generally defined as persuasive appeals containing sexual information (Reichert, 2003), sex in advertising traditionally contains verbal elements, such as suggestive language and double entendres, and visual elements, such as attractive models or some form of nudity. With the aim of drawing attention to their ads (Lang et al., 2003; LaTour and Henthorne, 1994) and creating a sexual brand persona, advertisers aim to link products with sexual thoughts and feelings, and to position brands "as cutting-edge, avant-garde, and even alluringly taboo" (Reichert, 2003, p. 24).

Regarding historical trends in the use of sex in advertising, sex appeals have become commonplace since the 1970s (LaTour and Henthorne, 1994). Severn et al. (1990) noted that while the proportion of ads using sexual stimuli did not increase significantly since the 1970s, visual elements did receive more attention. Indeed, they contend, "presentations have become more explicit by focusing on nudity, male/female contact and suggestions of sexual intercourse" (p. 15).

While Las Vegas has cultivated a sexual persona in recent decades (e.g., sexy showgirls, the "Rat Pack" era, and the "what happens in Vegas stays in Vegas" national ad campaign of the early 2000s), an increasingly competitive marketing environment has led to the use of blatant sexual content. Much of this content appears in advertising mainly among casinos "off the Strip," that is, casinos located away from Las Vegas Boulevard, the main thoroughfare and location of some of the world's most famous casinos. In general, mega-resorts along the Strip, such as Caesars Palace, Bally's, and the Venetian, use appeals that relate directly to what they offer inside: exciting games, dazzling shows, delicious food, and, more recently, shopping. Newer casinos, such as the Hard Rock, catering to a younger crowd, have taken the sexual appeal in new, less subtle, directions.

The case of the Hard Rock Hotel Casino serves as an ideal example of how the use of sexual appeals can enhance brand image, create publicity beyond the content of sexually charged advertising, and, in this particular instance, result in regulatory agencies' involvement in the way a business promotes itself. Here, I examine the Hard Rock's communicative approach to selling its image in a sexually-laden environment. By analyzing the issues surrounding the use of sex in advertising in such an environment, this research adds to the literature on the use of sex in advertising, as well as considerations advertisers should observe regarding unintended audiences and advertising tactics within the gaming industry.

RESEARCH APPROACHES TO SEX IN ADVERTISING

Overall, researchers have used two basic approaches to the study of sex in advertising: teleology and deontology. Teleology is concerned with the effects of sexual content in advertising on human behavior (Gould, 1994), such as the effect of sex on arousal and subsequent responses to both ads and products (e.g., LaTour and Henthorne, 2003). Thus, studies that measure the effects of advertising on brand recall, intent to purchase, and attitudes take a teleological approach. For example, experimental research shows that subjects consider ads with sexually explicit visuals as more entertaining, interesting, and original than non-sexual ads, but also potentially more offensive (Severn et al., 1990). Researchers also have found that sexual appeals in ads increase attention toward, and memory of, ad content (Lang et al., 2003). In early research, Richmond and Hartman (1982) concluded that their findings implied that "judicious use of sex appeals will produce acceptable and satisfactory results" (p. 60).

These generalizations regarding the use of sex require, however, qualification. While sexual ads attract viewer attention, ads that use sex do not always result in greater purchase intention, especially when a product already possesses arousing qualities, such as alcohol (Lang et al., 2003). Indeed, when an ad contains substantial information, sexual content can interfere with message comprehension and even serve as a distraction (Severn et al., 1990). Therefore, Gould (1994) contends that sexual appeals are most effective when used with products that relate to sexuality.

Furthermore, LaTour and Henthorne (1994) found that both men and women are ethically concerned about strong, overt sexual appeals, which can result in undesirable reactions. Advertisers, they warned, need to determine the point at which audiences might consider a sexual appeal as unethical, and, subsequently, result in negative evaluations. LaTour and Henthorne (1994) also contend, based on previous research, that controversial sex appeals present social statements about a society's beliefs, with advertising serving to mirror those beliefs. Thus, by using such appeals, advertisers already assume that it is ethically "okay" to use them.

The morality inherent in advertisers' use of sexual appeals illustrates the deontological approach to sex in advertising. Rather than examining individual effects, or even societal effects (such as the link between ad violence and violent attitudes or actions), when one views such messages in terms of deontology, he or she considers its "moral rightness or wrongness" (Gould, 1994, p. 75). Thus, deontological research "focuses on whether such appeals are morally appropriate, apart from their effects," and whether advertisers use sexual appeals with good intentions or in an "exploitive and degrading way to appeal to consumers' 'base instincts'" (Gould, 1994, p. 77). As Gould (1994) states, research employing a deontological approach "is used to consider the views, norms, and values of all parties concerned" (p. 77). These concerned constituencies include proponents of free speech and the First Amendment (which Gould termed "liberals"), feminists (who oppose sexual appeals that demean women), and religious and other conservatives (who advocate for moral, traditional values and seek to limit or eliminate sexual content from the media). Advertisers who constantly push the sexual limits with their messages, and these interested parties, thus perpetually try to control the "sexual agenda" of what the public sees in advertising, notes Gould (1994, p. 77).

In the case of the Hard Rock Hotel Casino, which regularly employs sexual appeals, other groups besides the targeted audience are affected by its advertising. These groups include the public, people who do not necessarily belong or identify themselves as free speech liberals, feminists, or religious or moral conservatives, and, in this particular case, the Nevada Gaming Commission, the state agency that regulates the gaming industry. Parents have a natural interest to protect their children from inappropriate messages regarding sex, while the Nevada Gaming Commission works to protect the state's main industry from detrimental publicity that potentially can affect profits.[1]

LaTour and Henthorne (1994) contend that one of the important implications of deontological research "is the need for advertisers to recognize the moral/ethical complexity involved in the use of strong overt sexual appeals and to incorporate that understanding with their strategic thought" (p. 89). Thus, deontology serves as the foundation for the current inquiry. Specifically, I elucidate how the Hard Rock's overt sexual advertising challenged moral and ethical standards that resulted in public, media, and governmental responses. The research questions posed here are: (1) How are sexual appeals used in the Hard Rock's advertising?; and (2) What consequences result when an advertiser fails to consider an unintended audience?

The case study method, the systematic investigation of a person, group, organization, or event based on the use of many data sources (Wimmer and Dominick, 1991), is used to answer these questions. As mentioned, data for this case study include content from three billboards that appeared in the Las Vegas area between 2001 and 2003, local media reports, and the Hard Rock's own website. First, I provide a background of the Hard Rock, its location, and self-description as found in its website content. Next, I present qualitative content analyses of several billboards that exemplify the Hard Rock's use of sexual content to create and maintain its image. I then summarize a series of news reports about the Hard Rock's advertising tactics that appeared in the local media from 2003 through 2004. I conclude with a discussion about the consequences of using overtly sexual advertising termed "offensive" by members of the public and regulatory entities in terms of media responses within the Las Vegas community.

THE HARD ROCK HOTEL CASINO: BACKGROUND AND TARGET AUDIENCE

The Hard Rock Hotel Casino opened in 1995. Located one mile east of the famous Las Vegas Strip and about a mile and a half from McCarran International Airport, it consists of a hotel/casino and detached Hard Rock Café restaurant, complete with neon-lit, guitar-shaped signs, one in front of the restaurant at the corner of Paradise Road and Harmon Avenue, and another in front of the hotel. Club Paradise, a "gentlemen's club" featuring topless (female) dancers is located across the street. The general locale consists of a busy area frequented by foot traffic, and other businesses, including restaurants, an AmeriSuites Hotel, Hofbrauhaus beer hall, and shopping plazas, with the campus of the University of Nevada, Las Vegas located within a short walk, approximately a block to the east.

In the overview provided in the resort's annual report filed with the U.S. Securities and Exchange Commission, the Hard Rock describes itself as "a premier destination entertainment resort with a rock music theme," "modeled after the highly successful Hard Rock Café restaurant chain" (Hard Rock Hotel Form 10-K, 2003, p. 3). Regarding its clientele, the Hard Rock differentiates itself from the rest of the Las Vegas market by targeting "a predominantly youthful and 'hip' customer base," which it believes consists "primarily of rock music fans and youthful individuals, as well as actors, musicians and other members of the entertainment industry" (Hard Rock Hotel Form 10-K, 2003, p. 5). The target customer base ranges between 25 and 34 years of age, those "who seek a vibrant, energetic entertainment and gaming experience" (Hard Rock Hotel Form 10-K, 2003, p. 3). Illustrative of its "hip," trendy, young, and sexy image, the Hard Rock includes a lingerie boutique called "Love Jones" and the "Pink Taco" restaurant ("pink taco" is a euphemism for female genitalia). The Hard Rock further established its sexually tinged image in 2002, when it paid a $100,000 fine in the wake of complaints of public sexual acts at one of its nightclubs the previous year (Simpson, 2004c; Velotta, 2003).

The Hard Rock serves as the venue for several music award shows and events hosted by entertainment industry notables. High-profile celebrities and sports figures frequent the resort, including former basketball star Dennis Rodman. According to its annual report, the Hard Rock Hotel Casino "is aggressively marketed" through public relations activities at the domestic and international levels, direct mail, print, radio, and television advertising, "internet blasts," and "various members of the entertainment industry," such as radio shock jock Howard Stern (Hard Rock Hotel Form 10-K, 2003, p. 26).

"Looser Than Your Girlfriend": Selling the Girl-on-Girl Fantasy

Though not specifically listed in its self-report, the resort also advertises with billboards located both on its premises and in other locations in the Las Vegas Valley. Benefits of strategically located billboards include the ability to reach a large numbers of viewers (Lang et al., 2003). In essence, advertisers who use billboards buy an audience who "circulates around the message" (Tocker, 1969, p. 14). However, the brief viewing time allowed, about six seconds (Tocker, 1969), forces billboards to rely on visual content, and on viewers to "apprehend a metaphoric or gestalt understanding" of that content (Marlow, 2001, p. 42). In this regard, billboards must "cram" a large amount of information into one frame, so to speak, making them the ideal medium with which to study sexual appeals.

McCarran International Airport, like airports in other large cities, provides a typical venue for billboard advertising; visitors serve as an almost captive audience as they travel from the airport to their hotel rooms along or around the Strip or downtown Las Vegas. Among myriad billboards greeting arriving tourists in 2001, as well as commuters who use the airport connector route which connects southern suburbs to the city, stood one directing viewers to "Play Slots at Hard Rock Hotel Casino." This line appeared below the larger headline reading, "Looser than Your Girlfriend" (Figure 1).[2]

In that billboard, the Hard Rock's signature guitar, extending beyond the physical border of the billboard structure itself, and a cartoon drawing of two young, thin, and Caucasian women embracing flanked the verbal anchorage. The women have their arms around each other; the one with long, blonde hair kisses and holds the other around the waist, while the other smiles (seemingly at the viewer), with her hand on the

FIGURE 1. Same-Sex Themed Billboard for Hard Rock Casino

Photograph by University of Nevada, Las Vegas Photographic Services. Used by permission

blonde woman's hip. Both appear scantily clad. The blonde-haired woman wears what looks like a tube top and has her abdomen exposed, while the other wears a tight-fitting dress, with one strap hanging off her shoulder. They don't appear to be wearing any supportive undergarments (i.e., bras), and their breasts appear to be touching, albeit through clothing.

Regarding the relationship between an ad's image and its accompanying text, Forceville (1996) observed, "the text of an advertisement is often deliberately ambiguous or enigmatic–no doubt to capture a viewer's attention longer than would otherwise have been the case–and requires information supplied by the picture to solve the riddle" (p. 73). The billboard contains the words "Play Slots at Hard Rock Hotel Casino," which explains in part the large, headlining text "Looser than your girlfriend." The term "loose slots," commonly used on casino signs, refers to the payout rate on slot machines, implying to casino players that they can make more money on certain machines. The word "loose" is used qualitatively; the implication of a 97% payout rate, for example, means that over the long term, a player can "get back" 97% of the money put into a machine. While 97% seems like a high percentage, in reality, the player will lose money, and the "house" still holds the edge.

By stating it has slots "looser" than one's girlfriend, the Hard Rock first tells the viewer it has loose slots. Juxtaposed to the pictorial information, this also implies that "your girlfriend," meaning a man's girlfriend, is so "loose" she will have sex (or at least make out) with another "girl." Past research has found images of "lesbian erotica" particularly arousing to men (Reichert et al., 1999). Thus, "men viewing women for pleasure" summarizes the audience for this type of sexual appeal (Reichert, 2001, p. 9). Consequently, one might see that the Hard Rock aims its message at men who enjoy watching women with women. An additional interpretation points to the idea of control and pleasure. As the slot machines exist for entertainment (playing a game), so, too, do the women depicted.

As one takes a deontological approach to this ad, the message is that the Hard Rock wants to attract persons, namely, men, or even women, with a certain ethical and moral attitude not only toward women, but toward themselves, that is, freewheeling, "loose," and unconcerned about general societal notions about propriety (that is, monogamy with one's girlfriend). Regarding the combination of the connotative meaning of the words "Looser than your girlfriend" and "Play slots," and the visual image of two women embracing, the resulting message about the Hard Rock Hotel Casino points to its own looseness (an interesting counterpoint to the intensity implied by the term "hard rock"). Thus, at the Hard Rock, one can indulge not only in watching loose women, but playing loose slots–a combination of sex and gaming without the rigid rules of society or the laws of mathematics.

In addition to saying something about the Hard Rock and its target audience, this billboard also reflects the advertiser's attitude toward women in general. Based on Gould's (1994) take on deontology, the mere existence of this message, that someone actually thought of it and that it was allowed to be placed on a large billboard in a very public and highly trafficked location, questions the views, norms, and values of those involved–the creators, the billboard company, and the people looking at it, whether the targeted or unintended audiences. Obviously, the creator(s) of the message, the Hard Rock Hotel Casino, and the billboard company, which provided the billboard structure itself, had no serious ethical or moral concerns about the "Looser than your girlfriend" message.

Similarly, the image of women as portrayed in the message appears not to be of issue. The billboard communicates the allowance in Las Vegas, in particular *de facto*, for women to be depicted with women in advertising, a practice which has become a "standard narrative device for heterosexual titillation" (Reichert et al., 1999). Regarding the moral implications of this ad, and the Hard Rock's advertising approach in general, it provides further support to Reichert, Maly, and Zavoina's (1999) contention that in the lesbian-chic device, "women are presented as sexual objects whose primary importance is wish fulfillment for men, and men's ideas and men's perceptions of what sex should be like constitute the status quo" (p. 129). The implication of loose girlfriends, or women who are unfaithful to their boyfriends or even girlfriends (should they be true lesbians), seems acceptable as well. Reichert (2001) found that female homoerotic advertising appeals are interpreted more sexually by men than by women, which suggests that this billboard and its counterpart print ad were created by persons who assume this message appeals to (heterosexual) men, as well as to women who are not offended by depictions of lesbianism or bisexuality.

Gould (1994) contends that deontological research also must address audience considerations. The audience of this particular billboard consisted of persons traveling from, near, or past the airport, with the Hard Rock hoping to attract them to its premises. However, one could certainly ascertain that others, namely, Las Vegas residents who use the route to get to or from work and home, saw it as well, and likely more than just once. These residents might have included children, who either simply saw a cartoon of two attractive women hugging and, if old enough, read the caption "Looser than your girlfriend." The meaning may have escaped them, but one must consider the possibility of effects on other segments of the public, such as those not included in the Hard Rock's targeted 25-to-34 age demographic.

The message to these groups echoes that of the message's source: Women exist for men's pleasure. In his critique of the print version of this billboard, Reichert (2001) noted that the lesbian-chic image used by the Hard Rock "may be sending 'instructions' or aspirational messages to women as to what men find appealing" (p. 19). In the reading of the written text combined with the visual image in the billboard, I concur with Reichert's (2001) initial assessment of the print version of this billboard: "It's difficult to discern any sign of female empowerment or liberation" in the ad (p. 19). While the possibility exists that the ad and its woman-on-woman image might appeal to lesbian women, the research holds otherwise, in that heterosexual women portrayed engaged in erotically charged homosexual behavior have little to do with the real lives of lesbians (Reichert, 2001; Reichert et al., 1999).

PUSHING THE LIMITS, EVEN IN VEGAS

The "Looser than Your Girlfriend" billboard did not incur any public or governmental ire. However, a series of subsequent billboards, as well as print ads, caught the attention of both the public and gaming regulators. The billboards featured photographs of nearly nude women and language that people from a variety of interested parties found offensive and local media found of sufficient newsworthiness to write about for more than a year. I describe the content of two of them here. A chronological review of news reports and eventual outcome of public and regulatory complaints against the Hard Rock follows.

"We Sell Used Dice"

During 2002, the Hard Rock began the "We Sell Used Dice" ad campaign. The visual component featured a photograph of a slender, topless female model wearing only some costume jewelry (a necklace and bracelet made of animal claws or teeth, and another necklace with a razor blade pendant), panties, and "belly chain," and holding a pair of dice over her nipples. The underside of both breasts were shown, thus giving the illusion that the woman was nude, except for the strategically placed dice. The accompanying text read, "We Sell Used Dice," with the hotel's name. The print version of the ad included the model's face; the billboard did not.

McCarran International Airport again served as the location of the billboard. While the "Looser than Your Girlfriend" sign was located on the northern side of the airport, greeting viewers who were going in the direction of the Hard Rock Hotel itself, the "We Sell Used Dice" billboard greeted motorists going in the opposite direction of Las Vegas proper, away from the Hard Rock and toward the southern area of the valley. The billboard was located on the airport connector that led to several car rental facilities, which provides much tourist traffic.

As Reichert (2003) noted, mainstream advertising rarely contains complete nudity. The content of the used dice ad, however, came close to it–with only the two dice, which, suggestively, were pink, just covering the woman's nipples. The verbal anchorage, "We Sell Used Dice," advertised the fact that the Hard Rock Hotel Casino sells used dice as souvenirs at its retail facilities. Indeed, one can purchase used dice and used playing cards at almost any casino. This ad links gaming with sexy women, thus furthering the association of the Hard Rock with sex in general.

As mentioned, the billboard provoked public response, illustrating that deontological concerns, especially in terms of advertisers' consideration of unintended audiences and the environment within which an ad appears, play an important role in the advertising process. The billboard had been in place for six months before the Clark County Current Planning Division and Public Response Office labeled it as "obscene," and told the billboard company leasing the space to take it down (Rake, 2003). Regarding the definition of "obscene," county zoning criteria specified that any part of a female breast below the nipple would qualify, with a larger context that billboards not include body parts that "are usually covered" (Rake, 2003). The public response office had received a written complaint from a resident several weeks before it made its request, which prompted an investigation resulting in the order for the billboard to be removed. Though taken down before any legal action ensued, the "Used Dice" billboard later served a role in the events leading to the financial settlement by the Hard Rock regarding its advertising.

"Buck All Night"

The National Finals Rodeo, commonly known as the NFR, held at the Thomas and Mack Center on the UNLV campus near the Hard Rock, serves as one of the largest annual events hosted in Las Vegas. In late 2003, a billboard on the Hard Rock premises featured a photograph of a woman from the knees down (see Figure 2). Wearing strappy high heels, her hand appeared to be either pulling on or taking off a pair of panties. Next to her feet was a cowboy hat on the floor. She appeared to be standing close to an unmade bed, which featured the covers pulled to the floor. In the print version of the ad, which appeared in the December 4, 2005 issue of the *Las Vegas Weekly*, a free entertainment-based publication, the woman's legs were shown from upper thigh down, and the bed sheets and pillows were in disarray, as if the bed had been either slept in or the location of sexual activity.

The visual image implies that a woman had been or was about to have sex with a man, supposedly a cowboy, based on the hat as a clue. The accompanying text read, "Get Ready to Buck All Night," a play on words both regarding the rodeo (bucking occurs on broncos), and the slang word for intercourse, which apparently occurs at the Hard Rock. As the photographic evidence implies, there had been, or would be, bucking "all night" in the bed. Additional text under the headline told viewers about the "2nd Annual 'Buck-Off' in the Viva Las Vegas Lounge" held nightly during the rodeo. In the print ad, additional text told readers, "If you've got the balls, we've got the prizes. If not, well, you can catch the Buck Off Girls take a buckin' wild ride." The print ad also listed drink specials for Coors Light and Jack Daniel's, and food specials for chicken and ribs, pork chops, and T-bone steak–just what a cowboy/"man" would want.

Obviously aimed at NFR participants, attendees, or rodeo fans in general, this billboard blatantly forwards the notion that sexual activity occurs at the Hard Rock, with no mention of gaming at all. Rather, the attraction here points to the promise that (male) patrons who visit the hotel need not even bother with the casino, but head straight to the lounge and get ready to have sex "all night." Hence, this ad uses sexual appeal to associate the Hard Rock with sex directly and advertises the Hard Rock as a place where getting lucky has nothing to do with the games of chance offered on the casino floor.

Located in the immediate vicinity of the Hard Rock and the NFR venue, the "Buck All Night" billboard, nevertheless, caught the attention of local residents and media as well. Called "unoriginal" in a *Las Vegas Review Journal* article on the use of suggestive advertising in Las Vegas (Jones, 2003), this billboard, along with the "Used Dice" ads, served as an example of a new push by advertisers to attract "overlooked young, affluent customers" (Jones, 2003, p. 1F). These billboards also attracted the attention of gaming regulators, the public, and the media in what became a highly publicized argument over the content of its advertising.

FIGURE 2. A Billboard Designed to Entice Rodeo Attendees

Photograph by University of Nevada, Las Vegas Photographic Services.

Used by permission.

CHRONOLOGY OF ADVERTISING COMPLAINTS

As mentioned, the three billboards described here, "Looser than Your Girlfriend," "We Sell Used Dice" and "Buck All Night" appeared between 2001 and 2003. The latter two were at issue in a formal response from the Nevada Gaming Commission and Gaming Control Board, which oversee the gaming industry on behalf of the public. Gaming license holders can be punished for "failure to conduct advertising and public relations activities in accordance with decency, dignity, good taste, and inoffensiveness . . ." (Velotta, 2004a).

In January 2004, the Gaming Control Board filed a complaint against the Hard Rock over its advertising; the complaint cited not only the "Buck All Night" billboard and "We Sell Used Dice" billboards, but two other print ads that the Board found "inappropriate" (Velotta, 2004a, 2004b). The print ads had appeared in the free, entertainment-based publication *Las Vegas Weekly*. One ad told readers, ". . . we believe in your Monday night rights: large quantities of prescription stimulants" and "having wives in two states . . . Tell your wives you are going; if they are hot, bring them along" (Velotta, 2004a). The other ad showed a man and woman at a gaming table surrounded by playing cards and poker chips with the caption, "There's always a temptation to cheat." The Board argued that the "temptation to cheat" ad conveyed the message that cheating was acceptable at the Hard Rock (Simpson, 2004a). The billboard version of this ad (see Figure 3), with the revised caption, "Keep your mind on the game," appeared near the entrance to the Thomas and Mack Center on the University of Nevada, Las Vegas campus, a venue for a variety of sporting and family-oriented events.

The Gaming Control Board cited the print and billboard ads for either "using lawbreaking activity" or for sexually suggestive content. The resort faced a fine of up to $300,000 for the three-count complaint. By this time, members of the community and the press expressed their concerns over the Hard Rock's advertising as well. For example, some 200 to 300 people, mostly mothers, attended a meeting of the Nevada Gaming Commission to support "a handful of foes of suggestive billboards" (Simpson, 2004c). In terms of media commentary, an editorial in the *Las Vegas Sun* cited the "Buck All Night" and "We Sell Used Dice" billboards as examples of "unacceptable images" ("Editorial," 2004).

For several months, a series of negotiations followed, including settlement rejections by the Gaming Commission and motions to dismiss by the Hard Rock, based on First Amendment issues (Smith, 2004a, 2004b, 2004c; Velotta, 2004c). Eventually, the Gaming Commission dismissed two of the three counts (Velotta, 2004d), but not before the Hard Rock had erected a billboard near its premises that pictured cartoon-like drawings of a cat, a beaver, and two rabbits with the caption, "Another clean and inoffensive billboard" ("Hard Rock billboard," 2004).

By October 2004, the Hard Rock agreed to pay $100,000 to settle the complaint, with the resort's attorney promising, "Going forward, we're

FIGURE 3. Another Billboard Using Sex Appeal to Sell Hard Rock's Entertainment Experience

Photograph by University of Nevada, Las Vegas Photographic Services. Used by permission.

always going to be mindful of our relationship with the regulators" (Benston, 2004). The fine paid as a "punishment" for its advertising practices served a symbolic purpose, but did not appear to dent the Hard Rock's profits. In 2004, the year of the complaint and subsequent settlement, net revenues reached $15 million. Indeed, revenues had steadily increased since 2000; between 2001 and 2004, net revenues increased by $3 million (Hard Rock Form 10-K, 2004).

DISCUSSION

Overall, the present study examines how the Hard Rock Hotel Casino in Las Vegas used sexual appeals in its advertising, specifically outdoor advertising, which was open to public viewing. Regarding the research question concerning the use of sexual appeals in the Hard Rock's advertising, the ads presented here reflect an overall brand image that associates gaming with sexual activity. Images of women appear repeatedly to attract attention and reinforce the idea that the Hard Rock promises entertainment on a variety of levels, with sex serving as a main attraction. The resort used lesbian-chic imagery to promote its "loose slots," and female nudity and sexual innuendo in two other billboards, which became part of a complaint filed by state gaming authorities.

As for the sexual ideology of the Hard Rock, these ads demonstrate that in its attempt to reach the "hip," once-overlooked customer, the resort appears to endorse casual sex, or, at least, non-monogamous sex. One of the print ads even told readers that they should bring "both wives" to the Hard Rock–if they were "hot." Though the "Looser than Your Girlfriend" billboard did not create the public stir as the other ads described here, one could hardly imagine a casino, even the Hard Rock, run the headline, "Looser than Your Wife."

The use of females in various stages of undress, or as implied lesbians, serves as a motif in the Hard Rock's advertising (as with other casinos in Las Vegas). The Hard Rock consistently offers the promise of attractive women, so much so that it directs (male) visitors not to be distracted by all the beautiful women as they partake in gaming, as the "Keep Your Mind on the Game" billboard demonstrates. Such images of female nudity and same-sex activity, in addition to normalizing the objectification of women, contribute to a "hegemonic discourse" regarding heterosexual pornography, perpetuating the notion to both men and women that women serve as things to be "used, abused, and discarded" (Reichert et al., 1999).

In this sense, the deontological perspective of advertising theory allows for the conclusion that the Hard Rock forwards a traditionally patriarchal view of women, in which women's value lies in their physical attractiveness and ability to please men. Morally speaking, if the goal of creating an egalitarian society, one in which women hold equal status to men, is considered a "good" thing, then the Hard Rock's advertising does not serve to advance that goal. This point becomes more salient when one considers the use of the female image in advertising in general, especially in terms of the objectification of women as a means by which media normalizes violence against them (Kilbourne, 2000).

The second research question concerned the consequences that result when advertisers fail to consider non-targeted audiences. While one consequence of the Hard Rock's overtly sexual adverting took the form of the $100,000 settlement, the ensuing public debate over the "We Sell Used Dice" and "Buck All Night" ads brought attention to the larger deontological issue of balancing advertisers' needs with community needs. According to media reports, in addition to the resort describing the ads as "humorous" and "satirical," the Hard Rock's president and CEO said of the "Buck All Night" billboard, "Sometimes you hit a single with an ad, sometimes a double. The rodeo ad, for us, was a home run" (Velotta, 2004b). For the Hard Rock, deontological concerns were outweighed by the "bang for the buck" this particular ad provided.

As mentioned, sexual appeals tend to be most effective when used to advertise products that implicitly associated with sexuality. In this case, sexual appeals were (and still are) used to sell the entertainment experience offered at the Hard Rock Hotel Casino. It is safe to say that Las Vegas, self-termed the "entertainment capital of the world," already connotes sexuality. The use of sex to advertise the city of Las Vegas as an entertainment venue, thus, for some audiences, may enhance its appeal and even be considered "ethically positive," to use Gould's term (1994, p. 75). However, as he noted, overuse of sexual appeals could be ineffective, with gratuitous sex contributing to a "cluttered environment" (p. 75). In terms of overt sexuality and less-than-subtle messages about sexual activity, the Hard Rock may be overselling its sexual image–resulting in negative responses from the public and the Nevada Gaming Commission.

CONCLUSIONS

As Gould (1994) concluded, "We know little about either the teleological effects of sexual advertising on consumers or the evolving deontological norms of a shifting and highly segmented population" (p. 79). Out-of-towners might perceive Las Vegas as a place where "anything goes," but residents in the Las Vegas area consist of residents that include families and children, and people who do not work in the gaming industry. Thus, while sexual appeals in advertising might result in short-term gains, the case of the Hard Rock, known as "the juvenile delinquent of the casino industry" (German, 2004), evidences the need to weigh the image of Las Vegas with the "real life" community of Las Vegas. One might argue that risqué advertising by the Hard Rock and other casinos is a fact of life in Las Vegas. However, in his *Las Vegas Sun* commentary on the "sexification" of the city, columnist Jeff German (2004) noted that casinos who use overly sexual advertising are gambling with the city's future:

The challenge here is to go back to what we used to be good at doing–striking a balance between the Las Vegas we want the world to see and the Las Vegas we see beyond the Strip. If we're not up to this challenge, we risk losing both worlds.

Thus, the ethical/moral considerations of sexual appeals encompass not only the rightness or wrongness of content, but the wider context of where those appeals appear, in terms of both physical and media environments.

LaTour and Henthorne's (1994) offer additional advice regarding sexual appeals: That it is "prudent to continually re-evaluate the assumptions on which strategic decisions are based" (p. 89). Their advice seems especially relevant for billboard advertising placed in full public view without regard to audience considerations. The need to understand one's environment and the use of certain persuasive appeals holds even greater significance when sexual appeals are used. In the case of "Sin City," placing messages intended for a specific adult demographic on billboards where local commuter traffic occurs needs rethinking. However, given the added publicity generated by negative public and governmental responses, this will happen only if the Hard Rock and other gaming businesses perceive that creating a positive image in the local community, and with those who grant their licenses, requires a more prudent utilization of the sexual appeal.

NOTES

1. The Nevada Gaming Commission and the State Gaming Control Board constitute the two-tier system that regulates the gaming industry in Nevada. Both "administer the State laws and regulations governing gaming for the protection of the public and in the public interest in accordance with the policy of the State" (Nevada Gaming Regulation website, 2005). The Commission acts on recommendations made by the Control Board, and holds ultimate decision-making capacity regarding licensing matters.

2. A reversed image appeared in a print ad for the Hard Rock (Reichert, 2001). The print ad included men shown around a craps table looking at the women.

REFERENCES

Benston, L. (2004, October 28). Hard Rock settlement won't affect operations. *Casino City Times.com.* Retrieved on October 18, 2005 from http://www.casinocitytimes. com/news/article.cfm?contentID=146275.

Editorial: Sex ads are subject to regulation (2004, March 22). *Las Vegas Sun.* Retrieved on November 21, 2005 from www.lasvegassun.com/sunbin/stories/sun/2004/mar/ 22/51656617.html.

Forceville, C. (1996). *Pictorial Metaphor in Advertising*. New York: Routledge.

German, J. (2004, July 27). Columnist Jeff German: Striking a balance in Vegas. *Las Vegas Sun*. Retrieved on November 21, 2005 from http://www.lasvegassun.com/sunbin/stories/sun/2004/jul/27/517240910.html.

Gould, S. J. (1994). Sexuality and ethics in advertising: A research agenda and policy guideline perspective. *Journal of Advertising, 23*(3), 73-80.

Hard Rock billboard appears to taunt gambling regulators (2004, September 23). *Reno Gazette-Journal*. Retrieved on October 18, 2005 from http://www.rgj.com/news/printstory.php?id=81103.

Hard Rock Hotel Form 10-K: Annual report for year ending December 31, 2003 (2003). Downloaded on October 5, 2005 from http://www.hardrockhotel.com/home_company_financial.php.

Hard Rock Hotel Form 10-K: Annual report for year ending December 31, 2004 (2004). Retrieved on October 4, 2005 from http://www.hardrockhotel.com/home_company_financial.php.

Jones, C. (2003, November 30). Calculated risqu. *Las Vegas Sun*, 1F.

Kilbourne, J. (Creator/Presenter), and Jhally, S. (Producer/Director). (2000). *Killing us Softly III* [Videorecording]. (Available from Media Education Foundation, 60 Masonic Street, Northampton, MA, 01060).

Lang, A., Wise, K., Lee, S., and Cai, X. (2003). The effects of sexual appeals on physiological, cognitive, emotional, and attitudinal responses for product and alcohol billboard advertising. In T. Reichert and J. Lambiase (eds.), *Sex in Advertising: Perspectives on the Erotic Appeal* (pp. 107-131). Mahwah, NJ: Lawrence Erlbaum Associates.

LaTour, M. S., and Henthorne, T. L. (1994). Ethical judgments of sexual appeals in print advertising. *Journal of Advertising, 23*(3), 81-90.

LaTour, M. S., and Henthorne, T. L. (2003). Nudity and sexual appeals: Understanding the arousal process and advertising response. In T. Reichert and J. Lambiase (Eds.), *Sex in Advertising: Perspectives on the Erotic Appeal* (pp. 91-106). Mahwah, NJ: Lawrence Erlbaum Associates.

Marlow, J. E. (2001). The last gasp: Cigarette advertising on billboards in the 1990s. *Journal of Communication Inquiry, 25*(1), 38-54.

Nevada Gaming Regulation website (2005). Retrieved on December 20, 2005 from http://gaming.nv.gov/about_regulation.htm.

Rake, Launce. (2003, January 10). County going after 'obscene' billboards. *Las Vegas Sun*. Retrieved on November 21, 2005 from http://www.lasvegassun.com/sunbin/stories/sun/2003/jan/10/514500613.html.

Reichert, T. (2001). 'Lesbian chic' imagery in advertising: Interpretations and insights of female same-sex eroticism. *Journal of Current Issues and Research in Advertising, 23*(2), 9-22.

Reichert, T. (2003). What is sex in advertising? Perspectives from consumer behavior and social science research. In T. Reichert and J. Lambiase (eds.), *Sex in Advertising: Perspectives on the Erotic Appeal* (pp. 11-38). Mahwah, NJ: Lawrence Erlbaum Associates.

Reichert, T., Maly, K., and Zavoina, S. (1999). Designed for (male) pleasure: The myth of lesbian chic in mainstream advertising. In M. G. Castarphen and S. C. Zavoina (eds.), *Sexual Rhetoric: Media Perspectives on Sexuality, Gender, and Identity* (pp. 123-133). Westport, CT: Greenwood.

Richmond, D., and Hartman, T. (1982). Sex appeal in advertising. *Journal of Advertising Research, 22*(5), 53-61.

Severn, J.; Belch, G.; and Belch, M. (1990). The effects of sexual and non-sexual advertising appeals and information level on cognitive processing and communication effectiveness. *Journal of Advertising, 19*(1), 14-22.

Simpson, J. (2004a, January 23). Casino advertising: Racy Hard Rock ads raise complaint. *Las Vegas Review-Journal*, 1D.

Simpson, J. (2004b, February 18). Hard Rock, Control Board talks continue. *Las Vegas Sun*. Retrieved on December 5, 2005 from http://www.lasvegassun.com/sunbin/stories/text/2004/feb/18/516374540.html.

Simpson, J. (2004c, March 19). Public protests suggestive billboard. *Las Vegas Sun*. Retrieved on November 21, 2005 from http://www.lasvegassun.com/sunbin/stories/sun/2004/mar/19/516556482.html.

Smith, R. (2004a, May 21). Advertising complaint: Hard Rock resolution rejected. *Las Vegas Review-Journal*, 1A.

Smith, R. (2004b, August 27). Hard Rock Hotel moves to dismiss complaint over racy advertising. *Las Vegas Review-Journal*, 2D.

Smith, R. (2004c, September 21). Gaming commission to hear Hard Rock dispute. *Las Vegas Review-Journal*, 1A.

Tocker, P. (1969). Standardized outdoor advertising: History, economics and self-regulation. In J. W. Houck (ed.), *Outdoor Advertising: History and Regulation* (pp. 11-56). Notre Dame, IN: University of Notre Dame Press.

Velotta, R. (2003, November 6). Control board raps Hard Rock on print ads. *Las Vegas Sun*. Retrieved on December 1, 2005 from http://www.lasvegassun.com/sunbin/stories/sun/2003/nov/06/515827175.html.

Velotta, R. (2004a, January 22). Casino hit with complaint. *Las Vegas Sun*. Retrieved on October 18, 2005 from http://www.lasvegassun.com/sunbin/stories/text/2004/jan/22/516220392.html.

Velotta, R. (2004b, February 6). Hard Rock exec mum on ad complaints. *Business Las Vegas*. Retrieved on October 31, 2005 from http://www.inbusinesslasvegas.com/2004/02/06/tourism.html.

Velotta, R. (2004c, May 21). Hard Rock deal rejected. *Casino City Times.com*. Retrieved on December 5, 2005 from http://www.casinocitytimes.com/news/article.cfm?contentID=142980.

Velotta, R. (2004d, September 24). Gaming commission dismisses two of three Hard Rock complaints. *Las Vegas Sun*. Retrieved on November 21, 2004 from http://www.lasvegassun.com/sunbin/stories/text/2004/sep/24/517566027.html.

Velotta, R. (2004e, November 16). Gaming Commission set to vote on Hard Rock settlement. *Las Vegas Sun*. Retrieved on December 5, 2005 from http://www.lasvegassun.com/sunbin/stories/sun/2004/nov/16/517834041.html.

Wimmer, R. D., and Dominick, J. R. (1991). *Mass Media Research*. Belmont, CA: Wadsworth.

doi:10.1300/J057v13n01_11

Index

DATE DUE

NOV 0 7 2008			
5-4-10			